A Cut

A Cut Below

A Celebration of B Horror Movies,
1950s–1980s

SCOTT DREBIT

McFarland & Company, Inc., Publishers
Jefferson, North Carolina

LIBRARY OF CONGRESS CATALOGUING-IN-PUBLICATION DATA

Names: Drebit, Scott, 1970– author.
Title: A cut below : a celebration of b horror movies, 1950-1980s / Scott Drebit.
Description: Jefferson, North Carolina : McFarland & Company, Inc., Publishers, 2023. | Includes index.
Identifiers: LCCN 2023045232 | ISBN 9781476691954 (paperback : acid free paper) ∞
    ISBN 9781476650388 (ebook)
Subjects: LCSH: Horror films—History and criticism. | Motion pictures—History—
    20th century.
Classification: LCC PN1995.9.H6 D75 2023 | DDC 791.43/6164—dc23/eng/20230928
LC record available at https://lccn.loc.gov/2023045232

BRITISH LIBRARY CATALOGUING DATA ARE AVAILABLE

ISBN (print) 978-1-4766-9195-4
ISBN (ebook) 978-1-4766-5038-8

Front cover images: © Lightspring/vm/Shutterstock

Printed in the United States of America

*McFarland & Company, Inc., Publishers
    Box 611, Jefferson, North Carolina 28640
    www.mcfarlandpub.com*

To my Michelle;
it isn't a ride if you're not along

Table of Contents

Acknowledgments   ix
Preface   1

Festival One: The Animal Killdom   3
Willard (1971) 4 • *Ben* (1972) 7 • *Grizzly* (1976) 10 •
Kingdom of the Spiders (1977) 13 • *Piranha* (1978) 17

Festival Two: Those Darn Kids!   20
The Bad Seed (1956) 21 • *Alice, Sweet Alice* (1976) 24 •
Who Can Kill a Child? aka *Island of the Damned*
(1976) 28 • *The Children* (1980) 31 • *The Pit* (1981) 33

Festival Three: The Blood on Satan's B-Roll   37
The Devil Rides Out (1968) 38 • *Race with the Devil* (1975) 41 •
The Devil's Rain (1975) 44 • *The Sentinel* (1977) 47 •
Fear No Evil (1981) 50

Festival Four: Chop Chop Till You Drop   54
Strait-Jacket (1964) 56 • *Popcorn* (1991) 58 • *Just Before Dawn*
(1981) 62 • *10 to Midnight* (1983) 65 • *Pieces* (1982) 69

Festival Five: Any Portmanteau in a Storm   72
The House That Dripped Blood (1971) 73 • *Vault of
Horror* (1973) 76 • *Asylum* (1972) 79 • *From a Whisper
to a Scream* (1987) 82 • *Creepshow* (1982) 86

Festival Six: Terror in Technotown   90
The Fly (1958) 91 • *Westworld* (1973) 94 • *Demon Seed*
(1977) 97 • *Evilspeak* (1981) 101 • *Videodrome* (1983) 104

Festival Seven: Back Bacon Bloodbath   107
My Bloody Valentine (1981) 108 • *The Brood* (1979) 112 •
Of Unknown Origin (1983) 115 • *Spasms* (1983) 118 •
Curtains (1983) 121

Festival Eight: If You're Undead and You Know It,
Clap Your Hand   125
The Plague of the Zombies (1966) 126 • *Tombs of the Blind*
Dead (1972) 129 • *The Living Dead at Manchester Morgue*
(1974) 132 • *Zombie* (1979) 135 • *Burial Ground* (1981) 140

Festival Nine: What the Film   143
The Baby (1973) 144 • *Phantom of the Paradise* (1974) 147 •
Eaten Alive (1976) 151 • *Hollywood Meatcleaver*
Massacre (1976) 154 • *The Manitou* (1978) 158

Festival Ten: Duct Tape and Stardust   162
Invaders from Mars (1953) 164 • *Plan 9 from Outer Space*
(1957) 167 • *Fiend Without a Face* (1958) 170 • *Basket*
Case (1982) 173 • *Things* (1989) 176

Festival Eleven: Potluck of Horror   180
The Incredible Shrinking Man (1957) 181 • *The Curse*
of the Werewolf (1961) 184 • *Messiah of Evil* (1973) 188 •
The Bees (1978) 191 • *Prince of Darkness* (1987) 194

Festival Twelve: Around the Weird in a Day   199
Blood and Black Lace (1964) 200 • *Quatermass and the Pit*
(1967) 203 • *Viy* (1967) 207 • *Evil Dead Trap* (1988) 209 •
Santa Sangre (1989) 212

The Past, Present and Future of Horror: Or, How to Hit
Your Word Count and Close Out the Book   216

Index   219

Acknowledgments

This book would not be possible without the following folk: Everyone at McFarland, including Layla Milholen, for their hard work and dedication to making this the best book ever. The team at the Linda Chester Agency has been amazing; thanks for taking me on as a client, and a very special thanks to my agent, Darlene Chan—I'm so glad something about my work caught your eye. Working with you on this has been amazing; thank you for making me a better writer, and for being the best agent ever.

Daily Dead. I have been writing for Daily Dead since April of 2015. That spring I decided to cast my net to some horror websites with a couple of samples. Of the many websites I sent to, Daily Dead is the only one that responded. Not only that, but they were very interested in my idea for a retro column on older horror films; this became my weekly Drive-In Dust Offs column, which has over 300 pieces in it and counting. In fact, several of those Dust-Offs have made their way into this book, albeit with a polish and a fresh update where needed; the rest are brand new!

All of this is due to Jonathan James, owner/operator of Daily Dead. (Thanks so much for allowing us to print the work, and for tracking down the posters!) He and Managing Editor Heather Wixson, Derek Anderson, Tamika Jones, Bryan Christopher, Patrick Bromley, and so many others in our ever-growing family have been nothing but supportive and helpful. I tell my friends at Daily Dead that I love them all the time, but here's one for posterity's sake: I love you guys, truly, and thanks for always backing me. Daily Dead 4 Life.

To my Family: my kids Justin and Renee, my wife Michelle, Jeff & Pat, Paul & Steph, Jennifer, Jesse, Madison, Amanda, some little ones, Norm & Jenny, Rob & Coriann, Deryk, Kassidy, Anna, Costin, Jaden, Noah & Ally, Auntie Jeanette, Shauna, Big Al, Dionne, Payton, and my mom Karen, who got me started down this path of debauchery. Love you, Mom.

To All My Friends: most of you are online, some not, but you all know who you are. Thanks for always being there and being supportive through the months, years, even decades.

To Readers: thanks for picking up this book! I hope you like it, and may it inspire countless conversations about horror, the greatest genre of them all. See you inside!

Preface

Welcome to *A Cut Below*. So you like horror movies, huh? Me too! Good thing you're here then. What you hold in your hands is just as the title says: a celebration of the odd, the off-putting, and low-budgeted fare that the horror film genre offered between the mid–1950s when drive-ins exploded, and the mid–1980s as these films were drummed from theaters to exist mostly in the cheaper and more convenient frontier of home video. (Does it say all *that* in the title?)

I'm drawn to this specific time frame because there's a lot of cultural symbiosis between viewing platform and viewer: radioactive monsters in the 1950s during the Red Scare, the more grounded approach of the 1960s, the societal chaos of the 1970s, and finally into the 1980s, when the censors *really* cracked down on our beloved genre. (And the other really big draw? I was born in 1970, and these are my surrounding touchstones.) For instance, teenagers were able to get away from Mom and Pop in the 1950s and head to the drive-in with their friends in a car—meaning a certain level of independence from their parents, meaning a "riskier" type of film to watch. The idealistic hangover of the 1960s gave way to an angry, progressive decade that saw its major milestones—the Vietnam War, Watergate, Women's Rights, and the Middle East—reflected in the films being made at the time. Some subversive, some progressive, and some just shocking for the hell of it.

So, what sets a "B" movie apart from an "A" movie? It started fairly simply: when a film studio in the 1930s sent out movies for distribution, they often paired it with a second feature—much lower budget, dimmer stars—to "fill out the bill," as it were. These pictures were called "B movies" because they were second; the headlining film would of course be the "A." So eventually, the "B" became shorthand for "inferior," and has stuck that way ever since.

Horror lovers, though, like you and me know better: B movies are for the most part where we live. These are the films often made under less-than-ideal conditions, usually with fewer funds and unproven talent. This

1

translates into a great idea, possibly unwieldy, made with passion, heart, and Cthulhu willing, some talent. Every B movie is just as hard to make as an A one; the benefit of the B can be a lot less studio interference and a lot more creative control for whoever takes the wheel, hence more room for madness.

My adolescence happily coincided with the rise of "home entertainment" at the dawn of the 1980s, and horror films transferred to videotape flooded these brand-new "video stores"—I don't even know why the quotation marks are in play; reflexively, those phrases already feel from a completely different and antiquated time. But there were no streaming services, and you were at the mercy of whatever films the vendor bought for his business.

Luckily for me then, my merchant bought them all—whatever came on the market. It was just that time; if it could be put on tape, it was. That meant a lot of horror, and especially a lot of "different" B stuff: the film-centric Band Family (Albert, Richard, Charles, Bobby Sue, Felton) had a company called Media, and first, they put out whatever they could get their hands on—*Night of the Living Dead*, *Tourist Trap*, *Reefer Madness*, and a whole lot of borderline softcore. It was the great equalizer for someone immersing themself in this new world; *Can I Do It 'Til I Need Glasses?** stood as much of a chance of winning me over as *Slithis*. (Okay, more so; *Slithis* is terrible.) And that's how a horror kid grows up to be an even bigger horror kid.

This brings us to now. We are here to *celebrate*—the horror films you had to beg your parents to rent at the video store. To the ones that none of your friends wanted to watch, but the story seemed so insane it was impossible for you *not* to. To those films that you saw at the drive-in or theater as a kid and never forgot seeing *those things* happen on a family-friendly screen. And to all the films in the festivals ahead of you? Give them and all the other B movies in your life the love they deserve; after all, they've never let you down.

---

* The onscreen card reads 'Til; the poster has til; IMDb lists it as 'Till. For sanity's sake let's go with the onscreen card.

Festival One:
The Animal Killdom

Here's the deal, as far as horror goes: The Animal Killdom will end you. Let's not mince words; from those adorable marching ants to the rotund hippo (they roll around in the mud, HOW CUTE), they will all cease your existence. And it's usually not their fault.

Overt social commentary reared its head in horror during the Cold War, with studios clamoring to follow up Toho Studios' brilliant *Godzilla* (1954), a very clear and powerful metaphor for the horrors of nuclear annihilation. The American releases that followed used the same template—atomic testing, perhaps a mutated lobster or such, and Stars & Stripes saves the day. And they did well—some were entertaining and will be featured later in this book.

Here we scale things down a bit. It was inevitable of course; by the end of the 1950s, those teenagers at the drive-in were maturing, and with it, the genre was pushing to tell more realistic stories—grittier, with a deeper appreciation for layers of personality, and relying more on the hubris of man, as opposed to the more one-note militaristic jargon of the previous decade. I'm reluctant to use the word "subtle" in a subgenre that hosts clusters of spiders, enormous telepathic snakes, and misfits of rats. Now, *these* films? They will be in this chapter.

Forget the 1960s, they were busy doing that reconstruction of horror: *Psycho*, *Peeping Tom* (both 1960), and an emphasis on the inner monster became the prime focus of the decade, at least through Hollywood's eyes. (The indies never forgot their zippered monsters, though.) So, we're bypassing that decade in this chapter too; sorry 1960s, but we're looking for a very specific type of film.

Let's roll a few numbers (old slang for marijuana cigarettes, kids), pull on our platform boots, and stumble into the bell-bottomed and bra-burning 1970s: Vietnam is still going on; the Women's Rights Movement sees women organize and fight for equality at home and at work; and conflicts arise in the Middle East. The 1970s were rife with discourse on any number of volatile topics. Horror has always been a genre that pulls from the zeitgeist, plucks the latest societal unease, and discards the rest. And one of the biggest that the genre latched onto was the environment.

Pesticides—DDT, and many others—were found to be … rather bad for the ecosystem. So by the end of the decade, those particular poisons were gone; this gave horror a whole decade to tap into people's not entirely unfounded fears. We can't forget the dissipating ozone layer nor the military weaponization of some toothy fish.

When horror wasn't busy using Silly Putty on a newspaper and stretching out the facts to suit its purpose, it simply used the unknown to its advantage: One rat may not seem scary, but a bunch swarming all over you? No thanks. Arack attack? Rather not.

As I said at the top of this chapter, The Animal Killdom will end you. But that's why we're here—to get ended, over and over, until we turn on those headlights and drive back to reality. But for now, keep all hands and heads inside the vehicle—or the theater seat—if you wish to make it to the next festival.

Let's start this festival off with a loving tribute
to that most welcome of pets, the disease-infested rat.
At least he's got a friend in…

Willard (1971)

"I was good to you, Ben!"

Well, that's true, Willard, up to a point. Daniel Mann's *Willard* makes a few good and satirical points, one being don't bite the hand that feeds you, especially as that "hand" might bite you right back. *Willard* kicked off the Animal Killdom subgenre, leading to such memorable fodder as *Frogs* (1972), *Food of the Gods* (1976), and *Day of the Animals* (1977). However, *Willard* stands out from the pack by keeping its thrills low-key and scurrying on the ground.

Produced by Bing Crosby Productions—yes, that Bing Crosby—*Willard* received good notices when it was released in June of 1971. Propelled by top-notch performances, *Willard* delivers the vermin to your doorstep. Watch your feet.

Our film opens at a warehouse. The work day is done, and we see

Willard Stiles heading to catch his bus. A car pulls in front of him driven by Al Martin, his boss, and owner of the company, which was started by Willard's deceased father. Martin hands papers to Willard that he forgot at the office, and due to the exchange, Willard misses his bus. As he arrives at his run-down mansion (they once were wealthy, you see), he is greeted by his mother and her friends, who are throwing him a surprise birthday party.

Sad and dejected at turning 27, Willard heads out back and feeds birthday cake to a rat. The next morning, there's another rat, this time with babies. Willard starts to communicate with the rats by imitating their sounds, and before you know it, he's training and teaching them tricks. Meanwhile, his mother keeps getting sicker and more demanding of Willard, so much so that he dreads being either at home *or* work. Salvation at the office, however, comes in the guise of Joan, hired by Martin to help Willard catch up on his work.

Willard becomes smitten with Joan, but without the necessary social skills to gain her favor, he continues to train his Happy Time Rat Brigade. This becomes easy to do, as Willard personally befriends a natural leader, an albino rat that he dubs Socrates. Before you can say Mickey Mouse, Willard is using his army to deliver vengeance against those who have wronged him, especially Martin, the man ultimately responsible for everything horrible in Willard's life. Can Willard find true happiness with Joan? Will Ben and the gang get tired of being treated like interns?

One of *Willard*'s greatest assets is its lighthearted approach to the material. The subject matter certainly doesn't bear this out, but sometimes genre fare can use an anachronistic tone to stand out from the crowd. For instance, the music by Alex North, sweeping and lively, even *jaunty*, seems at odds with the events on display—and yet it works, by disguising the film as a Disney-esque "lonely boy and his blank" lark. Except, instead of life lessons taught by an adorable lion or Golden Retriever, the alleged protagonists are a mischief of rats. Willard, tired of being used for his boss' gain, in turn, uses Ben and his "co-workers" for comeuppance against Martin. A sly dig at office politics, *Willard* proves that relations between employer and employee are tough above *and* below the floorboards.

The screenplay by Gilbert Ralston, and based on the novel *Ratman's Notebooks* by Stephen Gilbert, is rather episodic until Ben starts making his presence known, and then becomes a tightly wound tale as the stakes are raised. The only two characters completely fleshed out are Willard and Martin, which is fine, as the lean 95-minute running time plays well with a two-character showcase. Director Daniel Mann, while certainly not a stylist, is exceptional with actors. Here is no exception, as Elsa Lanchester and Sondra Locke register well even with such underwritten roles.

But as I said, it's a two-man show. Ernest Borgnine invests Martin with oily arrogance, exuding a con man's condescension with a smile. Bruce Davison's All-American Ken doll looks were a deterrent at the start of his career, making it hard for people to see below the surface. As he aged, the public focused less on his appearance and more on the amazing actor underneath. His youth works to his advantage here—at first, we feel unthreatened by Willard, and take great pity on him, as he tries to make a go at life with the cards stacking up higher against him. But look closer, and see the anguish play out in Davison's eyes, his face, his stature, as his dreams crumble like so much drywall in a dilapidated home. It's a great portrayal of a desperate loner, cornered and trying to claw his way up the ladder of success.

Willard spawned a whole subgenre that thrived in the 1970s, but while giant chickens, killer bears, and gargantuan ants flooded the drive-ins, we should never forget this simple tale of friendship and betrayal, between a man and his rat, that started it all. How popular was *Willard*? The year 1972 brought a sequel, *Ben*, with a title song of yearning performed by a teenage Michael Jackson. Now there's someone who could have used a friend.

═══════════════

Success breeds sequels, which also breed weird ballads
sung to rats. Why yes, there were a lot of hard drugs
going around in the 1970s, why do you ask?

Ben (1972)

Sometimes a successful sequel requires the filmmakers to tear apart what made the previous entry work, and piece together something new; perhaps just keeping the engine and the chassis, and other car stuff that I know nothing about. What I do know, however, is that when you rebuild a clever psychodrama like *Willard* (1971) and turn it into a "Rats Gone Wild" meets "Disney-Lonely-Sick-Boy" flick, the result is *Ben*. And that result is a model so endearingly odd I'm amazed it made it off the assembly line at all.

Released by Cinerama Releasing in late June stateside with a world-wide rollout in the fall, *Ben* was viewed by critics at the time as a laughable follow-up to a film that didn't exactly win over reviewers. They simply found the premise and execution silly and moved on. They're not wrong, but why does a horror film have to be scary to work? *Ben* is

weird, folks—especially for the mainstream—and that's always a win to me.

The film opens with the finale of *Willard*, as our titular antihero (Bruce Davison) gets his comeuppance from Ben and several of his friends. On to the scene arrives Detective Cliff Kirtland, who finds Willard's notebook filled with rants, ravings, and how-tos on training a squad of vermin. Hanging on his every action is veteran reporter Billy Hatfield, who naturally suspects something is amiss when Willard is covered in bites yet nary a rat is found.

As a group of onlookers watches the formerly warmer Davison being carted away, one family stands out: the Garrisons—mom Beth, daughter Eve, and young son Danny, a triple-threat composer, puppeteer, and heart disease sufferer. As it turns out, Danny has one more talent: he can talk to the animals! Specifically, Ben; as he plays with his marionettes in his garage/playhouse, Danny is befriended by our furry murderer even as Ben is amassing an entire army of rats within the L.A. sewers. Will Ben & Company take over the city? Will Danny's ticker hold out with all this to-do?

Ben doesn't have a lot on its mind, but what it does say speaks volumes about sequels. Completely ditching the power struggles and office politics of *Willard* for a strange mix of sentimentality and sewer soirees, it doubles down on the mayhem while shoehorning in a story that would make Uncle Walt proud.

There are scores of vermin below the streets and were they the sole focus of the story, it would be another entertaining, yet slight addition to our Animal Killdom festival. Where *Ben* flies is the union of the carnage with Danny's illness. Danny is a sick little boy who earns audiences' sympathy with his heart condition: lonely and facing his mortality, he asks his sister if he could die, and she says "maybe." *Wow*, Meredith Baxter, not cool. I mean, it was the 1970s; you wouldn't want a healthy child to be responsible for all the mayhem, would you? That could be misconstrued as too *uplifting*.

So Danny wiles away his days composing cloying songs for his puppet show, and the highlight of the whole shebang for me, writing a song on the piano for his new friend Ben. And yes, it is the same loopy love song that Michael Jackson sings over the closing credits and won a Golden Globe for. I've never felt a purer joy than watching Montgomery tickle the ivories as he comes up with *each exact line* of the song. I mean, it's a pretty well-put-together tune; to see Baxter sidle up and not even be surprised he wrote it is par for the course in a film that tampers with the conventional.

Bing Crosby Productions felt the need to supersize the infestation with a sewer-bound finale. Before that happens, however, the rats nibble here and there, including my second favorite moment in the film, when they take over a health spa that plays as much more comical than probably intended. Who's to say? Tonally, this film plays blindfolded darts like a champ. They must have assumed audiences were there for the carnage, and they were probably right.

Director Phil Karlson doesn't bring much visually to the table, but he pulls solid early performances from Montgomery and Baxter; Gilbert Ralston's script offers nothing profound for them to *say*, but holy moly does he give them interesting things to *do*.

Which is why we're here, right? It may not be as smart as *Willard*, but the odd mixture of Disney and danger is never less than fascinating, and easily as entertaining. And that's why I'll always have a friend in *Ben*. (*In Bennn*.)

After Jaws became the new summer ideal,
the B circuit went to work emulating. The following film
roared its way to the top of the box office...

Grizzly (1976)

Following the massive success of *Jaws* (1975), producers were chomping at the bit to replicate its grosses. Far too many movies to mention here, but suffice it to say that most were stinkers, and none could put a dent in the box office. However, one little film somehow managed to not only rake in big bucks—more than $39 million—in its wake but paid "homage" to the soon-to-be Universal classic. William Girdler's Bad Bear Bonanza *Grizzly* follows it so closely I'm amazed *Jaws* doesn't have a big black snout rammed up its gray-finned keister. No matter what its inspiration, *Grizzly* is a B movie blast.

Released domestically in May 1976, *Grizzly* was a surprise smash success, and critics derided the film as derivative, amateurish, and wholly without merit. Derivative? Absolutely! Amateurish and without merit? It beats dinner theater in the Poconos, folks, and merit is subjective. If your goal is to lean back and be entertained, *Grizzly* more than meets the criteria.

The story: We start with beautiful aerial cinematography of a Northwestern national park; campers are everywhere, backpacking and enjoying the outdoors in all its woodsy splendor. First on the menu are two female campers whose only crime is being chosen to kick off the carnage. With the swipe of a claw, limbs start flying and a wooden shed provides no

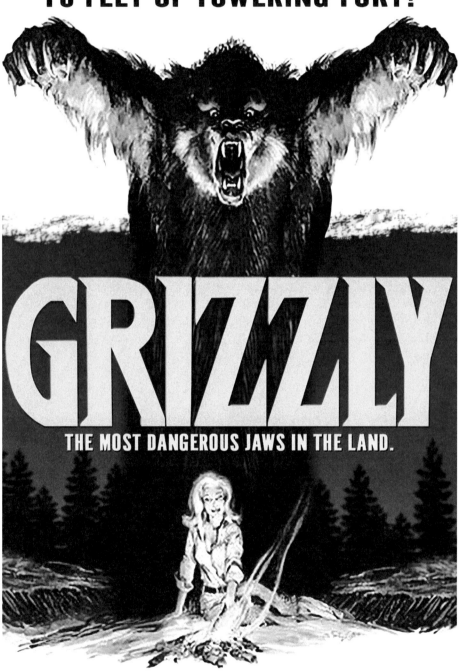

Grizzly, Film Ventures International, 1976

haven, but merely gives our antagonist an ample supply of toothpicks for post-consumption.

Chief Ranger Kelly (B legend Christopher George) searches for and finds the two dead girls. Presenting the evidence to his boss that it was a bear attack, Park Supervisor Kittridge bites his head off and tells Kelly to handle the situation. To do so, he enlists the help of Scott (B legend Richard Jaeckel), a naturalist, and Don (also B legend Andrew Prine), a helicopter pilot. When more attacks occur, Kelly wants to shut down the park, but Kittridge refuses, as he doesn't want to cause a panic.

When even more fur-bearing atrocities happen, Kelly is allowed to shut down two sectors of the park, I suppose in the hope that the bear will respect zoning divisions. Of course, this doesn't slow down the big fella so Kittridge sends out a group of drunken hunters to take care of business. Frustrated, Kelly, Don, and Scott take to the mountains to dispense of old Smokey themselves.

Now, take out the four main characters mentioned above and swap them with four from *Jaws*, and change the setting from land to sea. Tada! Screenwriting Mad Libs in reverse. Part of the appeal of *Grizzly* is playing spot the similarities between the two. I haven't even mentioned Kelly's girlfriend Allison, played by Joan McCall, who is married in real life to producer and co-writer David Sheldon, mirroring Lorraine Gary (*Jaws*' Mrs. Brody) and President of MCA Sid Sheinberg, who oversaw *Jaws*. And it goes on and on. Try playing it as a drinking game. If you're still standing by the third reel without keeling over from alcohol poisoning, you should be picking out a rehab center to visit.

Director Girdler is largely responsible for this ferocious forest tale. He previously helmed the Blaxploitation possession film *Abby* (1974) for American International Pictures (AIP), which Warner Bros. believed ripped off *The Exorcist* so much that they sued them and had it removed from theaters. Now, there were similarities between those two—but not nearly as flagrant as our fuzzy Landshark and *Jaws*.

Regardless, Girdler was a solid director who kept getting better at his craft with each film. He was good with actors, and here pulls spirited, relaxed performances from each of the headliners. His use of widescreen is also impressive, lending a sense of grandeur and scope to a relatively low-budget feature.

Considering how relentlessly silly the screenplay is, complete with painful dialogue, it's a miracle he was able to create such an entertaining creature feature. He followed this with only two more films, 1977's *Day of the Animals* and 1978's engagingly weird *The Manitou*, before dying in a tragic helicopter accident that same year. A pity—I'm pretty sure he was just getting warmed up.

Oh, and don't be scared off by the PG rating—as I said, the limbs are flying, heads are rolling (human and otherwise) and there's more than enough blood to keep a horror fan happy. It must have been nap time at the MPAA when this was screened for a rating.

Some films have ambitions, large in scope with a clear view of the big picture. Other films, like *Grizzly*, are content to provide a few smiles and cheap thrills while the images dance across the screen. Sometimes not seeing the forest for the trees works just fine for me.

Next, we're overrun with pissed-off pesticidic spiders?
Fear not, your favorite 1960s space cowboy will save the day!
Or not. This was the 1970s...

Kingdom of the Spiders (1977)

Full disclosure: I hate spiders. Like really, really despise them. God's creatures blah blah blah—save it. They are absolutely, without question, the most insidious, terrifying *things* on the planet. Now, horror films *about* arachnids? Well, that's different. They have a built-in creepiness factor that ensures they will hit the icky button with me—not my go-to sensation for horror, but still creating a sensation while I watch—which promises a memorable experience.

But when you add in a level of fun, and with *Kingdom of the Spiders*, a ridiculously high quotient of it, I pivot from respect to awe in the space of 97 minutes. Not for the spiders—that will never happen as long as I'm gulping air. But the film? I'm in awe, with every viewing. It's my favorite Animal Killdom film, my favorite John "Bud" Cardos directorial effort, and hands down my favorite William Shatner performance. It's a dang gone gem.

Released by Dimension Pictures in November, *Kingdom* was a surprise hit. Dismissed by most critics at the time as just another goofy B picture (guilty!), *Killdom of the*—oops sorry, *Kingdom of the Spiders* has survived and thrived for over forty years because it refuses to be anything less than entertaining, fast-paced, thrilling, and loaded with those nasty buggers that to this day have me checking over doorways and under sheets.

Our film opens with the title zooming at the screen, a screeching symbol that subtlety will hold no currency here. Then a soothing country ballad by rockabilly legend Dorsey Burnette informs us all we need to know about "Peaceful Verde Valley," as we see various beautiful, rugged

A LARRY WOOLNER / MICKEY ZIDE Presentation
starring **WILLIAM SHATNER**
co-starring **TIFFANY BOLLING** · **WOODY STRODE** · and introducing **ALTOVISE DAVIS**
LIEUX DRESSLER · DAVID McLEAN · NATASHA RYAN · MARCY LAFFERTY · Produced by IGO KANTOR and JEFFREY M. SNELLER
Executive Producer HENRY FOWNES · Screenplay by RICHARD ROBINSON and ALAN CAILLOU · Directed by JOHN BUD CARDOS
An ARACHNID Production · COLOR   ☰☰ **United Artists**
A Transamerica Company

"KINGDOM OF THE SPIDERS"

Kingdom of the Spiders, Dimension Pictures, 1977

Arizona landscapes. Cut to the Colby ranch, as their prize calf grazes in the field. A POV of something low and ominous crawling towards it ends with a startled look on the calf's face (not to mention a stock music cue courtesy of "The Twilight Zone"). Walter Colby (Woody Strode) calls in our protagonist and local vet, Rack Hansen (Shatner), to investigate his prized possession's sudden illness.

Back at the lab, Rack determines the calf's death was caused by an unknown venom. He sends away a sample to the city and in return the city sends Diane Ashley (Tiffany Bolling), their finest entomologist, to investigate. It was spider venom, you see, and off they go to find the nest at the Colby ranch. Miss Ashley offers up some exposition as to why the spiders would attack, and our 1970s horror bingo card proclaims that pesticides win out. Since the spiders won't eat the DDT-laced food, they've decided to find alternative sources.

After another attack on Colby's livestock, the decision is finally made to burn the spider hill to the ground. Naturally, the spiders don't take kindly to being driven from their lair and decide to visit good old Verde Valley, without a hint of peacefulness. Rack, Diane, and others hole up at Emma Washburn's lodge in the hopes of fending off the arachnid attack while the town is overrun with unwelcome guests. Can they stave off the invasion, or will they become Happy Meals to Go for the ugly critters?

While there is nothing new under the Arizona sun, *Kingdom* is packed with Saturday matinee goodness; from a dashing hero to a story that whips from one scene to another with a steady urgency, all thanks to the fluid editing of Steve Zaillian, who would go on to write *Schindler's List*. It offers everything that accompanies greasy popcorn and carbonated delights; the only problem is, *this thing is vicious*. It's one of those films that should have been rated R instead of PG just on tone alone, for you will witness people being cocooned for future consumption; animals suffering painful deaths; and for good measure, not even the kiddies are safe.

The film picks uncanny locales to hoist its phobia on the viewer; you probably would flip your gourd if tarantulas started crawling through your car vents, or perhaps a backyard where the only relatively safe place to stay is the swing set itself. Can I interest you in a discarded tire, or maybe a nightstand drawer? It's all here, and more. I've only told you about the outer webbing.

Credit director John "Bud" Cardos and screenwriters Richard Robinson & Alan Caillou for creating at least a semi-believable scenario—I mean, a desert town could be overrun by spiders, although I doubt the death toll would reach *that* high before many could make it to safety. They're on the ground; step on them! It's not like they're raining from the sky. No, that would be Australia.

Speaking of flattened spider cakes, real tarantulas were used in the production—a tenth of the budget, $10 bucks a pop, 5,000 live spiders crawling everywhere, and on everyone. Just remember these were different times; I'm sure many people would be saddened to know that a good amount of them didn't make it out alive. Today, every last critter would be computer generated, and fine, let them all live! Whatever! (I'm kidding, of course. Burn them all with fire.) The cast is game: Bolling and a lively bunch manage to keep a straight face which is really all one could ask for.

But you know damn well why you're here; first name Rack, last name Hansen, an imperfect hero for uncertain times. This film was made in between Shatner's *Star Trek* TV glory and the theatrical *Star Trek* renaissance. *Kingdom* was not his first 1970s stab at straight-up horror on the big screen; check out *The Devil's Rain* (1975) for chuckles and chills. That film was firmly rooted in the broader range of Shatner's palette; probably the most surprising thing about *Kingdom* is how restrained he is on the Shatner Scale, as he reins in the majority of his mannerisms and actively seems to be participating in the scenes instead of waiting for his turn to speak. This isn't to say there aren't more than a few classic Shatner-isms, but because he tends to go wide, the narrow stands out. A case in point is the ending. His reaction shots in the last thirty seconds are probably the most honest, wrenching work he's done. I wouldn't dream of giving it away, as it is one of the aptest endings of any horror film from the 1970s; but if you know the decade's propensity for playing on the downbeat, you'll dig the hell out of it.

Most Animal Killdom films are enjoyable; *Frogs, Grizzly, Day of the Animals*, and many others offer varying degrees of pomp and dire circumstances for the viewer. I suppose it depends on what ruffles your feathers. But at the end of the day, it doesn't matter if it's a swarm of rats, a posse of mountain lions, or a flock of seagulls; if the filmmakers can't convert that fear into an entertaining terror experience you might as well be watching Animal Planet. *Kingdom of the Spiders* offers that experience. And if those hairy eight-legged bastards *do* show up on National Geographic, I'll run the 40-yard dash out of my living room faster than Rack Hansen himself.

━━━━━━━━━━━━━━━━

And now, our final feature in The Animal Killdom…
Bradford Dillman has himself wrapped up in freshwater killers,
Keenan Wynn, and the best tribute to the little shark movie that could.
Never trust the government, especially when they're hiding…

Piranha (1978)

Homage in film can be a tricky proposition. Hew too close to the original, and you're just making copies with no new toner; veer too far away and folks will wonder why you bothered. Joe Dante's *Piranha* is that perfect beast then—a *Jaws* "homage" that bows to its source while winking at the audience, and yet still manages to be a wholly separate, wildly entertaining ride.

Released by Roger Corman's New World Pictures in North America in early August (capitalizing on *Jaws*' still undulating waves), *Piranha* was that rare New World phenomenon: It made some good coin AND was well received by critics. Steven Spielberg himself was so won over by Dante's take and talent that it led to collaborations on *Twilight Zone: The Movie*, *Gremlins*, and other projects. *Piranha* proves that you can hug someone, slap a "Kick Me" sign on their back, and they'll *still* take you out to dinner—as long as you mean well.

Our story opens with a pair of backpackers who decide to take a moonlit skinny dip in what they think is an abandoned swimming pool. Before you can say "Where's the buoy?" both are sucked under as the music swells and the credits roll. We then meet skip tracer Maggie, who heads up the mountain to locate one of the aforementioned missing hikers. She turns to alcoholic mountain man Paul (Bradford Dillman) for help, which leads them to a closed government treatment plant and a paranoid government scientist played by sci-fi totem Kevin McCarthy. Believing the missing teens to be in the pool, Maggie drains it, leading our titular creatures right into the river, and very hungry.

Of course, the fish were being bred with salt water as well, meaning they could eventually hit the open ocean. Regardless, our heroes have to head downstream and warn everyone at (a) the grand opening of Buck Gardner's (played by Dick Miller) aquatic amusement park, and (b) the local summer camp on the river which naturally houses Paul's daughter. Will he and the gang be able to thwart the toothy menace?

To call *Piranha* a cheap knockoff of *Jaws* is frankly, insane. If anything, it's a celebration of a type of film that Dante and screenwriter John Sayles (*Alligator*) grew up adoring: the aquatic monster movie. Make no mistake, clips on TV from *The Monster That Challenged the World* and *The Creature from the Black Lagoon* are very pointed references to the Atomic creature features of the 1950s. And really, the only differences between *Jaws* and these other films are its oversized but natural predator, the occasional government meddling, and $8 million. (Yes, I realize I'm grading on a talent curve as well. *Jaws* is pretty much flawless.) The opening scenes between *Jaws* and *Piranha* are *almost* identical, and that's intentional; the

very first image seen after the opening credits is someone playing the *Jaws* video game. *Piranha* knows the water in which it swims.

Sayles and Dante mount a love letter to these films; not only with direct links but overriding themes as well. *Naturally,* the government is involved in the development of the vicious species, and therefore mankind must pay for its transgressions. *Of course,* our troupe has to race against time to stop the menace after their warnings fall on deaf ears. But this is merely a skeleton for hanging a series of gags, gross-outs, and gleeful in-jokes shelled out for the B crowd. Dante's films are filled with plenty of goodwill and cheer, but it's all couched in a cartoonish, heightened atmosphere; it's even more pronounced in the second Sayles/Dante collaboration, *The Howling,* but then again werewolves offer a bigger playground, and a wider seesaw. So with fish, they choose to go *mean.*

Enter effects wunderkind Rob Bottin. He would later join the duo on the lupine bladder bonanza, and wow the world with his work on *The Thing* (1982) but here he revels in ripped flesh, gratuitous Keenan Wynn leg lacerations, and pools of bubbling blood accompanied by the high-pitched nibble noise. What I'm saying is this movie is *nasty,* and no more so than when Paul Bartel and his campers hold a day of watersports just as the piranhas are passing through; surprisingly, rubber dinghies are not the greatest safeguard against razor-sharp teeth. Not that Miller's water park fares any better—in fact, things get *much* worse—but flayed kiddie kibble certainly exceeds the Spielberg barometer of good taste.

And when you don't have Steven bucks, you don't get a Scheider, Dreyfuss, or Shaw; you get a Dillman, Menzies, Wynn, and Miller. I'm fine with that, and you should be too; because you also get a Barbara Steele thrown in for good measure as a sinister government expert. And they're all pretty great; I'm especially fond of Bradford Dillman as our mountain man, who comes across like Charlton Heston with a much smaller stick up his caboose, and New World regulars Bartel and Dick Miller provoke nothing but smiles.

But you don't need the money when you have the talent. Dante rose through the ranks at the Corman ranch editing trailers, so the filler quota is very low. Editor Mark Goldblatt cuts this thing within an inch of its life—even when the movie slows for sharp character beats it still *moves.*

Look, I saw both *Jaws 2* and *Piranha* in the summer of 1978, and there's no question which one earned my parents' hard-won money; the former reeks of desperation while the latter bathes in un-ironic, nostalgic inspiration. It's pretty easy to see why Mr. Spielberg thought *Piranha* was the better Catch of the Day.

Festival Two:
Those Darn Kids!

The moppets are our future, or so we've been told for decades; every generation touts the next as the Last Great Hope for the world, and that's as it should be. It's called optimism. It's pretty much the opposite of what we deal with in horror, and *definitely* what we're dealing with in this festival: What happens when good kids go bad? Real life has certainly mapped out the maze of a juvenile correctional path; usually a disadvantaged or abusive upbringing followed by a narrow life of roadblocks and temptation. Sobering stuff.

Hey, cheer up! In *our* dark and heightened corner of the world, the cherubs never face anything as mundane as incarceration, and the thought of recidivism isn't in their vocabulary. No, our kids run the gamut from rain-slicked slashettes to tourist trapping tinies. Over here, children don't always obey the rules. (Okay, never.)

Does this please us, fans of the absurd and shocking? You bet, because kiddie killers have always been taboo—not to our unholy brethren, but rather the pious pearl clutchers who believe little ones, on film as in life, should be seen and heard, but only to blow rainbows out their asses.

By the time the 1970s hit, kids dying on screen wasn't new; and if a kid was labeled "evil," they were usually taken away by the police, given a fitting punishment, and locked away. But making the children the antagonists—and getting away with it, often—immediately puts the viewer on edge, and left to face an uncomfortable question: If you can't trust your kids, who can you trust?

The filmmakers ahead all chose children to convey whatever their message was; it's no different than using Godzilla as a cry of atomic agony—it's just good old symbolism, folks. But we're not talking about a giant lizard, we're talking about innocent lambs. Whether they are being dispatched or doing the dismemberment, children playing around with death—close up and personal—simply wasn't thought about in mainstream entertainment.

People were *sort of* prepared when 1956's *The Bad Seed* hit the screen—smash novel, Broadway play, next stop Hollywood—but there was no turning back. The popularity of the film—even as a mild provocation—was enough to jumpstart a new subgenre that took full flight during the "everything goes" 1970s.

So hats off to this next group of films; when the show starts you will find huggable death dealers, troglodytes, sunbaked slaughter, and so much more. They may not *all* have an important message on their minds, but I can promise you this: No rainbows.

Let's start the show! Our first feature is in black & white,
which aligns perfectly with a morality lesson
not exactly built for subtlety or shading...

The Bad Seed (1956)

Killer kids started pulsating on the horror radar with *The Exorcist* (1973) and *The Omen* (1976). Horrific as these tots were, their actions were explained away by demonic possession and satanic lineage, respectively. Regardless of their cause, the sight of a youngster engaged in heinous behavior was still shocking. Now, roll back the clock a couple of decades and drop a sociopathic eight-year-old girl in the middle of apple pie–strewn *Ozzie & Harriet* America, and what do you get? *The Bad Seed*, that's what; a wonderfully odd ode to li'l murderers and the mothers who love them.

Released by Warner Bros. in September of 1956 and rolled out to the rest of the world over the next year and a half, *The Bad Seed* was an unqualified success. Not only that, it received four Academy Award nominations: Best Actress for Nancy Kelly, Best Actress in a Supporting Role for both Eileen Heckart and Patty McCormack, and Best Cinematography for Harold Rosson. That is quite the pedigree for a bizarre film about a killer kiddie with impeccable manners. Who says horror doesn't get any respect?

Little Rhoda (McCormack) is seeing her military big-shot daddy played by William Hopper off as he heads back to Washington. "Baskets of kisses" are cloyingly exchanged for "baskets of hugs," and so we know right off the bat that she's a daddy's girl, to the dismay of mom Christine (Kelly). Rhoda's closest confidant is landlady Monica, who also believes the child to be squeaky clean. Then a school picnic reveals that one of the children has drowned, and all the circumstantial evidence points to

Rhoda. Nobody would dare think an innocent cherub like Rhoda could be responsible until two things occur: First, the discovery that Christine's lineage may have some bats in the belfry, leading to several grown-up discussions regarding nature versus nurture; and second, the knowledge that Rhoda was quite insistent the penmanship medal awarded to poor little drowned Claude should have gone to *her*. As the evidence piles up, Christine must decide if punishing her with no dessert is enough of a deterrent to ending Rhoda's killing spree.

The Bad Seed had a meteoric rise in popular culture. William March's novel was published in April 1954; Maxwell Anderson's Broadway production opened in December of that same year, which was followed by the film less than two years later. And it's understandable—the subject matter was fresh and novel—what parent could fathom their child being a killer? Their *teenager*, sure—the 1950s brought about the rise of teenage culture and subsequent rebellion, but wee ones? Unthinkable.

Now, as subversive as the idea was, this was still the 1950s; the execution is all insinuation and description—audiences weren't even allowed to witness a toilet flush until *Psycho* in 1960. Different times called for different measures, and where the film version of *The Bad Seed* earns its weirdness stripes is in presentation.

Instead of taking a more naturalistic approach to the material, director Mervyn LeRoy essentially transports *The Bad Seed* from stage to screen with no change in tone whatsoever. Other than a couple of briefly shown artificial outdoor sets, all the activity is confined to the living room, kitchen, or Rhoda's bedroom.

Luckily, the skilled camerawork of Rosson keeps the tedium to a minimum, doing what he can to engage the audience visually. But it can't completely shake the staginess of the production, and I think that's done on purpose; by keeping up the wall of artifice (one entrance, one exit, hit your mark *here*) the viewer doesn't feel too close to the material—audiences still needed to be reminded that this was fiction, nothing more.

This opinion was shared by the producers and rating board as well—in the book and play, Christine fatally wounds herself with a gun after she gives her daughter an overdose of sleeping pills; yet Rhoda survives to kill another day. A delicious ending and one that bookworms and "sophisticated" Broadway audiences could wrap their heads around, but that wouldn't work for the Motion Picture Production Code—at that time in film, *criminals had to pay*. And I wouldn't dream of giving away their ultimate solution to those who haven't seen it yet, but it is amusingly abrupt and effective.

And if that wasn't enough to course-correct the moral turpitude of the material, the cast, as in the stage production, individually takes a bow for the camera, ending with Kelly putting McCormack over her knee and giving her a good spanking—*making sure the audience knows it's just pretending.* Jesus. I'm fairly confident the Production Code bought their reefer from the most hep teens in town.

It doesn't end there—most of the Broadway cast was ported over for the film, and judging by the results, no one told them they weren't still on the Great White Way. The performances are *very* melodramatic; the actors shoot for the rafters with each gesture and arched eyebrow. This isn't to say they aren't good—McCormack, Kelly, and Heckart (as Claude's grieving, alcoholic mother) all do well, just for the wrong medium. The film is all tell and no show, which is usually deadly on film unless the subject matter is as provocative as it is here.

Is evil bred? Is it born? It is the topic *du jour* amongst the adults here. Regardless, the plot keeps winding back around to Rhoda's behavior and her professed innocence, and when she finally explodes and confesses her irreversible sins to her mother, the effect is chilling. This is where McCormack earns her accolades, calmly detailing the horrific events as if describing the lunch menu in the cafeteria.

The Bad Seed, the play, was ahead of its time; it had the balls to put forth something taboo and groundbreaking for discerning audiences to absorb. By transposing the show directly to the screen, the filmmakers of *The Bad Seed* have created an oddly endearing melodrama that oscillates between the absurd and the thrilling. And regardless of which way the pendulum is swinging, the viewer is left hypnotized. Rhoda is psychotic and a liar—but she's so good at it, I think she deserves *some* kind of medal.

Let's move on from a naughty little girl
to a nasty little number from Alfred Sole
that does the Catholic Church no PR favors...

Alice, Sweet Alice (1976)

The Catholic Church—and religion in general—always seems to have a hard go of it in horror films. Whether seen as the last respite for the desperate (*The Exorcist*), or co-conspirators of evil (*The Omen*), the church has proven to be a wellspring of guilt and mistrust, useful tools for building a great horror tale. *Alice, Sweet Alice* is a sinister example of good old Catholic retribution, and the finest American version of a *giallo* to boot.

The film premiered in November 1976 at the Chicago International

Film Festival under its original title *Communion*. Columbia Pictures was originally supposed to distribute the film, but legal issues arose and they dropped it. Allied Artists, which stepped in but demanded a name change so people would not think of it as a religious film, came up with *Alice, Sweet Alice,* and released it in 1978. Reviews were very good, some critics even going as far as comparing director Alfred Sole to another Alfred, Hitchcock. But that wasn't the end of the road—the film was released again in 1981 as *Holy Terror*, this time to cash in on co-star Brooke Shields' popularity at the time (think *Endless Love*, Calvin Klein jeans, and *The Blue Lagoon*). The film didn't light the box office on fire under any of its guises but remains a startlingly effective slasher with a definite Italiano flavor.

Meet Alice, played by Paula Sheppard, and her younger sister Karen (Shields in her debut performance). Alice and Karen live with their mother Catherine, single and under the guidance of Father Tom, the kindly priest of the parish. Father Tom gifts Karen with his mother's crucifix as she prepares for her first communion. Alice, a genuinely creepy 12-year-old, scares Mrs. Tredoni, Father Tom's housekeeper, by wearing a translucent mask, then terrifies Karen in an abandoned warehouse wearing the same mask and a yellow raincoat. On the day of her communion, Karen is strangled to death by someone donning the same creepy outfit, in the back room of the church, and then put in a trunk and set on fire. Alice then shows up in Karen's place to receive communion as the body is discovered.

As the police investigate, Alice of course becomes the leading suspect in her sister's murder. The kids' father, Dom, arrives in town to be with his ex-wife Catherine and daughter Alice, as does Catherine's sister Annie (Jane Lowry). As the police look for more clues the body count rises, and Alice's behavior grows even more erratic. Is Alice responsible for the murders, or is there a larger tale of sin and sorrow at play?

Taking place in Paterson, New Jersey, in the 1960s, *Alice, Sweet Alice* uses its working-class surroundings to great effect, amplifying the horror amidst the mundane workaday life of its denizens, startling not only the victims but the audience with shock after shock. The backdrop of the Catholic Church, with its emphasis on ritualistic behaviors and obsessive worship, is the perfect juxtaposition, and a perverse parallel to the killings on hand.

The killer's motive is completely based on his/her belief system and is director Sole's heartfelt and heated response to being ex-communicated from the church after making an adult film, 1972's *Deep Sleep*. To say the film is anti–Catholic would be an understatement—however, you will find more religious iconography here than in the Vatican Gift Shop. The over-abundance of crosses and rosaries drives home the fervor by which the characters live their lives—which of course, blinded by their loss, leaves them open to danger.

It's very easy to see why Sole's work here was favorably compared to Hitchcock and Italian maestro Dario Argento in the press. He certainly shows a sure grasp of suspense—there are jumps here that Hitchcock would be envious of, as well as some unique camera angles that truly put the viewer on edge, unsure of when or where the killer will strike next. Sole also makes a calculated move that pays off brilliantly—he reveals the identity of the killer two-thirds of the way through, and in doing so makes the remainder even more suspenseful. Now *we* know who the killer is, and have to sweat out the rest of the film as the protagonists interact with the killer unknowingly. It's a great twist to a fairly standard revenge scenario.

As for Argento, we have the gloved and masked killer, a strong familial connection, and of course the religious backdrop—with the occasional hysterical bit of overacting thrown in for good measure. Sole was inspired to use the raincoat after seeing the killer in Nicolas Roeg's *Don't Look Now* (1973), a favorite film of his. It's a visual tactic that again, *seems* mundane, but paired with the mask, packs quite a wallop.

The performances are generally solid, selling Sole and Rosemary Ritvo's lines with a low-key earnestness that suits the solemnity of the material. There are a couple of rafter-shaking moments, but they are earned and appropriate to the story at hand. Being Catholic *does* lend itself to its fair share of drama. Ms. Shields acquits herself nicely in her debut, only onscreen for the first 20 minutes but making her mark in setting the tragedy in motion. Also of special note is Alphonso DeNoble as Mr. Alphonso, natch, the pedophilic landlord who has a very antagonistic relationship with Alice. He's sleazy, grimy, and in keeping with the virulent anti–Catholic stance, meets a suitable fate.

But the weight of the film truly falls on Paula Sheppard as Alice. How do you get a 12-year-old to convincingly play a detached, disturbed, potentially psychotic girl on the cusp of womanhood without going over the top? The answer is, you don't—you hire a *19-year-old* to play her. It's an amazing feat that Sheppard pulls off with aplomb—nuanced and disciplined, it's a shame that she only has one other acting credit on her resume, displaying an intelligence similar to a young Jodie Foster.

Alice, Sweet Alice will be more than a pleasant surprise to those seeking out fresh scares from the vaults. Smart, intense, and chilling, it provides the viewer with a sobering look at religious fervor taken to the blood-soaked extreme. The Sins of the Father, indeed.

Here's another perfect example of horror using children
as a narrative device in a forceful,
shocking, and suspenseful way;
ultimately arriving at the question…

Who Can Kill a Child?
aka *Island of the Damned* (1976)

Killer kids on film have been cyclical ever since *The Bad Seed*, as little Rhoda found that the best way to eliminate family problems was to eliminate the family; from that was born the blonde moppets in *Village of the Damned* (1960) and an attempt to attach a sci-fi explanation behind the killings. On to the turmoil of the 1970s then, as a political and philosophical bent was applied to *Who Can Kill a Child?* (1976) with devastating and lingering results.

WCKAC? was released in its native Spain in April under its original title *¿Quién puede matar a un niño?* and rolled out to various parts of the world under different titles thereafter: *Trapped, Would You Kill a Child? The Hex Massacre, Island of Death, Billy's Got a Sickle and He Looks Kinda Mad*, and most commonly *Island of the Damned* were all used to sell a film that is pretty hard to sell. This is a film filled with kids killing adults and adults returning the favor; tap dancing in a minefield would be a softer sell.

But that title and the film's protracted Mondo prologue create a somber mood that's hard to turn from: we open with nearly ten minutes of an ominous narrator showing us newsreel footage from Auschwitz, the Korean and Vietnam Wars, and others with the slaughter and devastation inflicted upon children. A somber start, to say the least.

Once that's over, we're on to the narrative. A married and expecting English couple, Tom and Evelyn (Lewis Fiander and Prunella Ransome) travel to Spain for a vacation. Their goal is to hit up an island off the coast that Tom had visited several years before. The couple rents a boat, and after four hours at sea, they arrive at their destination. It's a little quieter than Tom remembers it, however. A lot quieter, to be frank.

There are no people in the town at all; that is, except for the children. Laughing, playing, running, without a care in the world and wanting nothing to do with the visitors—for now. Soon, as Tom and Evelyn make their way through the deserted town front, they're faced with an inescapable truth: all of the adults are dead, and only the children remain—bloodied, smiling, and ready to play more games.

Who Can Kill a Child? is the truest version of this film, just as writer/

director Narciso Ibáñez Serrador intended: the evils of mankind lay waste to the innocent, and the narrative that follows is that reckoning. Take away that prologue, though, and it becomes a slightly different film.

I originally saw this in or around 1981 in the theater under the title *Island of the Damned* after AIP scooped it up for redistribution. The version I saw didn't have the prologue; what I witnessed was a straight-up killer kid movie. No less frightening, to be sure, but it was missing the solemnity that the audience feels with the extra footage. A pall, a sense of impending doom is cast with the prologue—you know retribution is at hand and deserved.

But the film manages to get Serrador's message across even without it: the loss of innocence. All children of war are forced to grow up regrettably fast (if they get to grow up at all); Serrador posits a world in which the victims become victors, the ghosts of every battle playing childhood games before laying waste to their elders in a sacramental lament. Evil begets evil, and karma wears the gruesome smile of a winsome child.

Who Can Kill dances under the bright Spanish sun, pulling the poison into the light to expose and kill it; cinematographer José Luis Alcaine gives Serrador a beautiful canvas to splay his twisted morality play across the screen. These picture postcards hold the moldy stench of regret in every tattered corner for the lost and the forsaken.

But the forsaken have a way of breaking through anyway; Serrador gives his children the outward appearance of normality, seemingly benign and naive—yet their actions are shown to be anything but. One shouldn't need a warning in a horror movie titled such as this, but the viewer needs to make peace with what happens; kids will die and they will kill—willingly, through mass hypnosis, or a psychic sea change without explanation. Fifteen years earlier, it would have been radiation; 20 later and it would have been a remake of a 35-year-old film.

Fiander and Ransome are responsible for making us believe in the unthinkable, and their journey from confusion to fear and anger is palpable; Serrador eventually puts them in a *Night of the Living Dead* corner that is as distressingly bleak and ironic as it is tense. The craft sells the story, lifts it from its roots, and plants it somewhere even darker.

Who Can Kill a Child? is a film that ultimately asks us what price we'd pay for peace in the name of idols and gold. The answer is hidden behind a smile and a sickle, but it's there.

═══════════════════

From the sublime to the silly where this film will always reside, it brings the kids into the '80s without anything to say or do but offer radioactive hugs…

The Children (1980)

The Children deals with the disintegration of the family unit, and the decay of modern society. Just kidding! *The Children* is about radioactive kids who like to give hugs and burn people up real good. Some horror films *do* have subtext, with layers peeled back to reveal inner truths about ourselves and the world. And some horror films are content to just show children having their hands cut off with a samurai sword.

Released in June 1980, *The Children* was actually quite a success for a low-budget film, playing to packed theaters and drive-ins alike. Not too shabby for a truly bizarre, high-concept scare fest.

Okay, here we go: Two workers at a nuclear plant get a reading that there's a malfunction. After a quick glance around the facility, and spent from their two-minute search for the problem, they lock up and call it a day. However, the viewer sees a leak from a nearby pipe, which can only mean one thing—yellow radioactive gas. Soon the school bus carrying five kids home goes through the cloud of yellow dust, as does the car driven by the protagonist's wife, Cathy, who happens to be very pregnant.

Intrepid Sheriff Billy Hart notices the bus abandoned by the cemetery shortly thereafter and begins a leisurely search for the children, including visits to the following parents. First, the local lesbian doctor, who hates men so much she just scowls and rolls her eyes. Next, we have the rich lady, who likes to bathe topless while her boyfriend pumps weights, and finds it delightful that there could be a kidnapping in Ravensback even though it involves her child. Last but not least, we have the protagonist John, who seems perpetually pissed off, and slightly inconvenienced that he has to help find his missing daughter. Our heroes search between the cemetery and three houses used for the entire film, hoping to find the missing children.

Meanwhile, the kids, looking a little pale, with black under their eyes and their fingernails, begin their journey home, one extra crispy hug at a time. Sheriff Billy and John have a final showdown with the tots at John's barn; discovering that the only way to kill them is to cut their hands off with the aforementioned samurai sword, they lay waste to the brood one pasty-faced, smiling munchkin at a time. Is this the end of the nightmare? Or will there be another generation of … *The Children*?

What do I love about this film? For starters—the adult characters in this film act so odd and removed from reality, I'm not sure if I would fear them or the kids more if I was passing through town. No one—with the exception of the sheriff, and occasionally Cathy, AND when John takes a break from yelling at his wife—seems to give a red hot damn about the kids. This extends to the unborn—in one scene, Cathy, stressed out by

Something terrifying has happened to...

the disappearance of the children, lights up a cigarette, looks down at her belly, pats it, and says, "Sorry!" Oh, there's plenty more where that came from.

This was director Max Kalmanowicz's first feature, and he shows no rapport with the performers here; he gets awkward performances from good actors (Martin Shakar, Gale Garnett, and Gil Rogers) and bad (most everyone else). No one phones it in though; these thespians give it their all, but where they put it remains a mystery. Having said that, Kalmanowicz shoots the death scenes very well—when the kids show up outside the general store, and their smiling faces are reflected in the window; and anytime they dole out one of their killer hugs, yellow plumes of gas envelop the parents as they are burned alive. Good stuff—ghoulish and delightful.

A good horror film can be elevated with an effective soundtrack, and horror fans were rewarded twice that same year because Harry Manfredini uses almost the exact same music for his score of *Friday the 13th*. Seriously—I was waiting for Mrs. Voorhees to pop out of the woods half the time.

The effects work by Craig Lyman is effective in the quick dissolves as the adults get fried, leaving their faces and bodies charred and scarred. However, pretending a hand is cut off by tucking it up a sleeve is something we used to do in elementary school. Fine, I still do it.

The Children didn't win any awards and it never makes any "best of" lists, but it holds a special place in my heart for following through on its taboo premise—kids being killed, radioactive or not—with a ton of (nuclear) energy, bad parenting, and warm hugs. Sometimes you just want to see children have their hands cut off with a samurai sword.

This is the proper way to end this festival;
a film so wrongheaded and bizarre
that the only defense I have is it's Canadian.
Sorry! Don't warm up the car just yet as we head deep into...

The Pit (1981)

What appears on the page is not always what appears on the screen. The screenwriter lays out what they *hope* to see translated, but that's not always the case. However, sometimes a film will morph from the pen to the multiplex in a post-faithful state that exceeds expectations. One such film is *The Pit*, a Canadian-made, U.S.-lensed flick that started out as a

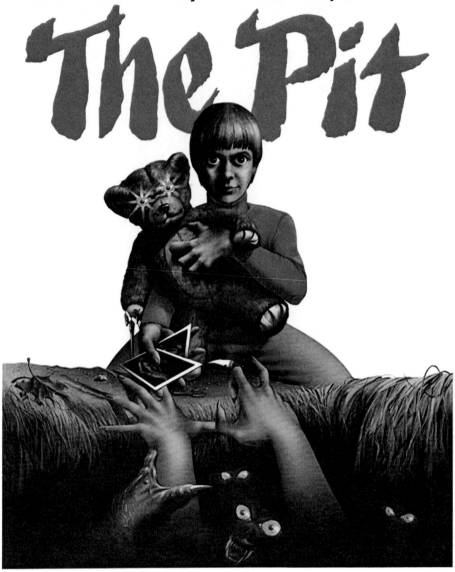

AMULET PICTURES presents "THE PIT" starring SAMMY SNYDERS and JEANNIE ELIAS
Original Screenplay by IAN A. STUART • Music by VICTOR DAVIES
Produced by BENNET FODE • Directed by LEW LEHMAN • Executive Producer JOHN F. BASSETT
Director of Photography FRED GUTHE • Editor RIK MORDEN / AN AMULET PICTURES RELEASE

The Pit, New World Pictures, 1981

psychological breakdown of a delusional little boy, and ended up in B Movie Heaven, where it is personally fanned and fed grapes by Ed Wood and William Castle on a daily basis. There's no other film quite like it.

The Pit, aka Teddy, was thrust upon an unsuspecting public on October 23 by New World Pictures in the States; it died at the box office and did not endear itself to the critical community. This makes total sense because *The Pit* is extremely compelling but completely insane; this thing is weird even by New World's standards.

How weird, exactly? Let's start in the middle since that's what the filmmakers decided to do. An adolescent bully and his girlfriend are led into the woods on a promise of hidden treasure by Jamie, the "hero" of our story. As soon as the bully sifts through the bag of promised goodies, he's pushed into the depths of the titular object where we hear him being eaten by *something*. We then rewind to the beginning of the story with Jamie's parents heading out of town, leaving him in the stead of babysitter Sandy, a local college student majoring in psychology.

Jamie confides in Sandy that there's a pit filled with, as he calls them, "tra-la-logs"—he means troglodytes, but I'm not sure the filmmakers do; they look like giant porcupines with glowing red eyes—and he feeds them butcher's meat to keep them satiated. Sandy thinks it's nothing more than the folly of a pubescent twelve-year-old. Before long Jamie is compelled to feed his tormentors to the denizens of the pit; will Sandy realize the truth before it's too late?

Okay, so far *The Pit* sounds like just a goofy, fun, B monster movie. However, we haven't even started to lacquer on the weird yet.

In Ian A. Stuart's original screenplay, Jamie is supposed to be eight or nine years old, not twelve. By changing his age, director Lew Lehman alters the tone of the film completely, yet preserves some of Jamie's pre-adolescent attributes. He still has a teddy bear that he converses with, wants Sandy to tuck him into bed, and in the film's ickiest scene, he has her wash his back during tubby time.

And yet significant portions of *The Pit* seem practically focus-grouped towards the adolescent male fantasy. Jamie is obsessed with the town librarian, Mrs. Livingstone (Laura Hollingsworth, I presume?). So taken is he with her updo and glasses that engulf her pretty face—a standard pubescent male dreamscape—that he (a) cuts out pictures from the library's book on nude photography, pastes on the librarian's head, and sends them to her; and (b) pretends he kidnapped her niece and blackmails her to strip in front of her window while he takes Polaroids if she wants to see her alive again. Not content with drooling over pics of Mrs. Livingstone, Jamie ogles Sandy as she sleeps and as she showers, professing his affections by smearing "I love you" on the steamed mirror.

But Stuart's vision fights for screen time too; Jamie is still portrayed as a sympathetic boy regardless of his borderline psychotic, leering behavior. Allusions to familial sexual abuse arise during the bathing sequence, and for whatever reason, Jamie seems to be the town punching bag. On the surface, he appears to be just an annoying twelve-year-old boy. It isn't hard to see the character study that Stuart was shooting for; but when Lehman externalizes Jamie's flights of fancy, it crashes any chance of being taken seriously, and the landing gear had already faltered on that approach.

In the screenplay, Teddy and the troglodytes are merely a figment of Jamie's diseased mind. On screen, Teddy is given a sentient moment where he turns his head towards the camera and of course, our troglodytes are not only *real*, they're unleashed upon the town when Jamie gives them a rope to climb out of the pit and fend for themselves.

So, in the struggle between the somber intentions of the page and the gleeful exploitation received, who wins? The viewer, that's who. We still get our monster munches and nudity, but it's the undercurrent of rippling psychosleaze that really sets this oddity apart. And hats off to adolescent Sammy Snyders for portraying Jamie, amongst the madness, like the protagonist in an ABC Afterschool Special—his aww-shucks dourness contrasting beautifully against the lurid shenanigans. Jeannie Elias holds her own as Sandy too; her megawatt smile standing out like a rose blooming in an outhouse, creating someone very likable *and* relatable. It's pretty important in a film this ungrounded to have someone to root for.

And yet all the disparate elements somehow come together; I suppose there's a willingness on behalf of the viewer to not only *accept* the events as they unfold but actively pursue a resolution that happily will *not* materialize—what you get instead wraps a giddy bow around the whole damn affair. Oh, I almost forgot! You get a ghost too. Was it in the script? Who knows? As the presiding Head Trog of The Pit Booster Club (Canadian Chapter), I have to tell you—if you're ever in doubt, you just need to recite our pledge: If it fits in *The Pit*, it must be legit.

Festival Three:
The Blood on Satan's B-Roll

We're going right to the top—or is it the bottom?—with our third festival's featured star... Satan! Get out your horns and pitchforks as we dive into the sacred and profane, all from the safety of a theater or drive-in, or the sanctity of one's own home. Festival Three, *The Blood on Satan's B-Roll*, is dedicated to films that bring baggage with them: a belief system.

What—or who—we believe in, spiritually, can influence how we see things; an extremely religious person may find a horror film with a direct line to God and the Devil so profound, it shakes them to their very core. Others, like the Catholic Church itself, will go out of their way to have this degrading "filth" removed from the public eye. Filmgoers were beside themselves when *The Exorcist* (1973) came out; fainting in the aisles, ambulances called, and William Girdler taking notes for *Abby* (1974). It was truly unprecedented.

Satanic horror can cut into and overwhelm a viewer's psyche, *especially* if their core beliefs are challenged or threatened; yes I believe in God, therefore... The Devil must be real too, right?

It's that seed of doubt in their minds: yeah, I'm willing to bet everything on God Inc., but what if Beelzebub gets me? You know, through the power of film. And some people will tell you that the temptation—the lure—of evil is *so* strong in satanic horror films that just watching them could send one to Satan's Grotto of Gonorrhea for eternity.

Pardon my French, but that's horse croissants. We bring our own preferences, biases, fears, and hopes to every film we watch; if we choose to engage those emotions, that's on us. If, however, we simply choose to view said films without any belief-clouding judgment, we will find much to love within the Evil Imp's Empire.

Why is that? Well for me, and I suspect several others, there are *serious* stakes at play; using the Devil is reaching back to the start of storytelling, and when filmmakers relish the opportunity to have the Behooved

One clomp around up here causing havoc—directly or through others—it speaks to the freedom of the genre.

It also reflects the overall nihilistic feel that permeates the films in this festival, with the exceptions being the first film featured, *The Devil Rides Out*, featuring a heroic (!) Christopher Lee battling a satanic cabal, and the last feature, *Fear No Evil*, which ends on a hopeful note. The three little piggies in the middle—*Race with the Devil*, *The Devil's Rain*, and *The Sentinel*—were all brought to you by the 1970s, the decade when the downbeat flourished in the culture, reflecting a time in society of great political upheaval, war, and Up with People. I get chills just thinking about them.

Personally, my three favorites in this festival are the middle ones, because of that pervading nihilism and mistrust associated with the Devil, who will do anything to get his way. It just sets the altar for spectacular mischief, is all; and who doesn't want that in their horror?

So let's light a candle, start a consensual relationship with a goat, betray our friends and family for eternal damnation, and get those devil horns in the air...

―――――――――――――

Our first entry is nothing but high-class, fast cars,
and an heroic Christopher Lee;
not your typical fare, especially for Hammer Studios....

The Devil Rides Out (1968)

It certainly took the movies a while to warm up to the idea of the Behooved One stepping across our screens. Looking to America, Hammer Films waited until Ira Levin's novel *Rosemary's Baby* was published and purchased for filming before going forth with their first satanic foray on film *The Devil Rides Out*.

Based on Dennis Wheatley's novel of the same name from 1934, it was Hammer's chance to move away from Gothic horror and prove that they could compete in an ever-changing market. But *The Devil Rides Out* did more than that—it provided Hammer with one of their very finest films, a chilling thrill ride that still delivers the devil-drenched goods.

Released in the U.K. in July 1968 by Warner-Pathé and December of the same year by 20th Century–Fox in the U.S., the film was commercially successful and, more importantly for Hammer, received very good notices. It showed that they could do contemporary features and not just period pieces. Now, contemporary in this case was the late 1920s, but castles were

The Devil Rides Out, Hammer Film Productions, 1968

replaced with mansions and horse-drawn carriages with automobiles, at least bringing them into the 20th century. Getting with the times, Hammer also enlisted the services of novelist turned screenwriter Richard Matheson, ensuring a screenplay that would play with modern audiences. And boy does it—*The Devil Rides Out* may not be as urbane and hip as *Rosemary*, but it showed that Hammer could put away the pitchforks and torches while still providing the terror they were so well known for.

Let's dive into the story, shall we? Nicholas, Duc de Richleau—Christopher Lee, playing the hero and loving it—picks up his friend Rex from an airport in England, with the intention of having a reunion with a third friend, Simon. However, Rex is told by Nicholas that Simon has not been heard from in months, and they speed off to his mansion to track him down. Simon is alive and well and is shocked to see his friends as he is hosting a "meeting" for a club to which he belongs—NOT the Knights of Columbus. Nicholas presumes something is amiss, which is confirmed when he peruses Simon's observatory and finds many signs of satanic activity; live fowl in a basket is a pretty good indicator. It turns out Simon is to be "re-baptized" into a satanic cult by Mocata, their suave and sinister leader.

The Devil Rides Out, which was released as *The Devil's Bride* stateside, still works today due to Hammer's resilience and pedigree harmonizing on a timely project. With horror tackling more realistic, gritty topics (a groundswell started by *Psycho* and others of its ilk), filmmakers looked for new ways to terrify audiences. Satanic cults and churches blossomed in the 1960s, and this proved to be new grist for the old mill. If you want to portray good versus evil, why not go right to the source and take on Ol' Scratch himself? Sensing the sea change, Hammer commissioned the novel, waited a few years, and then moved forward with production. They still hedged their bets a bit though. Unlike *Rosemary*, which comes across as cynical and jaded toward Christianity, *Devil* insinuates, okay *insists*, that God is responsible for the outcome of the story. So unlike most satanic films of the following decade, Hammer still wants you to believe everything will be all right in the end.

To this end, Matheson's screenplay doesn't leave you a breath to think about it until it's over. The film hits the ground running and barely lets up for 96 minutes. Car chases, fist fights, a pretty chaste implication of an orgy—we'll have it with our tea, thank you—and other assorted moments whiz by faster than most action films of *today*. Matheson also possesses an uncanny knack for making exposition sound interesting—it's practically all Lee spouts, and yet it doesn't drag the film, but rather adds to the atmosphere provided by the gorgeous Technicolor cinematography of Arthur Grant, and the razor sharp editing of Spencer Reeve.

Of course, the leader of the Hammer team is director Terence Fisher, whose *Curse of Frankenstein* and *Horror of Dracula* a decade earlier put Hammer deservedly on the horror map. He is clearly having a lot of fun here, with a chance to get away from bodices and candle filled hallways, and he makes the most of the opportunity. Of course, one of his great strengths was getting appropriate performances from his casts, this being no exception.

I say appropriate, as Fisher had a talent for modulating according to the material—where one of his *Dracula* films would lean towards the melodramatic, here he reels in the cast ever so slightly to fit the times and the material. The whole cast is fine, but the two main roles belong to Lee and Charles Gray, light against dark. Gray, with his magnificent, piercing silver eyes and disquieting smile, relishes the role of Mocata, imprinting with a whisper the dread of the unknown, even in what amounts to a not too considerable screen time.

The biggest delight, and the film's true selling point, however, is Christopher Lee. Rarely given the role of the hero, Lee digs in and owns the picture. Sporting a magnificent Van Dyke, with finely tailored suits and slicked back hair, he commands the screen with noble heroism that is in stark contrast to his hideous, pathetic turn as Frankenstein's monster a decade prior. He displays athleticism, and a calm litheness that shows maybe instead of fighting James Bond, he could have *portrayed* him. It really is a magnificent turn, and one of Lee's personal favorite roles.

Regardless of some dated effects, *The Devil Rides Out* still stands as one of Hammer's finest films, a firm reminder that old dogs *can* learn new tricks, and a glorious tribute to Lee. Even the most beloved villains, from time to time, deserve a chance to shine in the light of the virtuous.

═══════════════════

From sports and mansions to dirtbikes and Winnebagos,
our next film heads back across the pond to North America,
where their idea of satanic fun is to...

Race with the Devil (1975)

If you're going to race with the Devil,
you've got to be fast as hell!

Pull on up to the 1970s, when Satanic Panic fueled the nightmares of a horror-fed generation. Starting with *Rosemary's Baby*, exploding with *The*

Race with the Devil, 20th Century–Fox, 1975

Exorcist, and culminating with *The Omen*, hoofin' with the Horned One was a popular dance at the box office. *Race with the Devil* is a much less grandiose ride than its esteemed colleagues but remains a fun and interesting mesh of hot rods and Hell.

Released in June, *RWTD* came off the assembly line and was a sizable success for a modest B-flick. Car chase movies always turned a tidy profit on the circuit, exploitation filled with wheels and women perfectly suited for drive-ins across North America. By the time *RWTD* was released, satanic horror had saturated the market. But by crossbreeding it with a formula that still had gas in the tank, they were able to produce an energetic hybrid that could cruise for miles.

Let's pull out the map: Roger and Frank own a motorcycle dealership in good ole San Antonio, Texas. It's holiday time, so the boys gather up the wives, Kelly and Alice, for a ski trip to Aspen, Colorado. Their transport is a couple of motorcycles along with Frank's brand new, state of the art RV. Seriously, if you have a thing for vehicles, the decade is one big Auto Porn Emporium.

Camping in an empty field in central Texas, the boys sit outside the RV after a long day for several late-night libations. Across the creek, they see a group of hooded individuals performing a ceremony of some sort, culminating in human sacrifice. Scared, panicked, and drunk, Roger and Frank gain the attention of their new friends, who quickly give chase to our frightened travelers. From here on out, the gang is on the run from the cult, encountering menacing strangers at every turn, on the road and off, who won't let anyone be witness to their practices—and live to tell about it.

Most of the appeal of *RWTD* is on the surface, but it covers a lot of ground. You want exciting car chases before CGI made auto aviation not only possible but a requirement? You got it. Smiling Satanists who will stop at nothing to silence the heroes? Done. Cool rides and all the latest technology? Coming up. *RWTD* doesn't clutter up the proceedings with pesky things like character development and plot. And why should it? All the sacrifices to the B gods are met. (Well, most.) The movie is pretty chaste—with canine murder, vehicular violence, and of course, one nubile sacrifice to kickstart the action.

Director Jack Starrett provides little flash, filming in a flat style that reminds one of the dazzling camera work of "Quincy, M.E." But it doesn't matter, as he comes alive in the action set pieces, with kinetic stunt work and crashes. As well, he shoots with an economy that suits the material, paring it down to good versus evil in earthbound form—Heaven and Hell battling it out on the streets, metal on metal, tires burning with the hot smoke of Hades.

The screenplay by Wes Bishop and Lee Frost (*The Thing with Two Heads*—yikes) doesn't go deep on the cult angle, no heavy mythology is explored, which is probably the big reason why *RWTD* isn't mentioned in horror circles as much. The emphasis is on the action, with the sacrifice and subsequent pursuit merely a device to hang the car chases on. However, the script cleverly ratchets up the suspense by projecting paranoia at every turn—as the two couples make their way through the county, the smile of a child could be as insidious as the leer of an old man. It's a useful trope that always keeps the terror in our peripherals.

Casting Peter Fonda and Warren Oates as the double Alphas was a canny choice. Real-life friends, their bond easily translates to the screen, selling their plight with an easy charm. Loretta Swit and Lara Parker do what they can with the one-note roles, but never get to play with the boys' toys, resigned to screaming and cowering with fear. Personally, I think Swit could smack the Satan out of all of them.

Forty years on, *Race with the Devil* still resonates with horror fans in the know. Sure, there are no Castavets, Pazuzus, or Antichrists to be found, but sometimes the terror hides in the mundane, one lethal mile at a time.

The biggest problem with that last film
is that Texas is so big, there's no escape!
The biggest problem with the next one is trying to stay out of...

The Devil's Rain (1975)

"CORBIS! GOD DAMN YOU!!!"

Sorry, I just had to get that out of my system. The above quote is from none other than the mighty William Shatner, and I'm emphasizing it to let everyone know what amazing and fantastical delights await those who enter... *The Devil's Rain*. Released in 1975 to little fanfare, *The Devil's Rain* sits smack dab in the middle of a decade-long wave of satanic cinema. From *Rosemary's Baby* to *Damien Omen II*, the market was flooded with horror films dedicated to Old Scratch. It's a shame that audiences and critics alike didn't glom to this decidedly dour dance with the Devil.

Mark Preston (Shatner) and his family have been hiding Satan's Guest Book from Jonathan Corbis, Satan's earthly salesman, for centuries. Without the book, all of Corbis' converts cannot find their final resting place

Absolutely the most incredible ending of any motion picture ever!

BRYANSTON Presents A SANDY HOWARD Production • Starring ERNEST BORGNINE • EDDIE ALBERT in "THE DEVIL'S RAIN" • Also Starring WILLIAM SHATNER
KEENAN WYNN • TOM SKERRITT • JOAN PRATHER and IDA LUPINO as Mrs. Preston • with the Special Participation of ANTON LAVEY, High Priest of the Church of Satan
Written by GABE ESSOE, JAMES ASHTON, and GERALD HOPMAN • Produced by JAMES V. CULLEN and MICHAEL S. GLICK
Directed by ROBERT FUEST • Executive Producer SANDY HOWARD • A BRYANSTON RELEASE • COLOR

75/106

DEVIL'S RAIN

The Devil's Rain, Bryanston Distributing Company, 1975

down below; instead, they have to wait it out inside a funky looking TV set where it rains even more than in Seattle, hence the title of the film. As we find out in a sepia-toned flashback, the Prestons' ancestors, the Fyffes, were part of Corbis' original cult in the late 1600s. Deciding a life of hellfire was not for them, they ratted out Corbis to the village and the entire cult was burned at the stake. Corbis cursed Fyffe and his clan for all of eternity.

Back to the present day, Mark has a showdown with Corbis that doesn't go too well. His brother Tom, Tom's wife Julie, and Dr. Sam Richards all arrive on the scene after Julie has a horrific vision of trouble back home on the range. Will they be able to save the Preston clan and defeat Satan's minions? Or will Corbis have the last laugh?

I've never been able to take any of this satanic hokey pokey seriously—but apparently, the filmmakers did; they even had The Church of Satan's Founder Anton LaVey as "Technical Consultant." So I guess the ceremonies performed in the film are "accurate." Screenwriters James Ashton, Gabe Essoe and Gerald Hopman really want you to believe in this stuff; I say good on them for trying.

The Devil's Rain was helmed by the late Robert Fuest. He had a killer one-two punch in 1971 and 1972 with *The Abominable Dr. Phibes* and *Dr. Phibes Rises Again*, both starring Vincent Price as a mad doctor hell-bent on revenge, and both are great fun. Fuest directs *The Devil's Rain* with the same great rapport he's shown in the past with his actors. I'm assuming, however, that he took the chains off of Shatner and let him loose, because he plays not only to the cheap seats in the back but the parking lot outside the theater as well. There is a long sequence between Shatner and Borgnine in the desert that Fuest directs beautifully—suspenseful and well written. He was a great director who after this film—and maybe because of it—was relegated mostly to TV movies for the rest of his career. He deserved better treatment from the industry.

The makeup—and there's a lot of it—was created by Ellis Burman, Jr., and it's crudely effective. The protracted ending has Satan's minions moaning and groaning as they melt in the rain like psychedelic sherbet; messy stuff that goes on for a tad too long.

The great thing about this cast is they could simultaneously star in a low budget horror film and an episode of *The Love Boat* at the same time. From Keenan Wynn as Sheriff Owens to Ida Lupino as the Preston Matriarch to Ernest Borgnine as Corbis, they are all pros, always giving their all. They treat the material as they would any other project—with respect. Honorable mention goes to John Travolta—with a dubbed voice—in his film debut. Fun fact: Joan Prather (Julie) allegedly introduced Travolta to Scientology during filming. Not that there's anything wrong with that.

Here's the bottom line: *The Devil's Rain* is great fun. Well-directed and acted, full of satanic silliness, and Shatner hitting warp drive. Oh, and I didn't even mention that Borgnine turns into a goat devil...

"CORBIS! GOD DAMN YOU!!!"

━━━━━━━━━━━━━━━━━

From the ridiculous to the ridiculous and tasteless;
our next film oversteps a few boundaries, as expected from its director.
The ickiness here, though, works in its favor...

The Sentinel (1977)

In regards to his filmic output, director Michael Winner was wildly inconsistent at his worst and wholly divisive at his best, and vice versa. The remarkable thing is that those two extreme opinions can be about the same film; some find the kinetic sleaze of *Death Wish* powerful and disturbing, and others find its ham-fisted social grazing problematic and off-putting. But it was a big hit, so naturally Universal let him ride the satanic tide with *The Sentinel*, a Good vs. Evil, Portal to Hell potboiler that warms this Fulci-loving heart three years before Lucio even set foot in New Orleans.

Given a limited release in January stateside, *The Sentinel* wasn't a hit, and the critics *hated* it, deeming it lurid, reprehensible trash. It is, but it's also ridiculously entertaining and has a few truly haunting moments. Turns out Winner could do horror—and yet would never return to it (besides 1984's *Scream for Help*), riding out his film career with a series of *Death Wish* sequels before becoming a food critic for the remainder of his days. He was an unusual man, a peculiar talent, and for a brief moment, a fine purveyor of perverse horror.

Meet Alison, an in-demand model in New York with a clingy lawyer boyfriend, Michael, who's just itching for them to move in together. Alison has commitment issues, however, as a girl she witnessed her father cavorting with two women, and overwhelmed with grief, tried to take her own life. So she rents an apartment in a not-creepy-at-all brownstone from Ava Gardner, and in short order meets some of the residents: there's kindly old Charles and his cat Jezebel, who welcomes Alison with open arms and a crooked smile; Gerda and her girlfriend Sandra, who enjoy Alison's company because apparently masturbation needs an audience; and Father Halliran (John Carradine, in every movie made from 1930 to 1988), who watches out the top floor window with milk-toned eyes while clutching a crucifix. He doesn't get out much.

The Sentinel, Universal Pictures, 1977

Anyway, as much as Alison adores her new pad, things take several downturns in her life: blackouts, visits from her dead father, a secret Catholic sect that is *very* interested in her, and suspicions that point to her boyfriend as a murderer. Oh, and the brownstone happens to sit above a gateway to Hell. What does the Catholic Church want with Alison? Are the other tenants as friendly as they appear? If you die there, do you get your damage deposit back?

Make no mistake: *The Sentinel* is sleazy, demented, and crosses a line or two on the road to entertainment. However, it completely earns every frazzled frame of degradation because it commits to the material laid forth by Winner and co-screenwriter Jeffrey Konvitz, who wrote the novel upon which the film is based. Winner never shied away from the confrontational, and while he was not the most refined director, he always attacked a scene with tons of energy.

That's why the horror genre works for him—vulgarity is not only welcomed, it's embraced, and there's a real sense of palpable danger in the more horrific moments. Alison's late-night rendezvous with her father is terrifying, and the scenes with the tenants have a discombobulated feel, just left enough of normal to put the viewer at unease.

Of course, you'll probably solve the puzzle long before Alison does, but you'll receive no prize from me. *The Sentinel* is built to shock, not confound—the title alone holds most of the answers. The only element that bogs it down is the tired police procedural, but you have Eli Wallach and Christopher Walken investigating, so it's less painful than it has any right to be. Okay, maybe the fashion shoots are oh so Maybelline, but again, you have Jeff Goldblum and Jerry Orbach to pull you through.

What *is* up with this cast anyway? I haven't even mentioned Jose Ferrer, Martin Balsam, or Arthur Kennedy, and starring Christina Raines and Chris Sarandon. But this was still the heyday of Hollywood looking for the next *Rosemary's Baby*, *The Exorcist*, and *The Omen*; chasing that devil coin in the hopes of finding another phenomenon—*of course,* every actor working wanted to ride that train. But as hard as they try, it never left the station.

Why is that? I think it was just too weird and lurid for mainstream audiences at the time. *The Exorcist* championed the Church as saviors, and *The Omen* is pure, ghoulish popcorn fun made for the masses. Here, Winner simply doesn't flinch; if you're at all squeamish or uncomfortable, you *will* turn away before he cuts to the next scene. Having Dick Smith (*The Exorcist*) handling the effects only ups the eeriness, most effectively when paired with Albert Whitlock's (1982's *The Thing*) visual touch. Winner's idea of mainstream is a birthday party for a kitty and D'Angelo pleasuring herself while Miles fondles her breast. Universal execs must have seen their bonus checks flying out the window at the time.

As for the elephant in the room: Winner hired several people with real deformities for the gripping finale as denizens of the underworld, and it is a blight on the movie. Equating malformation with evil—whether that was the intention or not—is very sad and infuriating. It's the only misstep from Winner here—he was so close to making a perfectly tasteless film.

Pushing that aside if you can, *The Sentinel* deserves a place on any horror lover's shelf—make sure you file it in the "Satanic" section—as a primo 1970s oddity. As the saying goes: "May you get to Heaven a half hour before the Devil knows you're dead, or at least before he finds out you put nails in the apartment walls without permission." At least I think that's how it goes. I'm not good at sayings.

We close out this festival with a splashy, ambitious fight between Ultimate Good and Ultimate Evil ... soundtracked by Ramones, Talking Heads, and more.
Welcome to the 1980s!

Fear No Evil (1981)

As a first-time filmmaker, it takes a lot of courage to not follow the trends. The early 1980s were flooded with slashers, and for good reason—they were, for the most part, instant ATMs to the studios. Thank God then—or Satan, your florist, a masseuse, whatever floats your boat—for Frank LaLoggia, a New Yorker in his mid–20s who decided to go epic out of the gate with *Fear No Evil*, a parable on Good Versus Evil, capital letters, with a strong Catholic bent filtered through *Carrie*'s prom dress.

Filmed in 1979, this January release found little love from critics but did pick up the Saturn Award for Best Low Budget Film, which was well-earned indeed. *Fear No Evil* boasts high production values, more or less solid performances, and an ambitious concept beyond its means, but not its heart.

The film opens with Lucifer being chased through a castle on a New York bay before being vanquished by an old man with a golden staff. We hear a prophecy—three archangels, in human form, will band together to smite The Devil, paving the way for the return of Jesus Christ. BUT, it has to be the power of all three and so far only two have arrived on earth, meaning this particular conquest over Lucifer is only temporary as he promises to be reborn *soon*.

We then cut to the christening of newborn Andrew Williams which

doesn't go as planned, with Andrew bleeding from his wrists as he is anointed. Through a clever time-lapse of the dilapidation of the exterior of the Williams home, we learn that the maturing Andrew has taken over his parents' lives and left them defeated. School's no different—meek, effeminate Andrew is able to thwart his bullies through vigorous gym exercises (dodgeball is the *worst*) and expose their latent homosexuality.

Meanwhile, our third archangel has arrived in the form of fellow student Julie, and the final battle is fought at the castle during a production of the Passion Play, where all hell literally breaks loose. Will the triptych be able to defeat Lucifer before he can begin his reign on earth? Spoiler: There will be casualties.

I used to watch *Fear No Evil* a lot as an adolescent; it acted as a palette cleanser for the glut of slashers I was invested in. It was a reminder that not all horror had to be concerned with the everyday, mundane trappings of summer camps and sorority sleepovers. This isn't to say that it's better made or above the best of those, but the ambition was appealing and the execution stylish enough to overcome any shortcomings the film encounters, and there are a few. And as we've cycled through meta-slashers and monsters, plus a few films that owe a debt to this one—I'm looking at you, *The Prophecy*—it's these very same attributes that I'm inclined to cling to.

The notion of archangels inhabiting the bodies of the earthbound gives the film poignancy and grandeur, which is at odds with the high school "revenge" angle that Andrew pursues—but in doing so it also raises questions of faith and mortality. The archangels have to come to accept their roles as warriors in the name of God, and LaLoggia doubles down with some melodramatic but effective scenes between Elizabeth Hoffman and John Holland as two of the chosen. As the third and youngest, Kathleen Rowe McAllen has a clear-eyed freshness well-suited for her role as the newest guardian of good. As for our high school villain, Daniel Eden as Tony makes an effective sub-Travolta, although Billy Nolan was never impelled to kiss another man in the shower or grow a pair of breasts. (I *think*. I haven't watched *Carrie* in a while.)

Stefan Arngrim is an angst-filled Andrew and a suitable Antichrist; he's birdlike and curious, with a calm demeanor that explodes once it's time for the final showdown. Unlike Damien Thorn, however, Andrew prefers to *bring it* and shows up in an outfit akin to a Bob Mackie/Kiss collaboration. And why not? If you're going to rule the world, do it in *style*.

As far as a commentary on Catholicism goes, the film wants to have its sacred bread and eat it too. The Williams family certainly has all the *tchotchkes* on display, even though Dad seems to find his solace in spirits from the liquor store rather than the church. But the final stand at the Passion Play goes full out with a crucifixion that becomes bloodier than Mel

Gibson's due to Andrew's influence, and for some reason, he has a horde of zombies who do his bidding. This film is everything *but* a slasher.

So, *Fear No Evil* is a film that embraces, rather than ignores, its thematic inconsistencies. Whether Tony gets his comeuppance because he's still in the closet or because he's a hypocrite is unclear—I lean towards the latter—and between the earnest light shows signifying heavenly power and the desecration of sacred imagery, it's hard to tell if LaLoggia is going for solemnity or shock. His follow-up film, *Lady in White* (1988), certainly finds a consistent tone that this one never attains. But the fun in ambition is watching a first timer shoot for the stars; *Fear No Evil* may eventually end up earthbound, but it's a blast watching it rattle the pearly gates.

Festival Four:
Chop Chop Till You Drop

Now here's a subgenre that started late, yet has saturated the market for decades: slashers. Two of the most prominent films used worldwide when we think of this category are *Halloween* and *Friday the 13th*. These are the films, released in 1978 and 1980 respectively, that people see as epitomizing, or at least solidifying the hearty tropes of the subgenre: masked killer stalks (usually) teenagers in various settings—a house, the woods, apartment buildings. That's the general idea.

So what brought about this nastier, meaner, more visceral approach? Nothing less than the changing times, of course—by 1960 audiences were tired of rubber-zippered men clumsily running around chasing bikinied women, and filmmakers were keen to wade into more realistic waters.

This brings us to two films at the start of the decade: *Psycho* and *Peeping Tom*, by Alfred Hitchcock and Michael Powell. The former, based on the novel by Robert Bloch, was a massive, unexpected hit; the latter was a flop that pretty much ended Powell's career.

The former is an entertainment, albeit a perverted one; the latter is a much grittier—and sordid—affair. It's also an entertainment, to be sure; but whereas *Psycho* lets you know when the ride is finished, *Peeping Tom* will give you phantom motion sickness for years to come.

Naturally, *Psycho* was cloned: people with secrets—a couple of steady sinners in this particular story—converge on a remote location, where sins are committed and revealed. This is the basic slasher template, with multiple variations and vulgarities through the decades—talent not necessarily included.

The early part of the 1970s continued in this more realistic vein until a couple of films really tapped into something a little rougher, a touch … stronger. *Black Christmas* and *The Texas Chain Saw Massacre*, both in 1974, just hit harder. The first with its nearly invisible (yet never silent) antagonist who terrorizes a Montreal sorority house, while the second offers a deafening chainsaw roar as its mode of communication.

The vulgarities spouted by our unknown assailant in *Black Christmas* over the phone to the sorority sisters were shocking at the time, and still pack a punch now. The incessant whirring of the logging implement in *Texas Chain Saw* floods the viewer with fear and dread even when silent. The point is, these two "shocking" films show little in the way of visceral impact that the slasher subgenre would become notorious for, yet still pack a ferocious punch. A slasher can be much more complex and thrilling than just guts and grue—you can have some gasp to go with your gore.

Halloween in 1978 and *Friday the 13th* in 1980 set up the tried-and-true template for the slashers' "Golden Age" of let's say, 1978 to 1984; we can't use comic graders' objectivity, so this is my own demarcation starting with 1978's *Halloween* and ending with 1984's *Friday the 13th: The Final Chapter*. And in those six years, many teens (or alleged teens) get lost, go missing, inherit a house, rent a cabin, become camp counselors, join a fraternity/sorority, try to hide an accidental death, reopen a haunted theater, and get tricked into traveling to the Caribbean by Ben's son. Simple ingredients often work well enough for lovers of slasher films who embrace them like a warm blanket: a killer, a secret, pretty people having sex, and over-the-top, explicit violence.

Slashers are and have always been the most heavily criticized of the subgenres—in terms of sexual politics and misogynistic attitudes and narrative flaccidity, it's hard to beat them. The simple truth is that the formula is so thin that even the slightest variation in plot or characterization can feel like a bigger victory than it really is. The worst thing any horror film can do is bore the audience. It's death. And by the late 1980s, we were getting really bored. What you'll find below are some films that buck that trend and offer differences that range from subtle to over-the-top.

The films in this festival offer up a little bit of 1960s camp (*Strait-Jacket*); one of the best—and craziest—of the early '80s slashers (*Just Before Dawn*); one from the start of the next decade (*Popcorn*)—yes, I've broken my own time frame parameters, shocking no one—that is part modern-day slasher and part 1950s tribute; one where the subgenre flavors the action genre (*10 to Midnight*); and ends with the goriest, stupidest, yet somehow most completely loveable slasher of all. (Oh *Pieces,* I'll never quit you.)

So sit back, sharpen your weapon of choice, and enjoy the festival. Chopping is optional, but not a horrible idea considering the folks ahead.

━━━━━━━━━━━━━━━

Our first film features a movie star of old seeking cinematic relevancy.
Her rage put her in the bin once
but will she end up in yet another...

Strait-Jacket (1964)

It's 1964. It's been 19 years since Joan Crawford's Oscar-winning performance in *Mildred Pierce*, and you see she has a new movie opening this weekend: *Strait-Jacket!* "What could it be about?" you ponder, right before you see the ad of Joan swinging an ax with a maniacal gleam in her eye and tossing down your paper in disgust. "Horror nonsense," you mumble. "She'll never get my money again!" That's a shame, Winifred, because *Strait-Jacket* is a hot blast of campy delights that I'm positive your kids and grand babies will have a great old time with down the road. Now have a lay down and I'll tell you all about it.

Released by Columbia Pictures stateside in January, with a worldwide rollout in the spring, *Strait-Jacket* was a big hit for director William Castle (*The Tingler*) and Crawford, cementing her status as the queen of the "psycho-biddies," "Grande Dame Guignol," and other such derogatory terms. And it was a fast label too, as 1962's *Whatever Happened to Baby Jane?* made such an impression in mainstream culture that it seemed the clearest route to success for aging actresses at the time. Critics predictably murdered it, although some did single out Crawford for her commitment to the bit. And boy, does she commit.

Let's start with some story: a voice-over tells us of one Frank Harbin (an uncredited Lee Majors in his screen debut) who brings his ex-girlfriend home from the bar as his wife Lucy (Crawford) is out of town. He sneaks in his ex past their sleeping daughter, Carol, and begins his extramarital doings, when wouldn't you know it, wifey decides to take the train home a day early. Not surprisingly, Lucy doesn't take to the activities well, and proceeds to cut off the heads of her husband and his friend with an ax right in front of little Carol. Lucy is sent away to an asylum for 20 years.

Flash forward to present day, as an adult Carol anxiously awaits the arrival of the mom she hasn't seen since she was a little girl. Lucy arrives at the farmhouse of her brother Bill and his wife Emily, who have raised Carol since Lucy went on her extended vacation. Reticent at first, mother and daughter soon warm to each other and Carol convinces Lucy to have a makeover done, top to bottom, so she looks as she did in happier times. Once she transforms, Lucy begins to hear children's voices, and acts so strangely that she hits on Carol's boyfriend, Michael. When her shrink from the hospital pops by for a visit, heads literally start to fly. Could Lucy be taking a gruesome stroll down memory lane?

This story has been told many times before, but in the hands of the gifted writer Robert Bloch (*Psycho*), King of the Gimmicks William Castle, and Crawford, *Strait-Jacket* becomes an American Gothic tale writ large,

or at least certainly larger than Castle was used to. An opportunity for him, yes. A necessity for Crawford? Definitely.

Baby Jane was a major boost for her career, and savvy as she was, she had no problem hopping aboard the "psycho-biddy" train, as long as she received top billing. And script approval. Casting, too. And why not? She had earned that right, and she believed that her fans would come out to support her work. Perhaps the reception was strong to *Strait-Jacket* not because of *her* fans necessarily, but by the next generation's fascination with seeing someone of her stature swinging an ax with abandon. The film is pure kitsch; heightened melodrama that lets her loose in every scene until Castle has the good sense to yell cut. If she was embarrassed to play down to the exploitation crowd, you'd never know it from her performance.

It certainly helps that Bloch's script is pretty tight; as I've said, it essentially had been done before. Certainly since—possibly even in some of your favorite slashers—but the story moves along so quickly that any and all queries will have to catch up to you at the finish line. Besides, you'll be too caught up in the Grand Guignol-ness of it all to even notice.

Catering to the younger crowd, there are plenty of severed heads and one on-screen decapitation. While moored quite far from realism, the brief effects work in *Strait-Jacket* ups its camp appeal in a "hey, let's put on a show!" way. This is in no way a slight—it would be impossible to make a serious film with Crawford as a hatchet killer so Castle wisely plays to the balcony, where the kids occasionally break from their make-out session to see what's on the screen.

Castle was of course a huge Hitchcock acolyte, and while *Strait-Jacket* strains to rise to Hitch's level of *Psycho* sleaze, he's better off where he is. I'd rather have Dame Joan splashing joyously through a dirty gutter puddle than strutting down a paparazzi-laden red carpet any day. And that, Winifred, is why your kin will love it. Now go to sleep, dear.

═══════════

As we've seen, hell hath no fury like a woman scorned.
Our next entry has a killer gathering victims at a—wait for it—
horror film festival. Time to fire up the...

Popcorn (1991)

Welcome to horror in the 1990s: a decade that kind of floundered for its first half, unsure of which direction to take before *Scream* (1996) and its monster success brought masks and knives back into fashion.

Popcorn (1991), a nostalgia-laden, possibly supernatural slasher, goes in *all* the directions at once.

Yet it somehow manages to be more clever and entertaining than most of its brethren before the *Scream* floodgates opened and offered up variations (after variations) of self-aware and meta-textualized horror, and frankly better than a lot of what followed for the remainder of the decade. Why? Because *Popcorn* is smarter about which routes to take and which to mostly avoid. Helmed by a couple of stalwarts of the '70s, namely Alan Ormsby and Bob Clark (*Children Shouldn't Play with Dead Things, Deathdream*), they give the film a cohesiveness even while it tries to sell itself to you as a supernatural slasher *and* a cheesy, nostalgic '50s throwback.

Add in the fact that Ormsby was fired part way through, and cast member Mark Herrier of Clark's *Porky's* was brought in to finish directing, and the entire production had Kingston, Jamaica, subbing for Southern California. That it was even made and released is cause for celebration.

But the same can be said about any film—they're all miracles, and sometimes they're even good. *Popcorn* is one of those. It stands out in a rather scattered decade by targeting two very specific subgenres of horror: slashers and William Castle–style hucksterism.

So how does this Venn diagram intersect, if at all?

While they may seem disparate, a slasher and a gimmick-laden film often pull their levers from inside the same horror headspace: they both come with built-in preconceptions. The slasher fan wants totemistic, costumed killers (yes, Russ Thorn's Canadian tuxedo in *The Slumber Party Massacre* counts in my book) while the Castleheads need a plot—any one will do—that revolves around manipulation of the senses, which in turn creates a physical sensation in the audience members. For instance, rigging the seats to give off an electric shock during a similar event happening on screen, or filling the theater with obnoxious odors when released in the movie, both of which happen here. It's a potentially disastrous combination: each with their hoariest of tropes given free reign.

Yet *Popcorn* pulls it off, and it all starts with the story. Maggie (Jill Schoelen) is a film student at a Southern California education facility. As the film opens she has a horrible dream about a little girl, a mysterious man, and an altar. After she tells her mom Suzanne (Dee Wallace) about the dream, she heads to school.

To raise money for the cash-strapped department, Maggie's professor Mr. Davis (Tony Roberts), and her classmate Toby (Tom Villard) come up with a plan: Throw a grade "Z" film horrorthon at the old Dreamland movie theater set for demolition in a few weeks.

With little time, Toby brings in an old prop master (Ray Walston) who helps them set up shop (gratuitous cleaning montage included) for a first-rate show, even if the films aren't up to snuff.

While cleaning, the students come across an old, boxed-up horror short called *Possessor*. Belonging to a filmic cult leader named Lanyard Gates from the late 1960s, he planned on stabbing his wife to death on the theater altar to "complete" his film. He was shot before he had the chance. But the place caught fire in the ensuing excitement, and most of the cult perished.

As Maggie, Toby and the rest of the class count down to the feature presentations, the (possible) spirit of Lanyard (we'll see) haunts the hallowed halls of the Dreamland … and he wants to finish his movie.

I saw *Popcorn* in the theater with a friend when it first came out, and we loved the hell out of it. I really can't vouch for the other four people who attended, but we certainly enjoyed—and appreciated—the effort put in, and the results achieved.

But it didn't resonate with mainstream audiences, and I can't remember it making critics' year-end lists, although it probably clawed its way onto a couple of "worst ofs" by year's end. There wasn't a lot of theatrical horror at the time, and this low-budget flick with the reggae soundtrack would make an easy addition to some snooty critic's hit list.

And that is usually when most genre films will slink off to retirement on a video store shelf, lucky to be dusted off on the weekend, if at all. This was certainly the fate afforded *Popcorn*. It was as hard for some horror fans to see the appeal of a film that played in two disparate camps—slasher and hucksterism—with neither really in favor.

But anyone with an interest in the lineage of horror moviegoing should dig *Popcorn*; Walston has a nice little speech about how in the 1950s and 1960s the promotions helped to sell the experience, regardless of the quality of the film.

And within this film are three faux gems, created by original director Alan Ormsby: *Mosquito!*, *The Attack of the Amazing Electrified Man*, and *The Stench*. Ormsby was let go three weeks into production. The rumor mill simply says he was spending too much time on the fake movies and not enough time on the main one.

Enter actor-turned-director Herrier, in his feature film debut as well as his finale. He does a decent job, and weaves the two storylines pretty well for a film with reels seemingly flying everywhere.

That coherency is somewhat there in Ormsby's script. It's fairly tight if occasionally logic-resistant—what with the reggae band playing on stage *after* the power goes out, or the twice used trope of the killer somehow manifesting supernatural telekinesis abilities when the mood (or rather, plot) strikes. The former is low-budget amusing; the latter possibly a plot

point scrubbed along the way. Regardless, these are veterans of cellu-
loid wars, responsible for genuinely great horror such as *Black Christmas*,
Deranged, and *Deathdream* (all from 1974!).

So going in, I was already confident with *Popcorn*'s pedigree. What
I wasn't prepared for was how good natured it came across, and still does
today. This is a film that wants you to like it, without trying *too* hard. It has
a wry confidence in its delivery of B-thrills, its knowledge and affection for
horror cinema as social salve and/or religious experience, and above all, it
knows goddamn well that horror lovers adore backstage tales and lo-fi shenanigans. We're the genre that's obsessed with how the meat is made.

This cast finds the tone that works best for the material: light on its
feet, but playing it straight—and playing it dark when needed.

It won't be for me to reveal the identity of the killer—is it Lanyard
or someone with a vendetta—but suffice to say that it's probably who you
think it is, and it is the best performance of his truncated career.

Popcorn is a slasher, to be sure—taken in a different direction, The
Possessor could hang with Freddy—but the inclusion of and constant conversation with the moldy oldies at the center of the film makes it so much
more. It becomes a living testament to the power and allure of movies, and
to our glorious church.

By the way, our communion brings all the ghouls to the yard.

From incendiary film fests to campfire calamities,
where the best advice to take
is always get the hell out of the woods...

Just Before Dawn (1981)

Although he hasn't made very many films, Jeff Lieberman is a unique
voice in the world of horror. From *Squirm* (1976) through to *Satan's Little Helper* (2004), he's crafted only a handful of feature-length films, each
one different from the last. Watching him tackle a different subgenre is
like looking at a new painting by a great artist. *Just Before Dawn* is his
take on backwoods butcher clans, an inbred cross of *Deliverance* and *Friday the 13th*. Everyone should own a Lieberman or two; hell, collect them
all!

Released by Picturmedia in October, *Just Before Dawn* played the
grindhouses and drive-ins before shuffling off this mortal coil. Of course it
had a home video release, but slipped through the cracks there as well. It's

The nightmare has begun—

JUST BEFORE DAWN

DORO VLADO HRELJANOVIC
presents
A JEFF LIEBERMAN FILM
"JUST BEFORE DAWN"
Starring CHRIS LEMMON • GREGG HENRY • DEBORAH BENSON • RALPH SEYMOUR
and JAMIE ROSE • MIKE KELLIN and GEORGE KENNEDY
Executive Producers DORO VLADO HRELJANOVIC and V. PAUL HRELJANOVIC
Screenplay by MARK L. ARYWITZ and GREGG IRVING • Based on a story by JOSEPH MIDDLETON • Music by BRAD FIEDEL
Directed by JEFF LIEBERMAN • Produced by DAVID SHELDON and DORO VLADO HRELJANOVIC
Executive in Charge of Production DON STILLMAN   Released by *Picturmedia Limited*

RESTRICTED
UNDER 17 REQUIRES ACCOMPANYING
PARENT OR ADULT GUARDIAN

© MCMLXXXI Oakland Productions Ltd.   Lenses & Panaflex Camera by PANAVISION®

Just Before Dawn, Picturmedia, 1981

only been with the advent of the internet and social media that people are starting to discover the Lieberman hanging there the whole time.

We start in the woods of Oregon as a hunting uncle-nephew duo stumble upon an abandoned church. While they crack wise with the Lord in his dilapidated temple, a hulking figure has set their truck crashing into a tree. The uncle goes to check out the truck, leaving the nephew in the church, where a serrated machete to the groin ends any prayer activity. The uncle flees the scene, realizing his nephew won't be around for Thanksgiving dinner.

We cut to five twenty-somethings riding in an RV on their way up the mountain. The driver, Warren, has inherited property and so he brings his girlfriend Connie, friends Jonathan, Daniel, and Megan for a weekend of hiking and hijinks. They come across the uncle, who babbles on about demons and such; they throw him some food and drive off. Forest Ranger Roy tries to warn them off the mountain to no avail. Luckily the uncle finds Roy and tells him about the crazed madman in the woods, and the ranger mounts his trusted steed to save the five from certain doom. Will the forest ranger make it to the campers, hopefully *Just Before Dawn*? Duh, duh, DUH!!!

You really have to ignore the setup and realize it's all about the execution. Because story-wise, other than a late-in-the-game reveal which is fantastic, this thing is quite ordinary. But Lieberman is one of the kings of the slow burn; I have no doubt that Ti West is a fan. Lieberman likes to give audiences a chance to marinate in the characters so when bad things do happen, we care about them. Fair enough, but in making a movie that definitely plays by a lot of the same rules as a regular slasher, he leaves the viewer with several expectations. And it's not that he doesn't fulfill them, but he moves at a more measured pace than your average slasher fan may be accustomed to. Undoubtedly this was a major factor in its poor box office performance.

The screenplay by Mark Arywitz and Gregg Irving (Lieberman's nom de plume) reflects the popularity of the woods after *Friday the 13th*. The writers even elongate the scenario to allow the gorgeous Silver Lake Park of Oregon to become an imposing character itself. Awe inspiring cliffs, cascading waterfalls, and imposing, majestic trees play a large part in the story. Lovingly photographed by Joel King, *Just Before Dawn* is a blood soaked travelog that looks much better than a lot of its brethren from the same era. Arywitz's original script had a religious bent, with snake handling built into the clan's backstory and the "good" members of the family actually warn our heroes to get out while they can.

Lieberman hated it, and decided to pay tribute to *Deliverance*, and have Connie transform from meek and mild to hard-edged frontierswoman, who has to protect Warren in a nice turn of events. Connie has a great arc, and Deborah Benson carries it off with a steely-eyed determination. In fact, the whole cast is strong: Gregg Henry shows why he has become a go-to character actor through the years; George Kennedy underplays nicely as the ranger; Chris Lemmon—yes, Jack's son—has the same manic energy as his old man; and a special spooky hat off to John Hunsaker as the killer behemoth, who as it turns out, is a pretty versatile actor. And if you've seen it, you know what I mean.

Back in the gleaming machete, halcyon days of the slasher, the body count reigned supreme. *Just Before Dawn* certainly is no pretender to the throne; maybe half a dozen folk are killed. But know this when you look at a Lieberman: it's what he does in between the bodies that counts.

After the woodsy scent of our previous film, we head straight into the urban jungle, where Chuck Bronson faces a naked killer who always seems to be pointing...

10 to Midnight (1983)

Horror was so prevalent and popular in the early 1980s that even the action genre wanted in on the ... uh, action. Chuck Norris karate-chopped a Michael Myers wannabe in *Silent Rage* (1982), so next up it was granite-faced Charles Bronson's turn to take on slashers with *10 to Midnight* (1983), a sleazy yet fascinating trip through the mind of a serial killer. While it's never as deep as it thinks it is, it's smarter than it has any right to be.

Released in March, this Cannon production, co-distributed by MGM, was a mild success at the box office. It certainly didn't do *Death Wish* numbers, but it's not really a *Death Wish*–type of film (until it is). As for the critics, Roger Ebert called it "a scummy little sewer of a movie." He's not completely right though—the prevalent and misogynistic male gaze is upended long before the final credits roll. Besides, I'd have a lot less to write about if I didn't splash through the sewers now and then.

Our film opens on police detective Leo Kessler (Bronson adopting a similar moniker to *Death Wish*'s Paul Kersey, in case you needed a reminder, I guess) grumpily filling out a report when he really needs to be out on the streets mopping up crime. Cut to credits and then we're right in the thick of it as we meet Warren Stacy, doing typewriter repair in an office and thinking of the woman who spurned his advances. Before

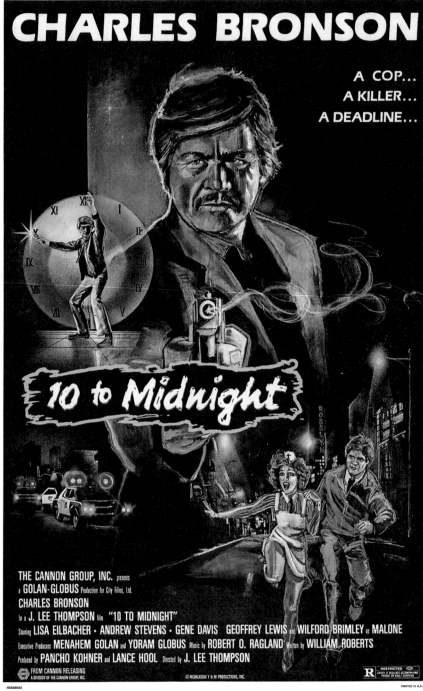

long, Warren is chasing her naked through the woods after disposing of her boyfriend mid-coitus, knife in hand. Kessler and his new partner Paul McAnn find connections between the victim and Warren, which leads to Kessler's estranged daughter Laurie, the victim's best friend, being put directly in Warren's path.

As Kessler and McAnn grow increasingly frustrated with Warren's ability to slip through the tenuous grip of the law, desperate measures are taken to keep the murderer behind bars. When that falls apart, Kessler must race against time to save the one person he truly cares about. But will he be too late?

10 to Midnight certainly lives in the shadow of Bronson's more famous property, even though the stone-faced actor turned not to Michael Winner but rather focused on another collaboration with director J. Lee Thompson. They had worked together previously on *St. Ives* (1976), *The White Buffalo* (1977), and *Cabo Blanco* (1980), and would finish out most of the 1980s together, including the final two dire *Death Wish* films. (Not the most dignified series, anyway; although the first has some social residue and the third is just a straight-up fun cartoon.) This and the eerie winter Western *Buffalo* are their best efforts together. I'd like to believe that these projects work due to the infusion of horror into otherwise standard Bronson action fare—but I think *any* steps away from Bronson's tired and dreary vigilante tropes could only lead to a more positive light.

But that light is still fraught with pinholes of darkness that threaten to eat through the very fabric and engulf the film. We start very firmly with Warren's angry gaze, contempt for not only *this* particular woman, but as we can see in his unblinking stare, for all women. He feeds this leering contempt with a full-on narcissistic streak, most evident not only in his insistence in forcing the women to view him as a (literal) male god laid bare, but in his total disconnect from communication. He does nothing but make proclamations, or if he does offer a question, he's already certain the answer will not be what he wants to hear.

Warren is a psychopathic monster, incapable of female interaction that isn't fueled by rage. The first half of the film *really* leans into his psychoses, and becomes almost a character study (mirroring Ted Bundy's behaviors somewhat—even driving a VW to give the film a faux realism it doesn't truly earn). The film makes no bones about fixating on the helpless female form, however. (To be fair, actor Gene Davis spends most of his screen time in the buff as well.) The first half has a greasy veneer that's hard, but not impossible, to shake.

Where the film upends the audiences' expectations is in the second half, when Warren is brought in after Kessler frames him with tainted evidence. Thinking he'll be in and out within 30 days on minor charges,

Kessler tells him about this "new" evidence prompting Warren to react with rage, which quickly turns to ... petulant whining. He's reduced to a toddler whose favorite toy has been taken away; brilliantly punctuated by shrieking "HE'S LYING!" into his lawyer's (an oily cameo from Geoffrey Lewis) face, leaving any traces of Warren's power crumbling on the interrogation room floor.

From this point on, *10 to Midnight* shrugs its shoulders, heaves a sigh of relief and turns into a slasher as Warren stalks Laurie and her roommates, all in various stages of undress for Warren to employ a robotic killing spree until his final showdown with Kessler. It earns its popcorn reputation at this point because Warren has been reduced to a shell of his delusional glory, at least to the audience. For his victims, it's business as usual with Horror's Greatest Hits, replay value offered to Screaming and Cowering, respectively. (Except for Laurie, who is fleshed out well by Lisa Eilbacher, and pushes back until the script says she shouldn't.) No longer complicit in Warren's actions, we can just enjoy the film from this point on as an efficient, bloody thriller.

It is notable that even in the more exploitative moments, there is a certain restraint in Thompson's approach to William Roberts' lurid screenplay. Which is to say he doesn't dwell on the seediness in any given scene for too long. Having said *that*, when your film is wallpapered with grime, it's hard not to run into it.

Would you believe me if I said this offers a good Bronson performance? Okay, would you at least buy that he's trying and animated compared to the very glazed over final act of his career? I think you should—he has a couple of terrific, subtle moments that certainly show up Andrew Stevens' stiff and underwritten McAnn. (A small victory, but it still counts.) Eilbacher is a strong and smart heroine, and god help them if they hadn't made her that way—balancing out Warren's misogyny is crucial to making the material palatable.

Which it most certainly is as soon as Warren (Davis' somewhat awkward and uneven take actually works in giving him an unpredictability) is stripped of his ability to shock and dominate. Once he's exposed as a physically strong but psychically stunted baby, *10 to Midnight* breezes by on showers and stabbings right up until the denouement. And if you're wondering how we got this far without any heavy-handed statements about the importance of due process, relax and let movie magic unfold before your eyes (and between Warren's) as a Kessler becomes a Kersey.

*This is the only way to end a festival on slashers; gratuitous in every way—
and it may even invent a couple of new ways—it's Boston via Spain,
it's Bava meets a meat-grinder, it's the goofy glory known as...*

Pieces (1982)

"It's exactly what you think it is!"

"You don't have to go to Texas for a Chainsaw Massacre!"

Indeed. It's not often that a film will tell you exactly their intention, with their mission statement right up front. With a film like *Pieces* (1982), it's a badge of honor worn proudly, a tattered and bloodied flag waving proudly from its mast on the seas of horror. Not only is *Pieces* exactly what we think it is, it's so much more—one of the most cheerfully odd, sleazy slashers to come out of the VHS era. Pull out your slickers folks, things are about to get messy.

Filmed in Spain and subbing for Boston, Massachusetts, *Pieces* did quite well, but critics were none too kind, and they were correct in a few respects—*Pieces* is laughably written, full of overwrought performances, and exceedingly gory. However, this is how it plays for the discerning horror buff: Fast paced, possesses a cartoonish silliness with memorable dialogue, and is gloriously gruesome. Chainsaws have a way of wooing the horror acolyte with their sweet, buzzing call.

Story time: Boston, 1942, and a little boy is putting a jigsaw puzzle together in his room. When his mother checks on him, she discovers that the puzzle is of a nude woman. Mom doesn't take too kindly to this bit of news, and chastises the boy. Clearly unstable, he decides that mother-son time is over and chops her into little bits. The police are called, and our little fella, believed to be the witness to an unknown assailant, is whisked away to live with a nearby aunt.

Cut to forty years later, and a series of murders are being committed on a Boston college campus by a black-clad rogue dubbed "Chainsaw Charlie" by the press. Lt. Bracken and former tennis pro turned cop Mary Riggs are assigned to the case, with Mary going undercover as an instructor at the college. Assisting them in their search for Charlie is Kendall, local stud on campus, the Dean, and groundskeeper Willard, who carries enough red herring for three films. It seems that Charlie is making his own puzzle out of girl parts. Will Charlie succeed in his nefarious scheme? Can Christopher George stay awake for the duration of his performance? Who will survive and who will fall to *Pieces*?

Here we have a Spanish slasher dressed up in Italian giallo wear,

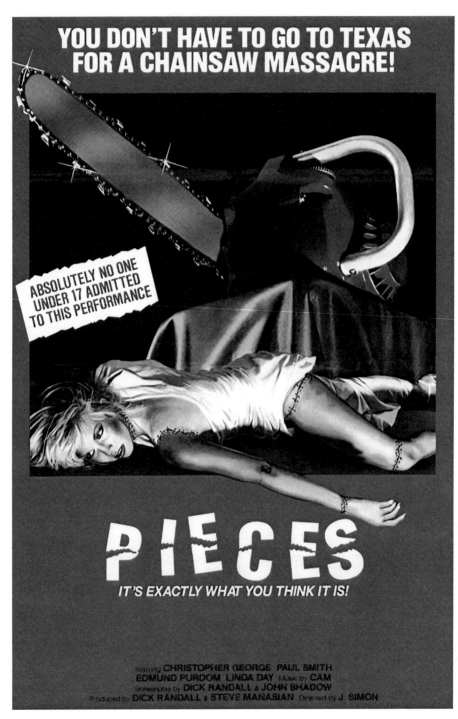

speaking with a muddled American accent, waving his saw in the air like he just doesn't care. It starts over the top and goes from there, dealing out all the tropes with a heavy hand and a song in its heart. I believe the filmmakers achieve a distillation of everything memorable about slashers. For a pubescent boy, that is. *Pieces* makes no bones about its goal—chainsaws rip through nubile young women, rinse, repeat. While the intention of the film may seem nasty and misogynistic, and plays to the adolescent male mind, the execution guarantees enjoyment for all. You see, by conventional standards this is not a good film. Nor is it a competent one. However, it is endlessly entertaining. *Pieces'* foibles are so outlandish that it becomes a grotesque parody of the genre, deflecting any criticism along the way.

Our MC, director J.P. Simon (1988's wonderfully revolting *Slugs*), doles out the sleaze by the bucketful, a drunken clown under the big top slopping confetti on anyone within his range. He shows a true zest for gruesome gore—painting walls, waterbeds, elevators and anything else he can get his hands on. Subtlety is not his strong suit, and it plays in his favor. While Charlie's look seems patterned after the giallo stalkers of yore (especially the gloves), the inspiration is actually The Shadow, the famous crime fighting physic character from the 1930s, with his scarf covered face and wide brimmed black fedora. Either way, it's a striking and unique look for the genre. A very special mention to the screenwriters Dick Randall and John Shadow (a pseudonym for Joe D'Amato, purveyor of 2,168 Italian sleaze fests, give or take). No spoilers here, but this beauty has some of the most bizarre, hilarious dialogue to ever float across the screen. Okay, one line: "The most beautiful thing in the world is smoking pot and fucking on a waterbed, at the same time." That's just the tip of the chainsaw folks; this film is loaded with them.

The performances are either so broad that they block out the screen or in the case of George, may cause drowsiness. By this point in his career, shortly before his untimely death, he starred in several horror films, notably *Grizzly* (1976) and *Graduation Day* (1981). He phones this one in, long distance and collect no less, but again this only adds to the fun on display. Take special note of his own dubbing, as it sounds like he hit the sauce before wobbling over to the recording booth. Remarkable. (By the way, I've always genuinely adored Christopher George—a unique and personable screen presence with legendary B status and star of several of my favorite films. Yes, this was to make me feel better, thanks.)

As slashers have ebbed and flowed in popularity through the decades, *Pieces* has managed to be the ship that has weathered every storm, beaten and battered by critics to and fro. Changing tides may persist, but one fact remains for horror fans: we know exactly what *Pieces* is, and we love it.

Festival Five:
Any Portmanteau
in a Storm

Webster's Dictionary defines *portmanteau* as "a horror anthology film with short stories of varying quality and tastes, ensuring a broad spectrum of viewers and perspectives. Something for everyone, unless it isn't."

Yes, it says precisely that. Don't even bother to look it up. Portmanteau, as you can clearly tell, is a fancy word for *anthology*. While horror stories have been prevalent since the writings of the Greeks and Romans, film embraced the anthology format early on. Germany released three between 1919 and 1924: *Unheimliche Geschichten* (Uncanny Stories), *Der müde Tod* (Weary Death), and *Das Wachsfigurenkabinett* (Waxworks).

Britain came out strong with *Dead of Night* (1945), a solid collection of five tales (plus wraparound) with an all-timer in *The Ventriloquist's Dummy*; I've always found those yakkin' mannequins creepy as hell, and this does nothing to stop the shivers.

Come to think of it, we're mostly sticking with Britain in this festival. Yes we have two American productions, *From a Whisper to a Scream* (1987) and *Creepshow* (1982), but for my money Britain's Amicus Productions—the first three films in this festival—has an unbeatable record for anthology films. (Not that we're ranking; it's not that kind of book. Besides, the answer is *Creepshow*.)

Look, anthologies used to be a hard sell. They were certainly out of fashion until some DIY spirit roared back in the last decade with the *V/H/S* series, which has proven to be very popular with horror fans. One of the great things about horror is the cyclical nature of the beast—wait awhile, and the odds of your favorite subgenre coming around again are pretty good. (And if your fave film series has the word "Amityville" in the title, you're good because those are endless and never going away.)

But these short stories, offering up tastes of man's fallacy towards man, are like delicious sampling from a glorious feast or a simple meat and cheese tray—the variety from segment to segment, film to film, can do a number on your digestive tract if you're not prepared. But my constitution has been steeled enough over the decades to embrace it all. The key is variety, but with enough commonality so there's a semblance of structure.

So what do our five films have in common? Well, the Amicus films have a unity as far as production values go, and the variables—cast, director, script—come from the usual reliable talent within Amicus' "house"; the American ones do not.

What I *know* all five share is this: good stories, well told. Is there anything else?

Let's begin our festival with an Amicus
at the start of the 1970s,
where all the tales revolve around...

The House That Dripped Blood (1971)

From the mid-sixties to the mid-seventies, anthology (or portmanteau if you're *really* fancy) horror films were big business. And Amicus Productions ruled the roost. Between 1965 and 1974 they released seven such films, starting with *Dr. Terror's House of Horrors* (not to be confused with *Dr. Tongue's Evil House of Pancakes*) and culminating with *From Beyond the Grave*. Today's film lands in the middle, *The House That Dripped Blood* (1971) showcasing a company just starting to hit their stride with anthologies.

Popularity of the omnibus format has ebbed and flowed throughout the last 50 years; after Amicus stopped making them, George Romero and Stephen King collaborated on one of the finest, *Creepshow* (1982), which didn't so much kick start a revival as have everyone afraid to compete. Throughout the late 1980s and 1990s there were pockets of inspiration, the syndicated, George Romero-produced *Tales from the Darkside* (1984–1988), *Tales from the Hood* (1995) and of course HBO's *Tales from the Crypt* (1989–96) mining the rich vein of dark humor prevalent in the old EC Comics. Now we have another renaissance upon us with the surprise success of *V/H/S* (2012) and its sequels, through 2015's *Tales of Halloween*, *Southbound*, and many more. Maybe the portmanteau will stick around this time?

Well, that depends. Quality control is job one with an anthology film

TERROR WAITS FOR YOU IN EVERY ROOM IN

THE HOUSE

THAT DRIPPED BLOOD

From
the author
of "Psycho"

Cinerama Releasing presents

THE HOUSE THAT DRIPPED BLOOD Starring Christopher Lee Peter Cushing

Nyree Dawn Porter Denholm Elliott Jon Pertwee Joanna Dunham Joss Ackland John Bennett John Bryans
Wolfe Morris also starring Tom Adams and Ingrid Pitt as "Carla"

Executive Producers Produced by Written by Directed by

Paul Ellsworth and Gordon Wescourt Max J. Rosenberg and Milton Subotsky Robert Block Peter Duffell Color **GP**

FROM CINERAMA RELEASING CORPORATION

71/89

The House that Dripped Blood, Cinerama Releasing Corporation, 1971

and today's crop usually bring in different talent to lay down the four-color vengeance for each segment. It's a dice roll to be sure, and the results are usually mixed. But the very idea is ensconced in the horror lexicon, and when a truncated tale works, it really works.

Which brings us to today's feature, and *Blood* certainly seemed to resonate with audiences when released in the spring of 1971. Let's take a trip to the house and see what we can find, yes?

Our wraparound story involves a Scotland Yard inspector (John Bennett) looking for a missing horror movie actor, last seen residing at the titular house. He meets up with realtor A.J. Stoker (John Bryans) to discuss the matter and is told that the house has a macabre history with former tenants. Of course, he wants examples, which leads us into our stories:

Method for Murder—A horror author (Denholm Elliott) is suffering from writer's block, so he and his wife (Joanna Dunham) move into the house looking for inspiration, and boy does he find it—he conjures up a hideous serial killer named Dominick. The only problem is Dominick starts showing up around the property. *For real.*

Waxworks—A recent retiree (Peter Cushing) rents the house to while away his time gardening and reading. Upon a visit to town, he comes across a wax museum that displays a figurine of a woman he thinks he knows. When his friend (Joss Ackland) pays a visit, they return to the museum, with deathly results.

Sweets to the Sweet—A widower (Christopher Lee) and his withdrawn daughter (Chloe Franks) rent the house, and soon thereafter he hires a tutor/nanny (Nyree Dawn Porter) while he does business in the city. He comes across as tyrannical toward his daughter, but is there a reason for his all-consuming control?

The Cloak—The missing actor (Jon Pertwee) from the wraparound tale rents the house with his co-star (Ingrid Pitt) as they film his latest vampire film nearby. Underwhelmed with the authenticity of the production, he procures an ancient cloak from a sketchy proprietor to add some realism to the film. Little does he know that the cloak possesses the power to make his performance *really* fly off the screen.

Once he has heard the stories, our intrepid inspector decides to visit the house (by himself, naturally) in an attempt to uncover the truth behind the disappearance. Will he like what he finds?

Writer Robert Bloch (the *Psycho* novel) had a longstanding relationship with Amicus producers Milton Subotsky and Max Rosenberg, starting with *The Skull* (1965) and ending with *Asylum* (1972), and I think the reason people tend to remember the Amicus anthologies he *didn't* write (*Tales from the Crypt* and *Vault of Horror*) with more fondness is because those were based on old EC Comics stories. Those films were more cartoonish by their very nature; with broadly drawn characters and narratives that emphasized the twist, the end game. Bloch's stories were of his own creation, and his emphasis was on the characters. So with the other films, the impact arrived with the destination; with Bloch's, the journey held the pleasures. There is only one tale here whose ending you won't see coming from a mile down the road, and that's okay. There's certainly plenty to take in before the next episode appears.

Director Peter Duffell had a lot of British television experience before this, and he would do more after, including two episodes of *Tales of the Unexpected*. He does a nice job here, creating a different mood for each tenant and story, and draws strong performances out of a first rate cast. Of course, Lee and Cushing deliver, as they were accustomed to this sort of heightened melodrama. Lee, in particular, gives a great turn in the finest story (*Sweets to the Sweet*), a tale intriguing enough that it could easily be expanded to feature length, emphasizing Bloch's strength. I wanted to know more about the widower, his daughter, the nanny, and the mystery of the mother. And Pertwee is hilarious in the final story (*The Cloak*) as the pompous B actor who even manages a couple of digs at the then-current actor who famously donned the cape and fangs (hint: he's in this movie). Ironically, this story is played for ghoulish laughs more in line with the non–Bloch anthologies.

When all is said and done, what's the final tally? That depends on the viewer. My favorite episode may not be yours (I know someone who thought my least-liked was the best), and that's part of what makes these portmanteaus so much fun. And probably why audiences are embracing them again—the chance to invest a little time in a short blast of terror, or a well-turned tale. So while we can all enjoy the current crop of omnibuses, let's not forget to pop over to Amicus' *House* (and other properties) for a visit. The furniture may be antique, but it's just as comfortable.

These are the British Rules:
if you leave a house that's dripping blood,
you must immediately check into the…

Vault of Horror (1973)

I've always had a great appreciation and fondness for horror anthologies, and I devoured horror comics as a kid; whether it was *House of Mystery* or *Creepy* magazine, they never failed to fire my imagination in short,

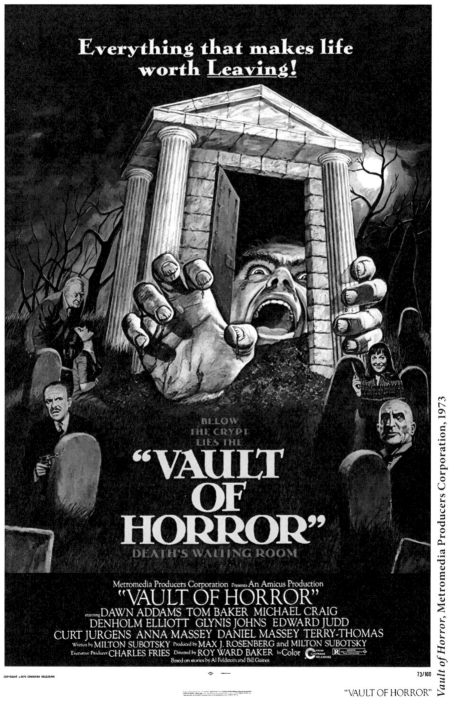

"VAULT OF HORROR"

sharp bursts. When the Romero/King collaboration *Creepshow* (1982) came out, my dream of seeing these kinds of stories translated to film was nothing but revelatory. I soon discovered it was not the first of its ilk, and began a journey through dusty video store shelves looking for its long-lost relatives. One of my first (and favorite) finds was *Vault of Horror* (1973), a five-fingered punch to my nascent, pubescent, omnibus-loving heart.

Produced by Amicus, *Vault of Horror* was not as well-received by critics as *Tales from the Crypt*, which is interesting, because I think it is the better effort—better stories, better performances, and better direction. Which isn't to say I'm slagging on *Tales*; it's very good. But *Vault* amplifies everything that worked in the previous film for a richer viewing experience—if that experience needed more vampires, mutilation, trickery, premature burials and eternal life. (And it should, don't you think?)

I'll break down each of the five tales, but let's start off with our wraparound segment: five British gentlemen board an elevator (sorry, a lift) which takes them to a private lounge where they gather around a table. One by one, they relate their last memory before they arrived at this particular destination. And yes, if you've seen any horror anthology, you know damn well where they are. But first, let's see how each of them got there:

Midnight Mess—Harold (Daniel Massey) goes looking for his missing sister Donna (Anna Massey), who has just inherited the family fortune. His plans are not completely honorable, so perhaps he should have left well enough alone...

The Neat Job—Arthur (Terry-Thomas) has very clear rules for his new wife Eleanor (Glynis Johns)—he's a neat freak, and he believes there's a place for everything, and that everything has a place. Will she be able to keep up with his fastidious needs?

This Trick'll Kill You—A magician (Curt Jurgens) travels to India in search of new tricks. When he comes across an act involving a snake charmer and a rope, he'll do anything to secure its mysterious powers...

Bargain in Death—An insurance scam goes terribly wrong for Maitland (Michael Craig) and his pal Alex (Edward Judd). It's funny how a little premature burial can come between friends...

Drawn and Quartered—An artist (Tom Baker) takes revenge on those who've wronged him through a voodoo spell that allows him to paint and then destroy the targets of his vengeance. Oh, and he does a wonderful self-portrait as well...

Yes, you can probably guess where each and every segment of *Vault of Horror* is going to wind up, but that's not where the fun lies. Instead pleasure is taken from the format itself: a premise, a turn, and a stinger, a *punch line*. This was precisely what drew me to those old comics—the comeuppance handed out to the villains of the piece was always apt and wryly humorous, often appropriately ghoulish, not to mention usually cruel. (It certainly tastes sweeter to the viewer that way.) This is why I prefer a lot of the older omnibuses (from Amicus mainly, but 1982's *Creepshow* probably does it better than all of them) to popular modern day buffets such as the *V/H/S* series or *The ABCs of Death*; I think it's terrific that people have taken to the multistory format renaissance, but sometimes the resolutions are disappointing, or drift away without making any point in a satisfactory way from a pure storytelling angle. I suppose it's just an ink-stained hangover from my childhood. Poetic justice tends to run red on the page.

It does here as well, albeit in a droll presentation from director Roy Ward Baker (*Scars of Dracula*, *The Vampire Lovers*), a Hammer favorite who liked to play in the Amicus sandbox as well. While Amicus was the hipper of the two and preferred to dwell in the modern day, *Vault of Horror* will not upset anyone beyond a PG sensibility. Which is fine, as it stays true to the comics (all adapted by Amicus producer Milton Subotsky from existing tales), which don't mind dismemberment but aren't so bloody messy about it. Having an A-list cast of British veterans selling the material with just the right tongues in just the right cheeks smooths over even the slightest of segments. I'm looking at you, *Bargain in Death*.

But … perhaps that's your favorite one? The great thing about the format is not being tied down or invested for too long before being whisked away to the next, with no commitment beyond 15 or 20 minutes to any particular yarn. The best really do feel like flipping through a good comic, turning the pages with the only certainty that someone's going to be in big trouble before too long; don't worry, they'll deserve it. And if you need a great anthology to pore over, you'll deserve *Vault of Horror* too.

―――――――――――――――

And if you somehow manage to survive the vault,
you'd best book yourself
a vacation at the…

Asylum (1972)

When it comes to anthologies, no one scratches my omnibus itch better than Amicus. From *Dr. Terror's House of Horrors* (1965) to *Tales from the Crypt* (1972) and to *From Beyond the Grave* (1974), time and again they served up slivers of ghoulish goodness, succinct and delectable. *Asylum* (1972) is no different—it probably has the best wraparound of any horror anthology, which sets it apart.

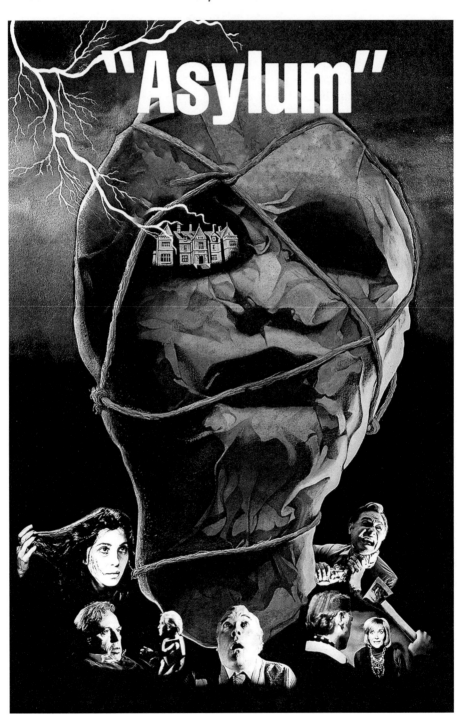

Asylum, Cinema International Corporation, 1972

Released in the U.K. in July with a rollout stateside by Cinerama Releasing Corporation in November, *Asylum* did well in its homeland, but fared less well with the critics. Roger Ebert's bizarre (yet humorous) two-star review focuses completely on producer (and Amicus co-founder) Max J. Rosenberg's obsession with coleslaw. Splayed cabbage aside, *Asylum* holds up as a witty multistory film with a wicked denouement and (as usual) strong work from legendary writer Robert Bloch (*The House That Dripped Blood*).

Let's start with that wraparound, shall we? Dr. Martin (Robert Powell) arrives at the Dunsmoor Asylum for the Incurably Insane for a job interview as the new headshrinker. He meets with Dr. Rutherford (Patrick Magee), who offers him the position on one condition: the former head, Dr. Starr, has himself been institutionalized. If Martin can identify Starr just by listening to the patients tell their stories, he'll have the job. And so, Dr. Martin, with guidance from Max the orderly (Geoffrey Bayldon), is shown around the asylum and meets the inmates:

First up is Bonnie (Barbara Parkins), one of the characters in "Frozen Fear." It seems in the outside world, Bonnie was having a fling with Walter (Richard Todd), much to the disapproval of his rich wife Ruth (Sylvia Syms). Walter's plan was to murder Ruth, chop her into pieces, and stuff her bits done up in butcher's wrap in the brand new freezer he'd bought her. He probably shouldn't have thrown in that voodoo bracelet of Ruth's though. She was very attached to it...

Next, Martin pops in to see Bruno (Barry Morse), the title character in "The Weird Tailor." In his previous life Bruno, behind on his rent, was gifted with a visit from the mysterious Mr. Smith (Peter Cushing) who would pay him $200 dollars to make a suit for his son out of a strange, glowing swath of cloth. When Bruno delivered the suit to Smith, he found the situation ill-fitting...

Then the doctor checks in on Barbara (Charlotte Rampling), a kindly young woman who tells him of a long ago visit back at home when her childhood friend "Lucy Comes to Stay." Barbara's brother George (James Villiers) felt very protective of her, but Lucy had other plans...

Finally, Dr. Martin is introduced to Byron (Herbert Lom), an ex-doctor who has a helluva lot of "Mannikins of Horror" in his closet. These creatures of his design, mechanized wind-up robots with humanesque faces (including one of himself) were ready to live, according to Byron— he just had to will himself into his own doll, which would really come in handy because Byron had a big old beef with the Asylum's Rutherford to settle...

Asylum simply has *the* best wraparound; it's organic, and relates to the stories, and is simply a very clever way to integrate everything seamlessly. The usual set-up for these involves people (dead), a mysterious stranger (Satan) who controls their fate, and a final reveal (they're in hell! Surprise!). Which is all well and good; it's what we expect from the pages of EC Comics, and the framing device has always been just that: an excuse to trot out the dirty laundry of some despicable folk, with dire consequences for all involved. Instead, Rosenberg and Amicus co-chair Milton Subotsky add a mystery element that draws you back in after every morsel, looking for clues as to who Dr. Starr really is. This brings a continuity and flow uncommon to most portmanteaus.

As for the stories themselves, my favorites are "Frozen Fear" and "Mannikins of Horror." Mileage will vary from viewer to viewer, but director Roy Ward Baker (*The Vault of Horror*) treats each tale with equal aplomb and (when needed) reserve. "Lucy Comes to Stay" fits the latter description. It plays due to his commitment to the bit, and the performances he gets from his cast. There is a uniformity to these films in terms of production that presents as admirable consistency; the biggest trend in anthologies at the moment is individual segments that showcase a different creative, which is perfectly fine. As long as the stories work—as they do so well here—that's what matters the most. *Asylum* miraculously holds it together—especially better than its patients.

━━━━━━━━━━━━━━━━

Once you're released from your padded cell, you'll hop across the pond to America. Except you'll find the hospitality there is just as bad; in fact, they'll make you rate it...

From a Whisper to a Scream (1987)

Ever since seeing *Creepshow* (1982) when it first arrived on video, I've been enamored of anthology films. Reaching back to Amicus' 1960s and 1970s treasures like *Tales from the Crypt* (1972) all the way up to *V/H/S99* (2022), omnibuses scratch a very particular itch for this viewer. Falling somewhere in the middle of my terrorline is *From a Whisper to a Scream* (1987), a proud and nasty addition to the subgenre. This bugger does *not* mess around.

Released by Moviestore Entertainment stateside and by Cineplex Odeon up in Canada the following year, *From a Whisper to a Scream* (AKA *The Offspring*, which is what I knew it as) made back its very small budget and the film received mixed reviews from critics in its limited release. Scrappy and mean, with a delightful turn from Vincent Price in

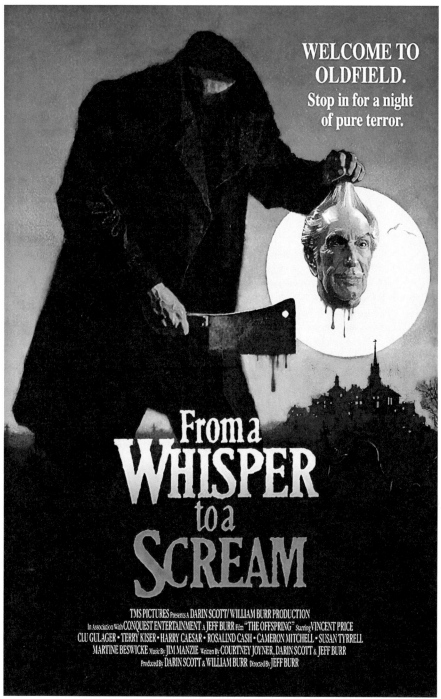

the wraparound, *From a Whisper to a Scream* delivers with four very solid tales of decadence guaranteed to hit at least a couple of your twisted pleasure points.

The film opens with the execution by lethal injection of serial killer Katherine White (Martine Beswick) in Oldfield, Tennessee. Witnessing her death is reporter Beth Chandler (Susan Tyrrell), who then tracks down her Uncle Julian (Price), the town's historian and librarian. Julian regales Beth with four tales that describe the evil that permeates the very soil of the town:

- Clu Gulager has the hots for a fellow worker (Megan McFarland), which results in (a) murder, and (b) an unexpected visit from beyond the grave;
- Terry Kiser is a hoodlum on the run from gangsters who is nursed back to life by a swamp-bound Samaritan (Harry Caesar), and soon learns what greed begets;
- A carnival glass eater (Ron Brooks) falls in love with a townie much to the chagrin of the snake woman (Rosalind Cash);
- A trio of Union soldiers (led by Cameron Mitchell) stumble across a group of postwar orphans that are anything but hospitable to the North…

From a Whisper to a Scream offers a lot of variety for the discriminating horror lover. Each tale is unique and offers up the "poetic justice" of the EC Comics of yore—with the exception of the third segment, which chooses to punish the protagonists for the mere fact that they're in love. While well-made and performed with some gruesome effects (you just know that glass will be in play), this plays as the least effective due to its lack of hook, i.e., Bad People Get Theirs, which I need, dammit all. Comeuppance is one of my very favorite dramatic devices in horror (and action—comedy too, come to think of it) and the anthology story is the perfect place to use it—setup to punchline in 20 minutes.

So four and a wraparound is a good ratio, even better when the majority of stories are so strong. It's not so much because the plots are complex—they're more or less simple revenge tales—but it's due to the conviction that the filmmakers bring to the material. This was director Jeff Burr's second feature, and his lean and energetic style would serve him well later with the much underrated *The Stepfather II* and the aforementioned *Leatherface*. (There's no need to bring *Pumpkinhead II* into this.)

It's this enthusiasm that fuels *From a Whisper to a Scream*. From the screenplay by C. Courtney Joyner (*Prison*), Darin Scott (*Tales from the Hood*), and Burr himself to the scrappily impressive practical effects by Rob Burman (*The Thing*). Everyone works well above the budget to provide a polished product for the horror-hungry. But it's not only "enthusiasm," which can sometimes in low-budget terms just be shorthand for "eager but meager"—this is no amateur hour, with all parties involved showing a level of professionalism (and occasional inspiration) uncommon for a film with low financial stakes.

And at this level, sometimes things can get nasty. In addition to corpse love, child zombies, and dismemberment, we're treated to fatal indigestion and pin the tail on … well, you'll see. This is all told with nary a wink to be had. Perhaps that's why the film's reputation stands apart from others of its ilk—punishment is served, but in a grimmer fashion than its inspiration.

The humor here is then mined from those in front of the camera, and a couple of veterans are definitely up to the task. First off, even getting Vincent Price was quite the coup for the filmmakers, and he reluctantly signed on for the wraparound after the segments had been filmed. (He was trying to move away from horror.) Nor did he care much at all for the finished product. His mere presence alone, however, adds a level of prestige to the proceedings that a big budget film never could—and that's horror royalty. And his scenes with Tyrrell are terrific—his sweet southern drawl lures her in closer as he introduces each succeeding segment, and he does the same with the viewer. Price may not have appreciated the final product, but he brings a joyful, sly energy to the part as only he could. Really, the whole cast is great and filled with names from horrors past (Cash) and future (Kiser) who all do their part to sell the dark material.

But no one seems to be on even the same planet as Clu Gulager. His Stanley Burnside is a sweaty, twitching mess of a human, with coke bottle glasses, slicked back hair, and a greasy undershirt to complete his ensemble. The stained shirt is a good metaphor for Stanley himself, who not only is obsessed with a co-worker to the point of murder (and beyond), but also hints at an incestuous relationship with his ill sister. (Watch out for those ice baths. Brr.) Gulager is never less than interesting in all his films, and his Stanley is mesmerizing—awful to the core, but utterly compelling. (Don't worry, he probably gets his.)

The 1980s have more than a few anthology films that aim for (and play with) the *Creepshow* model—none of them however lean into the mean like *From a Whisper to a Scream* does. I'm afraid it may even be too cruel for poor old Stanley, bless his greasy soul.

We wrap this festival with my favorite portmanteau of them all.
Leave it up to George Romero and Stephen King
to create the ultimate…

Creepshow (1982)

Anthology horror films offer up the same pickle every single time out: is the goal cohesiveness—and by extension, uniformity—or is it one-up-manship? Do you want modulation … or overstimulation?

The answer is both I think, if done right. *Creepshow* (1982) is done right. It just may be the most done-right horror anthology of all time. It certainly was (and happily, still is) for a kid who voraciously tore through *Creepy* magazines and DC horror comics like *House of Mystery*.

It's all about the panels, you see—those glorious, splattery four-color panels that plaster each page with retribution, comeuppance, and … a heaping dose of gnarliness. The panels demand justice within their four walls, delivered with terseness and economy.

Creepshow understands this better than most, due to its main creative forces: George Romero and Stephen King. The late and legendary Mr. Romero (d. 2017) was coming off the excellent medieval motorcycle drama *Knightriders* (1981); Mr. King was in his seemingly perpetual ascension as the most popular horror writer of all time. When the cinematic stars align and the minds do too, you get *Creepshow*—the ultimate tribute to horror comics from creators who devoured the same ghoulish material as the next generation of horror kids *they* inspired.

And lo and behold, it hit some sweet spots for the public *and* intelligentsia. Praise was given to the ripe performances, brightly garish cinematography, and most importantly, the tongue-in-cheek tone beautifully shepherded by Romero and King. I've always believed tone was key to a great anthology—all the films featured in this festival steer a sturdy ship through sometimes disparate material to resolutely land on safe shores. They simply don't shit the bed before the curtain falls.

But *Creepshow* is different from the other portmanteaus in this festival. Better is subjective, but while the wonderful Amicus films discussed earlier carry the comic's tone very well, *Creepshow* does that *and* drowns in their gorgeous, goofy aesthetic. This is a literal comic book movie—it's framed with comic panels at certain crucial moments that power the story at hand. *Creepshow* is specifically created for any and every kid-at-heart…

… assuming you're that kid who always looks deep down every darkened corner and can't resist seeing what's behind that damn door.

The film has five segments, plus a wraparound featuring none other than Tom Atkins as the World's Worst Dad. Let's start flipping pages!

In our wraparound, an asshole of a dad (see above) smacks his kid—played by King's real kid, Joe Hill—because he's been caught reading the *Creepshow* tie-in comic for the very film in which he's appearing. (Very meta) After the animated credits, we dissolve into our first tale…

Father's Day—Pity poor Aunt Bedelia (Viveca Lindfors). Her horrible father had her fiancé killed in a hunting "accident" years ago—and Bedelia repaid the favor by offing dear old dad with an ashtray to the head on Father's Day. Every year she visits his grave and taunts him; he never did get his Father's Day cake—perhaps this year he does…

The Lonesome Death of Jordy Verrill—When a meteorite crashes in his field, dimwitted dirt farmer Jordy (King himself) pours water on it, causing it to flame out, split open, and emit a glowing green ooze. He also burns his finger on it, leaving a fluorescent, bubbling blister that immediately takes over his (drastically shortened) life.

Something to Tide You Over—When a rich and controlling millionaire (Leslie Nielsen) finds out that his wife (Gaylen Ross) has taken a younger lover (Ted Danson), he buries him up to his neck in sand on his private beach. And his wife is buried the same way on another part of the beach. As the millionaire watches the waves and his property through a state-of-the-art surveillance system, he wonders: Will the lovers be reunited? And will they be pissed?

The Crate—Two college professor chums (Hal Holbrook, Fritz Weaver) find their friendship constantly challenged by one's overbearing wife (Adrienne Barbeau). When the other discovers an ancient Arctic creature inside a dusty crate, he decides to help his friend with his marital problems.

They're Creeping Up on You!—It's back to millionaires and megalomania, as a cranky, reclusive germaphobe (E.G. Marshall) finds himself with a slight cockroach infestation.

And we finish back with our crappy dad, who gets his comeuppance via a clipped coupon and a rightfully pissed off 'lil King.

You can and will pick your number one—it's human nature. And then the following week you might switch that up. It's one of my favorite built-in features of the anthology format—when firing on all cylinders, there are no wrong answers.

I mean, there are no wrong answers *anyway*; I won't be that type. Your fave is your fave. What I'm saying is the quality of *Creepshow* is so high that it bypasses lows. There isn't a stinker in the bunch for me, but a favorite is *Something to Tide You Over*. It's mean, funny, very macabre, and has an all-time EC-style classic ending.

Yet here you come, foaming at the mouth and bullhorning the appeal of *The Crate*—especially Adrienne Barbeau's hysterical, over-the-top boor, Wilma. ("Just call me Billie, everyone does!") And another will trap you in a corner to tell you *Father's Day* has Ed Harris doing one of the wildest, weird white man dances in cinematic history. You get the idea. We're all correct.

The stories are good-humored, in that heightened (and compact) sense of delicious retribution that 20 minute grasps will allow. Nuance and subtlety hold no sway when the clock is ticking. And while King (with his first screenwriting credit) is not always known for terseness, here he has no choice in a regimented format. The straitjacket fits, and the stories move with precision and purpose.

Cinematographer Michael Gornick (who would take over directing duties on 1987's *Creepshow 2*) gives Romero and King's vision life, with primary-colored panels that pop and explode in canted angles behind the actors during surprising or horrific moments. For a lot of horror lovers, this will translate into nothing but smiles, as the likes of Leslie Nielsen becomes hysterical shooting at the water-logged zombie lovers.

There are some who don't particularly cotton to the comic or even the whimsical in their horror—just the scares, thank you very much. That's okay. *Creepshow*'s tagline "The Most Fun You'll Ever Have BEING SCARED!" may be the most honest claim in advertising history. Well, as honest as one can get, I suppose.

Festival Six:
Terror in Technotown

Welcome to Festival Six, Terror in Technotown. In this festival, I'm throwing down some serious PSAs about the dangers of technology, and I don't mean anything lame like figuring out how to get the remote to turn off the picture-in-picture mode. I am talking about serious matters, like Clint Howard getting zapped with the vengeful spirit of Bull from Night Court through an Apple II computer, or a futuristic resort for rich people, where one can fornicate with a robot and not only not be judged for it, but you also get courtesy wake up calls. Let's not forget some very artificial insemination from Robert Vaughn's super smart and horny computer. Movies are weird!

Sure, it's easy for this generation—Z, right?—they were born practically marinating in it from birth. But ... imagine a time when computers weren't in every home and in your phones, too. (Sorcery, I say!) As a Generation Xer, it has been fascinating to watch—and participate in—the ever-changing, shrinking world. My fear of technology—and I think I'm not alone—isn't that man will use it for ill, but rather that something irreversible will occur, where no cancel codes and fail-safes can stop it. Like setting the timer wrong on the coffee pot.

The protagonists in this festival are a mix of the smart using tech to ill-effect: the slow using it for revenge; the rich using it for vacations; and whatever the hell *Videodrome* is about. (I'm kidding. It's clearly about remembering to rewind your vagina tapes.) But what the *films* have in common is a severe distrust of machines, especially computers, and those who wield them.

The fear is always there in the unknown, and these films all lean into it. Essentially what you get are "What if?" scenarios that made futurists' heads explode at the possibilities. (I have no idea if they were even upset. Follow up question: What's a futurist?)

What if ... a man crossed his DNA with that of a fly?

What if … robots rebelled at a fantasy resort and started killing people?

What if … a sentient computer impregnated a woman?

What if … a computer was a portal used to conjure a demon as an instrument of vengeance?

What if … a chest cavity vagina could play video tapes but only Betamax? (Ew. Not the vagina; the Betamax.)

It makes complete sense for filmmakers to put that paranoia and fear to good use. Horror is so much fun when it pulls the zeitgeist kicking and screaming in its direction.

When I was a kid in the 1970s, computers were room fillers, and very far from home: NASA and Kurt Russell's Dexter Riley Disney movies, and that's about it. So they were a mystery to most of us—machines doing math quicker than the human brain seemed impossible. Now we have self-driving, electric cars—you don't even have to drive to get yourself in an accident. Progress!

And look, the computers almost took over during Y2K, right? We were this close to being the robots' bitches just like James Cameron predicted in *Terminator 2: Judgment Day*. Honestly, I'm fine with all of that; but if we could skip the impregnation, that would be wonderful.

We start with a film that for most, was eventually eclipsed
by its admittedly superior remake. But forget that for a moment,
and enjoy the many-eyed charms of…

The Fly (1958)

"Charming" is not often a word associated with horror films; it's counterintuitive to what the genre usually stands for. It's usually, you know, terror and tension, followed by release and a sense of ease, then repeat. Yet here we are with a romantic tale about a boy, a girl, a teleportation device, and the insect that comes between them. Welcome to the world of *The Fly* (1958), where the hosts are welcoming, the police polite, and the monster bug-eyed.

Released by 20th Century–Fox in July, *The Fly* pulled in $7 million against its $300,000 budget, enticing audiences with a tale often told at the time. Sold as another Atomic Age Monster Mash, *The Fly* instead uses a much smaller (and human) canvas to convey a message of obsession and the love that ultimately ends it. Having said that, you also get a man with a

THE MONSTER CREATED BY ATOMS GONE WILD!
IN CINEMASCOPE AND TERROR-COLOR BY DE LUXE!

20th Century-Fox

starring
AL HEDISON · PATRICIA OWENS
VINCENT PRICE · HERBERT MARSHALL
Produced and Directed by KURT NEUMANN Screen Play by JAMES CLAVELL Based on a Story by GEORGE LANGELAAN

FOR YOUR OWN GOOD
WE URGE YOU
NOT TO SEE IT ALONE!

The Fly, 20th Century-Fox, 1958

fly head and some neat-o transportation sequences, lest we forget where we are and what the hell we're talking about.

Which would be this: as our film opens, a night watchman comes upon one Hélène Delambre (Patricia Owens) fleeing from a running industrial press in an electronic factory (Radio Shack?) owned by her husband, André (David Hedison) and his brother François (Vincent Price). His *living* brother that is, as it turns out to be André chillin' under the flattened press, which we discover when Helene phones François immediately after and confesses to killing her husband.

Under occasional police supervision in her home (this takes place in Québec, and there's no need for your ill-mannered arrest procedures, thank you very much), Hélène recounts to François and Inspector Charas (Herbert Marshall) the events leading up to her inventor-spouse's demise—such as his experiment with transporting matter, which works great until a fly climbs into the chamber with him and they swap body parts. Now, if they can only find that darn fly with the white head…

In the light of David Cronenberg's 1986 classic re-imagining, the original *The Fly* is often viewed as a somewhat quaint relic of its time. Pleasant, a few decent effects, and a good evening to you, sir. And I myself was certainly guilty of this; having grown up in the Shadow of Seth with its perfectly doomed romance, state-of-the art effects, and finely honed suspense, how could it be taken as anything but a diversion, a trifle?

But … that's not really fair, is it? We have to judge it by its peers, I think. Back in the day, in the middle of nuclear sea creatures, giant lizards, and gargantuan arachnids, *The Fly*, much like its namesake, is small, but purposefully so. The easiest way to frighten a kid or teen in the 1950s was through the Red Scare, which was tangible, palpable, and all too real. The horror/sci-fi movies of the day dealt in that fear and paranoia and brought the kids in. Perhaps, then, *The Fly* was meant to sway the parents, even though there's just enough sugar to tempt the youngsters. Whoever the target demographic, it manages to set itself apart due to its intimate nature.

This was writer James Clavell's first film credit; he would go on to write the novel and TV adaptation of *Shogun* (1980), among many others. It's a solid first script that goes easy on the melodrama, perhaps to a fault. The kids want big moments, but other than André's shocking third act reveal, it tends not to get *too* excited. Clavell seems to be aiming for a *Phantom of the Opera* grandeur filtered through the pages of *LIFE* magazine, and he gets it in his unmasking to Hélène. André's multi-paned POV of her screaming amplifies her fear, cushioned in the lushness of Cinemascope's anamorphic widescreen.

The script is the true star here; director Kurt Neumann (*Rocketship*

X-M) stays out of the way, with little flourish, but a good feel for the characters—Price is always a delight, and here he offers a sympathetic turn as Andre's brother who secretly pines for Hélène. Speaking of, Owens keeps it grounded until she can't resist the urge as the stakes are raised. But it really is the love story between her and Hedison that, as I said, gives the film a real charm considering the subject matter. Hedison, while consumed with his experiments, dotes on his wife and child when he can, lending weight to the scenes when she tries to communicate with him post-transformation. And Hedison, who spends most of the runtime concealed under black cloth, is terrific at conveying the sadness and anger inherent with his condition.

The effects hold up very well, too. The transportation scenes give the film some wanted (and needed) action and are filled with color and wonder, again appealing to the kids who need the eye candy to stay invested. (I'm not averse to it, either.) And while the ending has been shown in countless clip shows over the decades, it still holds a macabre charm for a reason: it's incredibly creepy. (Plus, fuck spiders. All of them.)

So, is the remake better than this? It doesn't matter; they both come from different times, technologies, and temperaments. But for me, the biggest draw of the remake, the thing I keep returning to, is the romance between Seth and Veronica. It's the human element, removed from the latex and toxic bile, that is the heart of the film. And while it borrows the basic plot from the earlier version, Cronenberg, in his most emotionally open film, draws on what makes the original work so well: a tragic love story with a real sense of resolution. And all the bloodied bells and whistles in the world can't disguise the fact that Neumann and Clavell did it first. Whether it does it better is irrelevant. The world can always use more love stories (even with tragic endings), and I'm glad both exist.

―――――――――――――――

Well, that was a stressful situation, wasn't it?
You need a vacation! Why not grab a friend
and book a relaxing trip to...

Westworld (1973)

As a kid, you can't be picky where you find your fix of sci-fi and horror. Sometimes it's the big screen, but often it was that living room landmark, television. I remember being seven and watching a western where a couple of guys are on vacation at a resort where you can be a cowboy and

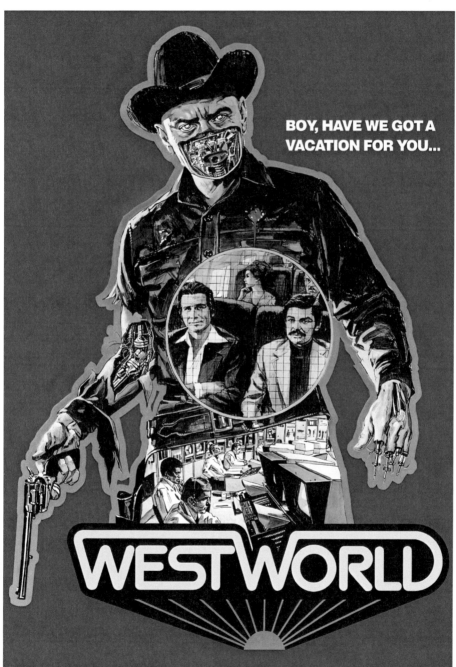

BOY, HAVE WE GOT A VACATION FOR YOU...

have gunfights with androids (sci-fi, sweet!). And then … bad things start to happen. The androids break down, and now they're killing the guests (Ooh, horror!). My head reeled from this magical swirl, a mesh of circuitry and chaos. Welcome to *Westworld* (1973), and its parent resort, Delos. Their slogan: *Have we got a vacation for you.*

This was a pretty good year for sci-fi. *Soylent Green* made a splash ("It's Peeoople!!!"), the latest installment in the Apes franchise, *Battle for the Planet of the Apes*, and Woody Allen's *Sleeper* were the leading contenders for futuristic fun at the theaters. *Star Wars*, which many people dubbed a Western in space, was still four years away from blowing up the box office. Michael Crichton's *Westworld* beat *SW* to the punch, and brought sci-fi (and horror) kicking and screaming to the Western genre.

Released in November, *Westworld* was an unqualified success for MGM; this was author/doctor Crichton's feature film debut as writer and director, and it is an assured and thrilling debut.

The story goes a little like this: John (James Brolin) and Peter (Richard Benjamin) take a trip to Delos, a multimillion dollar resort that lets guests live out their wildest fantasies at three different parks: There's Medieval World, Roman World (or as I call it, the Caesarian Section), and Western World, or Westworld. Each offers a unique experience to the guest, whether it's jousting, bedding a maiden, ruling an empire or in John and Peter's case, becoming desperados in the Wild West. The novelty of the resort (and the reason for the $1000 a day price tag) is that, except for your fellow guests, all the participants in your costly charade are androids run by a team of scientists and engineers with computers the size of Buicks.

After a shootout at the saloon with The Gunslinger (Yul Brynner) in which Peter puts him down, the boys continue to hoot and holler, enjoying the down and dirty Western experience (including bedding two salacious saloon "workers"—side note: who draws the short straw to clean the machines?). And then events take a turn for the worse. Minor malfunctions grow into glitches until the androids become … sentient. Sure the price is almost the same, but at least at Disneyland, Donald Duck won't plug ya with a belly full of lead. It's at this point the film switches gears from fascinating sci-fi to ruthless horror.

It's the tonal shift that is so intriguing. The first two-thirds present an amusing romp, following John and Peter on their escapades. At this point Crichton starts putting little nicks in the android armor to make us uneasy. And then…. THE moment. It involves Brolin, Benjamin, Brynner, and a deserted street. This is where Crichton *really* turns the screws, and doesn't let up until the credits roll. From here on *Westworld* induces rewarding robogasms for the viewer, propelling us headlong through a place where Asimov's three rules need not apply.

Technology gone wrong. A Crichton hallmark and legacy that is woven through the very fabric of science fiction. *Westworld*. *The Terminal Man*. *Jurassic Park*. All Crichton creations in one form or another, relaying a crippling technofear (computer viruses are hinted at in *Westworld*) to the viewer through a cracked computer lens. Crichton knowingly trots out the Western clichés to lull the viewer before shaking up the sawdust on the barroom floor.

Crichton shows an affinity with actors too, getting relaxed and entertaining turns from Benjamin and the magnificently maned Brolin. Benjamin is a revelation, showing that he can give a more restrained performance as opposed to his manic comedic forays down the line. Casting Brynner as the Gunslinger is inspired; it's clearly a mirror image of his character from *The Magnificent Seven*. Here, Brynner exudes a steely, coiled evil that when released, shatters your expectations of him forever. After this, you can call him The Malevolent One.

If you can't afford a vacation this year, fire up the entertainment system at home and visit the fine folks at *Westworld*. Come for the cowboys, stay for the slaughter. And if someone sends you a discount code for Delos—tell them thanks, and hit delete.

Okay, maybe that wasn't the ideal vacation. Why not head back home, relax, and let your insane husband's insane computer impregnate you with the...

Demon Seed (1977)

Demon Seed (1977) was the latest in an ever growing subgenre of science fiction film: Technodoubt (okay, I just made that up). But as the world started to catch up with its imagination (Apple Computers was born in 1976), and technology raged forward like a silicon locomotive, Hollywood searched for ways to exploit mankind's natural fear of progress. From the dangerously malfunctioning HAL in *2001* (1968), to the murderous androids of *Westworld* (1973), rich veins of cybernetic carnage were mined for maximum cinematic paranoia. *Demon Seed* upped the ante by downloading the menace right into the home.

Released in April by MGM, the film was not a commercial success by any means, but certainly drew attention from critics due to its unusual (and quite absurd) high concept story, a showcase performance from Julie Christie, and a piqued interest in director Donald Cammell. Regardless of

the gateway, *Demon Seed* remains a unique genre treatise on dominance and loss.

Dr. Alex Harris (Fritz Weaver) and his wife Susan (Christie), a child psychologist, are separating. Alex is distant and cold, apparently incapable of human connection, a situation which Susan has grown weary of. She chooses to stay in their state of the art, computerized, voice-activated (and fully secured) home, while Alex stays at his lab at ICON, a scientific corporation. After eight years, Alex and his team have perfected their supercomputer, Proteus IV (voiced by an uncredited Robert Vaughn), make it sentient, and instill in it the power of reason—with the belief that this will make Proteus more amenable to any requests that ICON might have. After four days of going live, Proteus has discovered a cure for leukemia (a plot point featured later on in the film), but soon grows bored (and insolent) with Alex's requests.

Of course, Proteus has bigger plans—it wants to study man, from top to bottom, and demands to be "let out of his box." Alex refuses, so Proteus takes matters into its own hands (so to speak) and plugs into the vacant computer terminal at the Harris residence. Discovering that the house is almost completely automated, it takes over the system, sets up shop in the basement and builds, via a remote controlled robotic arm, a tetrahedron that acts as its physical representation. (Hold tight. We haven't hit weird warp drive yet.) Deciding that Susan will be its subject, Proteus puts the house on lockdown, and after resistance from Susan, informs her of the real plan—to father a child with her, and experience life as a human. Okay, you can hit the weird button now. We're there.

The plot of *Demon Seed*, by any standards, is insane. However, fleshing out the fractured relationship between Alex and Susan gives the film a gravitas (especially in heartbreaking details revealed late in the film) that pushes it towards believability. Their relationship is one side of the triangle, the other one between Susan and Proteus. The supercomputer means her no harm, but sees no issue (physically or mentally) with (a) holding her against her will, (b) essentially raping her, and (c) making her go full term (in this case 28 days) with the baby, concocted from her egg and its bionic batter. The battle of wills between the two is the main thrust of the film, with the return of Alex leading up to a possible rebirth of their nuclear family. All is shattered and twisted with a late reveal proving the old adage about never going home again.

The horror angle (we wouldn't be here otherwise) is played up in a couple of ways: There is no demon in *Demon Seed*, but this was the 1970s, when Satanic Panic was in full bloom (don't blame the studio—the title comes from the 1973 book by Dean Koontz) and everything Lucifer–like was flying off the shelves and the screen. As well, the film plays into our fears of isolation and the unknown—trapped in the house by Proteus,

Susan is alone and scared as to how her baby will turn out—successfully mined earlier in *Rosemary's Baby* (1968).

So here we have a touch of *2001*, a sprig of *Rosemary*, with enough caution thrown towards technology to send the timid Amish-bound. What's amazing is how much of it works, considering the story line. A large part of the credit should go to Cammell, a former painter who used his 1960s London sensibilities on the Mick Jagger–starring *Performance* (1970), and after this, the bizarre (even for the 1980s) thriller *White of the Eye* (1987). This is his *normal* film, probably due to the fact that he had no hand in the screenplay, which was written by Robert Jaffe (*Motel Hell*) and Roger Hirson. Are there parts that play more to his sensibility? Sure—when Walter (Gerrit Graham), Alex's coworker, checks on Susan and does battle with Proteus, the film nestles down for a bit in WTF territory. Or Proteus' light show, generously provided for Susan during impregnation, will take one back to the good old days of Pink Floyd at the local planetarium (bong hits not included). What makes it work is that Cammell commits to these scenes and the quiet ones the same, with a steadfast resolve to see the story through from conception to birth.

Christie seems an unusual choice for Susan—at first. Known for more highbrow fare like *McCabe & Mrs. Miller* (1971) and *Shampoo* (1975), she made only seven films in the 1970s. But take a closer look at Susan and you'll find a wounded woman searching for closure and dealing with tragedy, all while fighting a heartless being looking for his own rebirth. She plays Susan with a somber dignity and a quiet pride. She's a fascinating character and Christie gives a remarkable performance. Weaver imbues Alex with a detached pomposity befitting the husband; right to the end, his alliances are quite clear. Graham turns in a sympathetic performance as Walter, showing more care towards Susan than Alex ever does. Finally, uncredited but impossible to ignore is Robert Vaughn as the voice of Proteus. His naturally robotic intonations work perfectly here—calm and flat at first, becoming increasingly turbulent as its sense of reason is questioned and vilified. It's one of his most energetic and sly performances.

Demon Seed. Beyond the sensationalistic title lies a film that attempts to outgrow its pulpy origins through solid direction, strong performances, and a hard-wired will to *be*. Proteus would find that very reasonable.

And now for something a bit tamer.
Ron Howard's little brother Clint gets his ass kicked
Carrie-style until he summons an ancient demon with an Apple II computer
to help him fight back. Okay, forget what I said about it being tamer...

Evilspeak (1981)

Vengeance is mine, sayeth the Lord—and many horror films to boot. Payback has always been a constant theme, whether it's a sinister spirit avenging murder, or a maniacal parent repaying camp counselors for not watching her handicapped child. The meteoric rise in popularity of video games and personal computers at the turn of the 1980s, married with ancient evil, brought a modern edge to this shopworn trope. A sympathetic tale of comeuppance, *Evilspeak* (1981) serves up its revenge under the computer screen's warm glow.

Released by Moreno Films, first in Japan in August 1981, and February 1982 in North America, *Evilspeak* nearly made back its US$1 million budget opening weekend stateside. A few good reviews trickled in, comparing it favorably to the high school horrorfest *Carrie* (1976). Regardless of comparisons, it stands as a unique antique of a burgeoning time in technology and a potent payback tale.

Our story begins with ex-communicated Catholic Father Esteban (Richard Moll) holding court with his satanic followers on a beach in Spain, when he is told in no uncertain terms by a member of the church that he needs to renounce Satan in order to receive salvation. One beheading later, we flash forward hundreds of years and we land at West Andover Military Academy, where cadet Stanley Coopersmith (Clint Howard) is helping his teammates lose another soccer game. Stanley is Mr. Can't Catch a Break, bullied by his peers, and looked down on by the school officials as a useless, orphaned, government charity case. Sent to the church basement to clean as one more form of punishment, Stanley comes across Esteban's diary and some how-to books on performing devilish duties. Stanley takes his goodies and has the Latin translated on one of the school's PCs (sorry, Apple II—but hey, at least no viruses, right?), revealing a message from Esteban about his impending return.

Of course, a sacrifice is needed, which our sheepish Stanley is unable to provide until he is pushed too far by his classmates. When Esteban does finally return via Stanley, swords are swung, pigs get real hungry, and our hero gets his revenge on everyone who has wronged him. (Don't worry, it's a sufficient cast for maximum carnage.) Can anyone stop Stanley from fulfilling Esteban's devilish destiny? Will cooler heads prevail? Are there any heads left?

Evilspeak has a lot in common with *Carrie*, including sympathetic performances from its leads, taut direction, and soggy middle acts. While both films use this downtime to further flesh out the characters, it's unnecessary as the opening acts give us all we need. What sets the film apart from Brian De Palma's Girl Gone Wild extravaganza is a gonzo sensibility

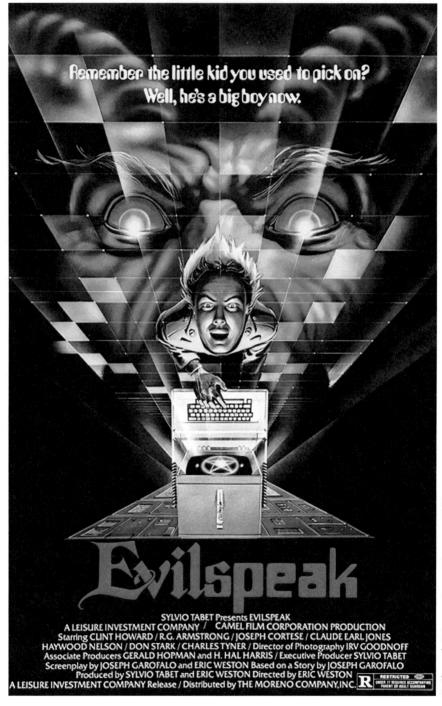

in the final third that makes *Carrie*'s prom look like a no hands—no touch junior high mixer. The final showdown in the campus church is well worth the wait, as Stanley goes on an unprecedented chopping spree with some help from Babe's carnivorous cousins. It all culminates in a frenzy of bacon and brimstone, trimming the graduating class (and faculty) down to a more manageable size.

Orchestrating the schoolhouse rock is first-timer Eric Weston (*Hyenas*), who doesn't show a lot of flash behind the camera until the third act, where he lets loose with a manic display of fire, wind, and blood. (Is that an element? It should be here.) It's a promising debut, showing a fine B-movie sensibility and a solid rapport with his actors. The script by Weston and Joseph Garofalo does ladle on the abuse to Coopersmith a little thick (I can appreciate the bullying from classmates, but how the hell is this faculty still employed?), however it serves to sweeten Stanley's retribution come the home stretch.

A fine cast of newcomers and vets fills the halls of West Andover. Don Stark brings a low-key menace to Stanley's chief rival Bubba. And every adult, with the exception of Luca Brasi himself (Lenny Montana) as nurturing cook Jake, is rotten to the core. But look at these rogues! First we have Claude Earl Jones as Coach, whose obsession with winning every soccer game at an all-American academy is misguided at best. Next up is the Reverend Jameson, played with a smarmy piousness by Joe Cortese, who spends more time on his knees pleading for donations from the political elite than he does praying. Last but far from least is R.G. Armstrong as drunken caretaker Sarge, delivering a wild-eyed, psychotic performance proving that you don't have to be satanic to make the people panic.

And then there is our Stanley—Clint Howard. The film cannot possibly work if we aren't on his side, but not to worry. Between his adolescent pout and wounded puppy-dog eyes, Howard breaks your heart as the put-upon, downtrodden Coopersmith. He goes through so much that by the time he gets his due, you'll almost feel a sense of pride. Hey, at least he's finally good at something! As for Howard, it would prove to be his finest starring performance.

Evilspeak still resonates with horror fans decades after its release. Why? Because bullying should never be tolerated, and anytime the repressed can make a stand through actions, protests, or blogs, it is a cause for celebration. And if help comes in the form of a demonic priest via computer, accept it—it's worth the storage space.

Our final entry has James Woods fisting himself. Welcome to...

Videodrome (1983)

"Long live the new flesh."

Welcome to David Cronenberg's *Videodrome* (1983). The above is the last line uttered in the film, and it's a hell of a capper for one that is by turns gross, perplexing, intriguing, and always weird. Of course I love the film; it's a Cronenberg wild ride that I can't resist. This was his follow-up to *Scanners* (1981), which was a surprise hit. *Videodrome* ... was not a hit, nor did it break even at the box office; but that's okay, because the critics also hated it.

I don't think it's a matter of understanding—the themes are there, but it's his delivery system that causes people to need fainting couches and smelling salts for revival. What gets me about Cronenberg and critics of his work—and there are many—is that words like "repulsive" and "disgusting" are used as shields to deflect the material completely. Guess what? It's both of those things and much, much more. Those who dislike his work will use those words to simply shut out the material and not engage with it.

And what I've found through the decades is that Cronenberg *wants* the viewer to be engaged—to not would be the antithesis of filmmaking, wouldn't it?—but it must be done on his terms and his playing field. He might make you feel *bad*, but he will make you feel.

Let's start this show at CIVIC-TV in Toronto (modeled after real life media giant CITY-TV) as cable programmer Max Renn (James Woods) is on the search for fresh shows for his late-night viewers—titillation and violence are the catch of the day, as always.

Someone shows Max a pirated show out of Malaysia called "Videodrome," an early reality show that has people engaging in sadomasochism, which eventually leads them to be murdered on camera. With no commercial breaks! Finally a show that entices Max! He begins a search that first leads him to an S & M radio host Nicki (Blondie's Debbie Harry), who after sleeping with Max watches a broadcast of "Videodrome" and becomes very aroused. When Max discovers the signal is actually coming from Pittsburgh (not exotic, but nice I guess), Nicki takes off to audition.

The more he watches, the more Max hallucinates. Enter the chest vagina—thanks to the amazing Rick Baker and his effects crew—which becomes a handy storing place for a gun. Max's journey takes him to a homeless shelter run by Bianca (Sonja Smits), the daughter of media analyst Brian O'Blivion (subbing for Canada's own guru of media affairs, Marshall McLuhan).

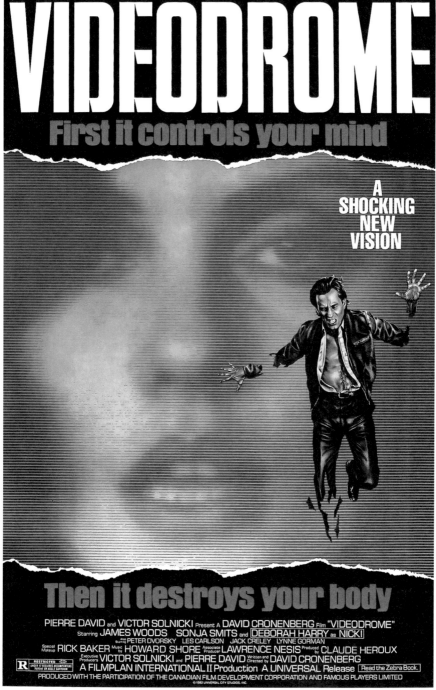

Videodrome, Universal Pictures, 1983

At the Cathode Ray Mission, the homeless are made to watch endless hours of TV as a type of therapy. Brian O'B's philosophy is that television is a cure all. But that's only the beginning; is Max hallucinating, or is his body—his very nature—being controlled by "Videodrome"? Stay tuned...

It's a Cronenberg, so the odds of its occurring are close to 100 percent. He revels in side-door realities where the implausible fits in because everything is just a little off, and accepted as such.

As the decades pass, it becomes more obvious that the salacious nature of the film—pleasure and pain entwined in desperate transactions and new horizons—will never sit well with Mom & Pop America. And he had Universal pick up the tab, the cheeky bugger. But sex—and all of its fleshy and messy connotations—was front and center in early Cronenberg films like *Shivers* (1975) and *Rabid* (1977). Here he swaps out venereal diseases for a different kind of virus but the effect is the same—the destruction of the flesh.

Or is that a rebirth? It's hard to say—if you follow the story, then Max's dissolution is merely the beginning of his journey; if you don't then that way madness lies. It really isn't so much a story, as it is a questionnaire for oneself: Are you obsessed with sex and violence? Does overexposure to TV and films lead one to commit horrible crimes? If you sit too close, will you go blind, or will your head be sucked through the tube in a static tsunami? All very important questions—and it should be noted, without a hint of judgment.

I've come to appreciate Cronenberg's outlook the older I get—the body decaying is a part of life, but that decay can also be considered change. Pragmatism of the flesh leads to flights of the mind. It's not "the medium is the message," but it's all I've got.

Festival Seven:
Back Bacon Bloodbath

Seeing as how I am in fact Canadian, it only seems right to have a festival dedicated to the Great White North: Welcome to *Back Bacon Bloodbath*, ya bunch of hosers! We've always taken our horror to heart up here, even if they may appear to come from somewhere else. Truth be told, this book would have several Canadian films in it whether I created a festival for them or not. Some of my favorite horror films from this era—and maybe yours too—*are* Canadian made.

They were probably financed by money men from the States, but Canadian-made all the same, with a healthy percentage of talent in front and behind the camera. And if you're talking about the history of Canadian genre films, you can't avoid the glamour and sex appeal of tax breaks—none of these films would be around without it.

Here goes: from 1975 to 1982, you could come from anywhere and finance a film in Canada and write off the entire production on your taxes, 100 percent. There were strict rules, of course; we're not *complete* pushovers up here. The films had to be at least 75 minutes long; two-thirds of the "above the line" talent and a minimum of one producer had to be Canadian; and 75 percent of production (including post) had to be completed on our soil.

Needless to say, filming boomed up here; some of the films were even good—like the ones we're featuring in this festival. We've got slashers (*My Bloody Valentine* and *Curtains*), rat-catchers (*Of Unknown Origin*), and an "accidental" Oliver Reed double feature! (*The Brood* and *Spasms*.)

Fine—there's no such thing as an "accidental" Oliver Reed *anything*, not least in my world. *Burnt Offerings* (1976) was my first recognizable excursion into terror at the age of six; a public display at the Orpheum theater in Estevan, Saskatchewan, joined by my Horror Partner for Life (and mom), Karen. Reed's performance as beleaguered head of the Rolfe clan was nearly as frightening as Anthony James' pasty chauffeur. Nearly.

I suppose that's my way of wrapping up this particular introduction—tying it to my first theater experience in Canada is crucial to my horror journey, even if *Burnt Offerings* is an American production. It's all about that connective tissue, stretching back and forth through the subgenres like so much maple taffy.

While we wait to see from the Canadian government if I've covered *my* percentages with this introduction, let's get on with the festival!

My god, the bacon. It's everywhere...

===============================

We start with the tale of Harry Warden,
who swings an ax
like he's Lizzie Borden...

My Bloody Valentine (1981)

"What becomes a legend most?"

When Lou Reed talked-sang those words in 1984, he may as well have been pining for 1981's slasher *My Bloody Valentine.* The man knew a thing or two about meanness after all, and *MBV*'s one-and-done status gives it a certain integrity separate from the corporate mill. (Not *too* much integrity though; this is still a Paramount pickup.)

So why is *MBV* held in such high regard today? It only made a couple of million more than its low budget, and then shuffled quickly off to home video shelves. (To mine, specifically. I had the videotape.) Time has been kind to *MBV.* There's something to the small-town setting that makes it immune to outside trends that would date the material. It has an easygoing coastal charm in between the pickaxing and the uh, pickaxing.

As the legend goes, five coal miners became trapped in the Hanniger Mines after two negligent workers—on their way to the Valentine's Day dance—didn't check the methane levels and there was an explosion. All died in the mine except for one: Harry Warden, who was discovered mad and resorting to cannibalism. (How long *were* they down there?)

At the following year's Valentine's Day dance, Harry donned his miner gear and killed the two responsible for the mine explosion, with a warning: Never hold another Valentine's Day dance again. But that was 20 years ago, and the next generation wants to party ... no matter the cost.

I think that's a great setup for a story, in that it has worked many times before; "tragedy plus time" will net you ... every successful revenge

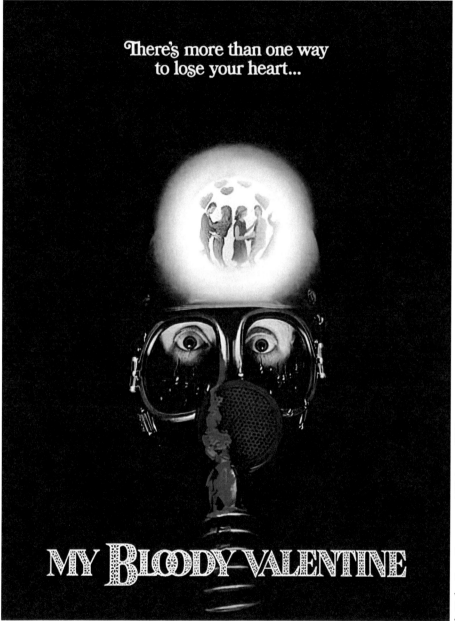

story, really. But the mythology has a working class vigor that doesn't quite come through in tales of camp counselors and babysitters. *MBV* understands small town life better than most; when everyone knows everyone's business, the killer could be closer than you think.

T.J. Hanniger (Paul Kelman) has returned to Valentine Bluffs after trying to find himself. Instead he finds himself back home in his mayor dad's coal mine, and not in the arms of Sarah (Lori Hallier), the squeeze he left behind. Closing out the triangle is T.J.'s best buddy Axel (Neil Affleck), who's been seeing Sarah since T.J. left town. Is this shit soapy? You bet your ass!

Hanniger Jr.'s, prodigal son status is upended as it coincides with the return of the Valentine's Day dance—and by all appearances, Harry Warden along with it. People are dropping—and occasionally spun dry at the laundromat—leaving both Chief Newby (Don Francks) and Mayor Hanniger (Larry Reynolds) on the hunt for the gas-masked marauder..

And wouldn't you know it? The miners and their mates decide to move the party to work, unaware that Harry has come back to Valentine Bluffs to make good on his promise: hold another Valentine's Day dance… AND YOU WILL MORE THAN LIKELY PERISH!

I may be paraphrasing, but the point stands: Harry warned them. He warned them all.

A standup guy if you ask me. Would Jason do the same? No, he has Crazy Ralph for that, doesn't he? Michael isn't particularly big on offering courtesies to potential victims, either. At the very least, Harry has *manners*. Until he doesn't. (Harry covers his bases—he issues his own warnings, *and* he has barkeep Happy offering up proclamations of doom.)

Or, hear me out … it isn't Harry at all, but someone pretending to *be* him! No, you shut up! Twenty years is a long time, and Harry wasn't in the best of shape when they found him. All I'm saying is let's watch Chief and the Mayor spend a good portion of screen time traveling to morgues and police stations searching for Harry clues while everything is happening back at Valentine Bluffs.

Yes, *My Bloody Valentine* adheres to all of the familiar tropes as in previous slashers—dense authorities, wise bartenders, and horny young folks—all there and trotted out with efficiency. But there are a couple of major components that differentiate *MBV* from the pack—The setting, and the people who populate it.

I spent a good portion of my childhood in small-town Canada—just swap oil drilling for mining—and went back for a couple years as an adult. I can vouch for that pall of emptiness that hangs from every busted neon letter or shuttered business, that makes one search—sometimes frantically—for the imaginary exit forever.

This could be a "me" thing, I suppose; I have friends still living that small-town life and loving it. But through T.J.'s experience—leaving the nest to make his own—we can see the restrictive, insular structure of the town. It isn't for the restless; it's for the settled, which makes the attacks all the more horrifying.

And inhabiting the town are a likable cast that bring a lived-in believability to *MBV*. These people seem like little town lifers—mostly content with their lot in life. Well, until Harry's return of course. The only characters who don't register are Chief and the Mayor. It isn't the actors' fault; it's that they're given only the most unctuous and cliched drivel to say. (I understand the need narratively to have them move away from town, I just wish their moments were more than unintentionally funny.)

Let's talk fashion; a madman is only as fit as his kit. Harry Warden comes outfitted in a loose yet shapely dark jumpsuit—he accentuates the O positive with curb-stomping construction boots, a gas mask, and a pickaxe that just won't quit. One has to remember that Jason was in his potato sack stage, and wouldn't don his hockey mask until 1982. This gave horror fans a year to appreciate Harry's sartorial choices before everyone started doing variations à la Jason, and Harry's quickly cemented itself as different—and very creepy.

MBV also drew attention due to the amount of gore footage cut before the MPAA would grant it an "R." Minutes were shorn, but guess what? This is the version we lived with for decades, long before the lost footage was found and reinserted for home release. Which is better? I enjoy watching both, but the rhythms of the original flow are so tight and smooth that the "unedited" version seems almost unnecessary—a testament to the great job that special makeup effects artist Tom Burman (*The Beast Within*) and his crew do. It's amazing grue—I'm glad it exists, and you can't go wrong either way. The foundation is sturdy, unlike say, Hanniger Mines.

MBV has always stood out, for various reasons at different times: as a victim of the MPAA's slaughter; as a film unburdened by competition with itself; always as a slick and competent thriller (director George Mihalka, take a bow); and as a late-in-the-game special effects showcase.

Like any conscientious (and somewhat honest) citizen, there are things in my country to be ashamed of and others to be happy for. I've stood beside *My Bloody Valentine* for over 40 years, and Warden willing, I'm hoping to do it until my last, coal-crusted breath.

═══════════════

Do you like divorce dramas? No? How about one with Oliver Reed, Samantha Eggar, and a bunch of murderous mommy monsters? That's what I thought...

The Brood (1979)

The Dead Zone (1983) is where director David Cronenberg started turning from the horrors of the body to including the torture of the soul. But before that, he made tentative steps towards adding a layer of vulnerability to his work in the very personal and frightening *The Brood* (1979). It's still rooted in the tactile, but listen closely and you can hear whispers of humanity piercing the skin.

Which is to take nothing away from his earlier works; *Shivers* (1975) and *Rabid* (1977) are both potent allegories (and gory allies) on class warfare and sexual promiscuity. But *The Brood* was written by Cronenberg while going through a divorce and nasty custody battle, and while it mostly maintains a safe distance from emotional investment for the viewer, the beginnings of a sympathetic point of view start to take shape.

Released by New World Pictures in May, *The Brood* made decent money but no love was lost by critics at the time, with Roger Ebert calling it "reprehensible trash." This sentiment was echoed by many; it wasn't until the emotional thawing of *The Dead Zone* that they took notice of the latent talent behind the grotesqueries. Their loss—*The Brood* is easily Cronenberg's most traditional horror film, and scariest—it's built for terror along with the marital material.

Frank Carveth (Art Hindle) is picking up his daughter Candice (Cindy Hinds) from the Soma Institute, where his estranged wife Nola (Samantha Eggar) is undergoing treatment. Nola is under the care of Dr. Hal Raglan (Oliver Reed), who has pioneered "psychoplasmics," a way for patients to manifest their pain through intense therapy, which results in blisters, lesions and other such pleasantries. When Frank returns home with Candice, he notices bruises and scratch marks on her back, and vows to Raglan that Candice will never visit her mommy at the Institute again, shared custody or not.

As Frank delves more into the methods used by Raglan at Soma, a connection begins to emerge between Nola's repressed memories of an abusive childhood, and the brutal deaths of loved ones at the hands of malformed kids who bear more than a passing resemblance to Candice. As Soma appears to be a place that gets results, will Frank be able to stop Nola before her rage destroys them all?

On the surface, *The Brood* appears to be just the next Cronenberg body horror, and it is certainly in line with his previous work. *Shivers'* featured oral parasites, *Rabid* had phallic armpit terror, and here, turmoil is made real. But *The Brood* tells a story that could only come from a maturing filmmaker ready to put a little bit of himself on the screen. Now, as personal as Cronenberg says the film is (and knowing the backstory certainly gives

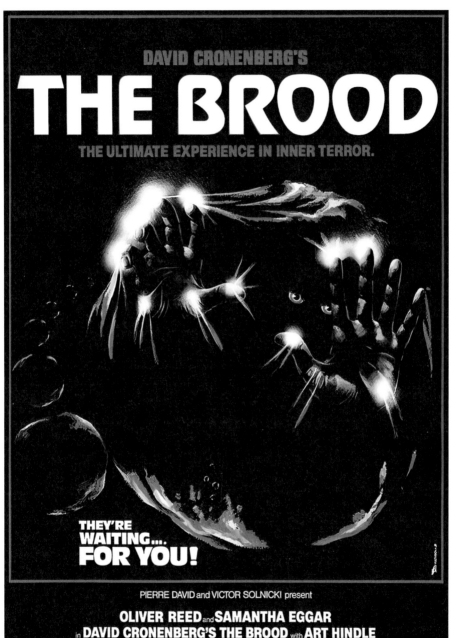

it considerable context), it still feels closed in, cramped; there's not a lot of emotional *release*. If we are to believe that Frank and Nola represent Cronenberg and his ex-wife, she's the only one truly expressing herself. Some critics feel the film is misogynistic by painting Nola as the mother monster, but Cronenberg is very clear that Nola is a victim in a cycle of abuse. He paints her with sympathetic strokes that finally bleed through the canvas and give the viewer a glimpse at the man behind the artist. And while it isn't from his character's point of view, humanity is on display nevertheless.

Nola's pain and unraveling is writ large by Eggar, who gives a brave, vulnerable performance. When she finally shares a scene at the end with Hindle, Eggar truly shines as a woman who has clearly moved onto a different phase in her life, which not only doesn't include her husband, but any semblance of reality as well. Hindle and Reed square off in several scenes—Hindle, standing in for the audience, is horrified by the idea that his wife may be beating their daughter; and that the institute should be her permanent home. Reed is the "new beau" in effect, acting ultimately as protector of Eggar, even though for the majority of screen time he's painted as the overlord pulling the strings. His brusque, hushed intensity is most effective in the many moments of role playing with his patients; he possesses a narcissistic streak that turns compassionate come film's end, and he ends up making the most selfless gesture in the whole film.

Cindy Hinds does good work as Candice, but in a move mirroring real life, she inadvertently becomes a spectator in the conflict between her parents. She's definitely not the focus of the separation, but is merely there to be put in harm's way. So while there are many complex familial dynamics going on, the kid in essence gets ignored, which would be ironic if it wasn't so depressing. That is a sad and horrifying reality worse than any on-screen death.

But this is early Cronenberg, and there *are* many deaths. And they really have a visceral impact, due to the fact that they are supposed to be carried out by children (as ugly as they may be), and by the way Cronenberg films them. As I said, this is the most straightforward horror structure he's ever used: foreshadowing, set up, and then punchline, helped immeasurably by Howard Shore (*The Fly*)'s tension filled score. These factors force the film to play as a thriller, although I promise you, your Netflix queue of "killer kid clones in custody battle" will be a short one.

That "traditionalism" translates into a palpable third act with confrontation, and genuinely suspenseful moments. His earlier films had horrific scenes meant to sicken and scare; with *The Brood* he hones those features and winds up with something truly terrifying.

Essentially we're left with two elements: a horror film built on a twisted premise with a razor sharp edge to its suspense, and a tale where the stakes are higher than the ephemeral. It would still be a few years (and films) before Cronenberg found that filmic balance, but *The Brood*'s confident crawl through the darkened macabre is more than enough until the light breaks through.

━━━━━━━━━━━━━━━━━━━━━━

Here's one a little lighter:
Man Vs. Rat,
fighting for the keys to the castle...

Of Unknown Origin (1983)

Man versus Nature, Man versus Beast, Man versus Food—all mythical in status to varying degrees and most represented on the silver screen. *Of Unknown Origin* (1983) tackles the middle myth with a tongue firmly planted in its giant rat-infested cheek and is an obsessive tour through a domestic hellscape.

Released in November by Warner Bros., and produced in conjunction with some of the last of that glorious Canadian tax shelter money, *Of Unknown Origin* was not a hit. It didn't wow the critics either, although Peter Weller (*Robocop*) was singled out for his wry performance as the put-upon vermin victim.

Bart Hughes (Weller) has it all: the perfect wife (Shannon Tweed, in her feature film debut) and son, a high paying job, and a beautiful brownstone in New York. (Read: Montreal. Tax coin. Beauty.) Wife and child head off for a vacation while Bart toils away on a big project. But don't worry about him getting lonely; company comes in the form of a bulldog-sized rat with a temperament to match. Of course, he thinks he has a normal infestation issue at first. Going from minuscule traps to exterminators to larger traps and larger issues (our friend chews through the dishwasher wires first and works his way up to the electricity) until the inevitable showdown happens between homeowner and home wrecker.

Of Unknown Origin deals in absolutes—this is Man versus Beast in capital letters, and is unapologetic in its intent. The film is pared down to essentials, as it should be. The only lateral story thread is his work, and it is presented to make obvious correlations to the chase-the-cheese "rat race" environment. There's nothing subtle going on here story-wise, because this is mythology—even the filmic and literary nods (Bart is reading *Moby Dick* and he's watching *The Old Man and the Sea*) are overt, and lets the audience know that nothing here should be taken *too* seriously.

Of Unknown Origin, Warner Bros. Pictures, 1983

This was director George P. Cosmatos' fifth film, making mainly action/espionage films such as *The Cassandra Crossing* and *Escape from Athena* before this. *Cobra, Leviathan,* and the ever-popular *Tombstone* came after. His natural affinity for movement serves him well here—after all, besides the office scenes, *Of Unknown Origin* plays out almost entirely in Bart's sanctuary (except for a few phone calls from Tweed) and Cosmatos keeps the action from feeling repetitive or passé.

It certainly doesn't hurt that he uses the *Jaws* template and shows us the critter sparingly—only later during a visit to his bed do we really get a sense of scope for what Bart's up against. And to be frank, most of the damage to his beautiful abode is done by Bart himself. The rat acts as a conduit for his domestic rage, and it culminates with Bart regaled in full-battle mode with stuffing, pads, and a modified baseball bat. He becomes a man driven to war to defend his turf.

Bart's journey is the soul of the film—a sane, competent man whose life and security are turned upside down by a single intruder. But as the exterminator tells Bart: "He's a rat. He's got nothing better to do." This of course makes the film even funnier; while Bart slowly descends into madness with attempts to catch his prey. The rat does what it does; it eats, shits, and kills. Sure the scale may be bigger—it eats almost the entire pantry and through all the electrical, and kills the cat—but it doesn't act against its nature, and remember, it has *nothing better to do.*

Bart, on the other hand, has to act against his civilized status until by the very end he's reduced to a makeshift warrior with a marbled moat. As the film progresses, we witness Bart go from clean shaven and organized, to disheveled and late with his project, to sleeping in chairs or perched like a squatting sentinel on the top of his staircase. Bart's experience turns primal when the modern world collapses on him and he becomes Home Hardware Hannibal, and it's a role that the normally taciturn Weller leans into *hard.*

If you're a fan of Canadian horror (and I bet more than a few of your favorites were at least made up here), this cast is a dream team: Lawrence Dane, Louis Del Grande, and Keith Knight all give the film that distinctly maple-y NYC flavor. This was Weller's first starring role, and he was more than ready for it. His deadpan expressions slowly give way from annoyance to desperation and end up at an exasperated resolve that is truly funny to observe. The film acts as a 90-minute sizzle reel for Weller, and deservedly so; it shows he could handle comedy and drama all in one weird thriller.

Whether *Of Unknown Origin* is thought of today as a mythical treatise on survival of the fittest or a humorous take on office and personal politics, at the end of the day it just holds up as a terrific giant rat movie. And trust me—those are as rare as an affordable brownstone in New York.

What's scaly and sweats a lot?
That's right, Oliver Reed is back!
And this time he's fighting a giant snake in...

Spasms (1983)

As a child, I first saw a snake with my own two eyes when one of the garter variety slithered through our front lawn and my mom, with a deep abiding fear, called my dad home from the office to slay the beast. (Or shoo it away. Probably that.) I maintain a healthy relationship with snakes: leave me alone and I'll leave you alone. (I *promise* I'll always leave you alone.) Of course, I love to see them in horror movies—the safety of the screen provides nothing but thrills when I know it won't be coming for me. This brings us to *Spasms* (1983), a disjointed-yet-fun film in which a big snake in a big Canadian city wreaks big havoc.

With a troubled production as serpentine as its subject, *Spasms* saw little theatrical love (or release for that matter) but nested comfortably on video for a while. Its white Thorn-Emi hard shell case was ubiquitous— before being forgotten, or at best a footnote on how painful it is to birth a film in the first place. Regardless of its considerable seams, *Spasms* still works due to some great effects from the late and legendary Dick Smith (*The Exorcist*) and an international cast of the finest troublemakers that a B-film will allow. Well, two anyway; we'll get to them in a bit.

First, some story: on an island off of New Guinea, a tribe is raising literal hell as they invoke a snake god responsible for taking souls down to hell. Once the serpent demon rises, it causes quite a bloody ruckus before being trapped by outsiders. A call is made to retired hunter and millionaire Jason Kincaid (Oliver Reed) that the beast has been captured and is on its way to his home.

You see, Kincaid and his brother tracked the snake years before; his brother didn't make it and Kincaid was bitten yet somehow survived. Ever since then, he's had a psychic link with the reptile and plans to face the demon down once and for all. To this end, he hires psychiatrist Dr. Tom Brasilian (Peter Fonda) to monitor the interaction, if possible. The only kink in the plan is our slithery friend escapes from its crate at the university and goes looking for snacks on the mean streets of Toronto. Will Kincaid finally get his one-on-one meeting with the monster, or is he just a delectable British snack?

Spasms is essentially *King Kong* for the 1980s, mixed with a dose of

The Animal Killdom. It's unapologetic in its goofiness, or at least isn't self-aware enough to wink at the audience. Director William Fruet (*Funeral Home*) has certainly assembled the right talent to keep the tittering to a minimum. The film is shot by Mark Irwin (*The Dead Zone*), has a snake theme written and performed by Tangerine Dream, and of course Dick Smith in charge of snakes 'n' bladders.

In front of the lens he gives you not only Reed and Fonda, but also Canadian legends Kerrie Keene and Al Waxman, whom many of you will know as the head cop on *Cagney & Lacey*. But us Canuckleheads will always cherish Al on TV as *The King of Kensington*, essentially a much nicer Archie Bunker. But I digress. Up north we tend to fly the flag when we see our countrymen and women bumping up against bright lights like Reed and Fonda.

As it is with many productions, there were problems set upon *Death Bite* (the original title, loosely based on the novel of the same name)—tales of rotating producers and vanishing funds plagued the work until Fruet came on in 1981 to film. It sat on the shelf for a year before yet another producer scooped it up. And then there's the snake, with a last-minute switch to go animatronic instead of real reptiles. Some of the action was scrapped due to time constraints and/or funding running out. They simply had to piece together what they had and hope for the best.

The best, as it turns out with nearly forty years of hindsight, is still pretty good. Yes those seams are glaring (the truncated ending, the subplot with serpent cult worshippers that goes nowhere, the puzzling focus on Kincaid instead of the ostensible hero Brasilian to name but a few), but what's left is ninety minutes of snake attacks (all practical) and a glorious turn by Reed.

There are more attacks than I initially remembered—and if you're cobwebbed like myself, probably more than you think as well—and the ones highlighted are beauts: a bathroom door blowout and the Fangoria cover death of Waxman (which was personally handled by Smith, as he hadn't done this type of bladder work before). There are other serpent slayings too, not to mention the obligatory POV shots of the creature chasing down folks. Hey, to these withered eyes, the snake looks decent enough—I mean, at least it's *there* in the shots with the actors.

Perhaps the most unbelievable thing in the film is that the snake would be any kind of match for Reed. Sweating profusely, eyes bulging, fingers on temples—these are the latter-day Reed staples, which he trots out here in full commitment to the performance. He even throws in a few quiet moments for those who can remember him capable of such. You get The Full Ollie, is what I'm saying.

Films are such a delicate balancing act. It's a minor miracle when a film like *Spasms* can still hold it together enough to entertain (go sssit over there with *Curtains*, will ya?) without completely shedding its skin.

═══════════════════════════

We wrap up our Canadiana with a film that features a very famous
ice skating scene; but it's much more than that.
It's time to raise the...

Curtains (1983)

When one looks back at mid–1970s to early 1980s horror, it's quite surprising to see how many Canadian made films are nestled among fan favorites. Titles such as *Black Christmas, Shivers, Prom Night, Happy Birthday to Me*, and *My Bloody Valentine* continue to delight and shock veteran horror lovers or those just starting their jagged journey down the terror path. There is one, however, that due to a troubled production and poor distribution, seems relegated to the discount bins of time. Today, we're pulling back the curtain on, uh, *Curtains* (1983), an unsung slasher weirder than a sackful of rabid beavers.

Released by Jensen Farley Pictures in March 1983 (U.S.), and September 1984 by Norstar Releasing in my home and native land, *Curtains* received a very limited release in both countries, but coming as it did at a time when the Canadian film industry had all but collapsed (see below), it's amazing it saw the light of day at all.

A brief history then. From 1975 to 1982, Canada essentially whored itself out (hey, we're not always proud) and offered filmmakers abroad a rather large tax incentive to film in Canada—100 percent of the cost of the film became deductible if one followed certain guidelines. Two-thirds of the cast and crew had to be Canadian and 75 percent of production and post-production had to be done up in the Great White North. This naturally resulted in a boom for the Canadian film industry, leading to the nickname Hollywood North. By 1982, however, they cut the incentive back to 50 percent and that was that. So you're asking, "Hey, Captain Canuck—what the hell does this have to do with *Curtains*?" And the answer is, everything—this production was so fractious that without the tax breaks it wouldn't have seen the light of day.

Before we delve into the behind-the-scenes disturbance (which is an all-time corker), let's try some story: Samantha Sherwood (Samantha Eggar) is a faded actress who has bought the rights to "Audra," a melodrama about a scorned woman confined to a mental institution. As our

Curtains, Jensen Farley Pictures, 1983

movie opens, she is acting out a scene for her director and paramour, the pompous tight-sweater patron Jonathan Stryker (John Vernon). Unconvinced she's ready for the part, the two connive to have her admitted to a mental facility so she can immerse herself in the experience. However, Samantha becomes a little *too* immersed and Jonathan decides it's best to leave her there.

She escapes from the institution when she reads that Jonathan is recasting "Audra" and holding auditions with six actresses at his estate. Mayhem ensues as Samantha shows up to reclaim her role—but first she must deal with a troupe of wannabes so thirsty for success, they'll do *anything* to get the part. Is Samantha picking off her competition, or is one of the ingénues stabbing her way to the top?

What we have, not by design, but by necessity, is two films fighting it out in *Curtains*. Director Richard Ciupka was hired by producer Peter Simpson (*Prom Night*) after helping Simpson finish directing a previous project. Ciupka was at the time a very well respected director of cinematography, having shot Louis Malle's *Atlantic City*. Armed with Robert Guza, Jr.'s, (*Prom Night*) script, he set off for the outskirts of Toronto with a parcel of Canadian actors (Vernon, Linda Thorson, Lynne Griffin, Lesleh Donaldson, Michael Wincott) and a plan to make more of a psychological thriller. The problem was, being a first time director, Ciupka fell way behind schedule. Simpson thought he was getting a slasher, not something so "arty," so he fired Ciupka and shut down production.

The project stalled for well over a year before Simpson started up production again, this time with a whole new crew and some of the cast, and he took over the directorial reins. So what we end up with is roughly this: the first 20 minutes or so are Simpson, the middle 45 is Ciupka, and the final 20 are Simpson again (and don't clock me on those, I'm just guesstimating).

Here's the thing though: Both directors create some really strong moments, enough so that the viewer with an open mind won't care that the seams show from a hundred yards away. Simpson's footage starts off strong, with Eggar, Vernon and an extended visit at the institution—setting the scene for Samantha's descent into madness quite effectively (without a massive dollop of silver screen "insanity" on display). His finale also has a fantastic sequence backstage in the prop area of Stryker's mansion, as one of the actresses is pursued by the killer—Simpson clearly shows a knack for generating suspense, especially considering how enclosed the space is.

Ciupka's footage is more difficult, and ambitious—it's clear that he was going for a heightened melodrama, a cross between *Ten Little Indians* and *Halloween*. Does he succeed? Well, the material is very movie-of-the-week, with the ladies arguing about ambition and sacrifice but not really displaying either (other than bedding down the loathsome Stryker). However, what the material lacks, Ciupka makes up with beauti-fully-framed, eerie camerawork (courtesy of DP Robert Paynter—*Super-man II*) that shows given the time and experience, he could have proven himself a horror contender. The most famous moment in the film is a mur-der that takes place on an outdoor rink. The killer, who wears an old hag mask (courtesy of Greg Cannom—*Dracula*), skates across the frozen pond, with a scythe behind his/her back in broad daylight. The blinding white of the snow juxtaposed against the black garb of the killer is unique and chilling. Even people who haven't seen the film are aware of this classic scene. It's one for the ages.

The performances are solid, with headliners Vernon and Eggar com-manding the screen over their younger costars. Lynne Griffin is the stand-out among the wannabes, with a loose, quirky style that sets her apart from the group, helped by the fact that her Patti is given the most back-story in the finished film (others were filmed but cut by Simpson when he resumed filming).

So how does *Curtains* miraculously manage to keep it together? First off, the setting and characters are different for a film of this type. Having adults in a slasher is always an eye-opening change, and while that doesn't necessarily guarantee better writing, it can lead to different behavior than we expect in films of this ilk. The snow drenched surroundings add a sense of chilling detachment as well, far away from the normal summertime slayings. The film also has a sense of humor about itself (which I'll credit to Simpson since he finished it), with onscreen curtains pulled back to signal scene transitions. It's unexpected and fun for a film like this to remind us not to take it too seriously.

What's refreshing about *Curtains* is its persistence to exist. It's an impressive feat for *any* film to be made, and then be released—given life. For a film to be made over a two and a half year period, with two different directors, and still manage to impress viewers with its stitched together corpse (and a beautiful corpse it is), is a cinemiracle. As a final note, direc-tor Ciupka was so displeased when Simpson sent him the end product that he wouldn't sign off using his name—he submitted it as Jonathan Stryker. A fitting tribute to the process of make believe, and the land, however fleetingly known, as Hollywood North.

Festival Eight:
If You're Undead
and You Know It,
Clap Your Hand

Zombies: you love them; you hate them. Sometimes you tolerate them and perhaps wish they would sit out a couple of horror cycles, maybe a decade or so—just long enough to refresh and re-animate their rotting corpses.

As a longtime watcher—and lifelong fan—of zombie films, I have felt all of the above emotions, and maybe you have too. Or not—zombies have become decidedly mainstream and very successful, especially on television. It's fair to say that zombies have survived—and thrived—in the modern world.

Cable TV has played the biggest part in this seemingly permanent resurgence of the undead; specifically, AMC's *The Walking Dead* franchise. Begun in 2010, it is based on the popular comic book series created by Robert Kirkman and Tony Moore.

And it really is a franchise, with successful spinoffs (*Fear the Walking Dead*) and film sequels exploring the show's more popular characters. It's very unusual for a subgenre to dominate for such a length of time, and according to its legion of fans, the interest has remained at a consistently high level.

But those zombies didn't just get up, groan, and shamble without some inspiration, and that honor falls upon the late—and truly great— George Romero. His *Night of the Living Dead* (1968) upended the quaint iteration of zombiedom, the voodoo-procured malady of *I Walked with a Zombie* (1943) and several others. He replaced these benign images with viscera literally torn on screen. The undead displayed an unquenchable hunger and a strong resistance to staying dead. These zombies, flesh hanging from their lips, were not instruments of terror—they were terror itself.

125

The films in this festival are all of the post–*NOTLD* era, with the exception of *The Plague of the Zombies* (1966), whose Hammer elegance gives way to decaying cadavers in anticipation of the grittier approach of Romero (without all that icky flesh-eating). But it's nice to have the contrast before the carnage *really be*gins: a trip to Portugal in the early 1970s yields beautiful, eerie results; then over to Britain for a rather ripping yarn; off to Italy for my favorite zombie film *ever*; and finishing in the same with one of the *funniest*.

This wasn't intentional on my part, but the majority of these films are not interested in the allegorical (and political) aspects of Romero's work, instead focusing on scares, and in the case of a couple films, the gross-out. The British *The Living Dead at Manchester Morgue* uses ultrasonic radiation as the boogie-man catalyst for resurrection, but the rest are more than content to press the flesh with the more sordid side of cinema.

So throw on your slicker and grab your umbrella; it's a messy festival, and all the better for it....

***

We're not quite in Romero territory yet,
but this Hammer offering is a great bridge
between the old ways and the new age to come...

The Plague of the Zombies (1966)

One can suppose it was inevitable for Hammer to take on a lesser celebrated (at the time) yet influential subgenre such as zombies. The 1930s and 1940s were certainly a heyday, with such films as *White Zombie* (1932) and *I Walked with a Zombie* (1943) setting a template of voodoo curses with unwilling (and undead) subjects. By the 1950s, they were already used for comic effect, until Hammer took their chance with *The Plague of the Zombies* (1966), an atmospheric yet rousing period piece that would help set up another template for zombiedom's biggest sea change two years later.

Part of a four-picture co-op with Seven Arts Productions, *Plague* was released stateside by 20th Century–Fox in late January to better than average reviews; mind you, Hammer usually found a somewhat appreciative press, if even just for set design and production values alone. But critics at the time liked the fact that Hammer added some new colors to its palette, even if the canvas was pretty familiar.

To wit: we open on a subterranean voodoo ritual, complete with tribal drummers and a masked leader who's busy pouring blood over a cloth

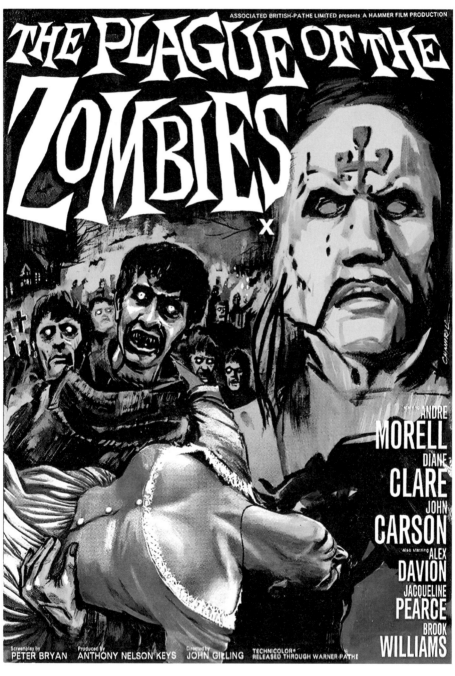

doll, while in a bedroom young bride Alice (Jacqueline Pearce) wakes up screaming. Cut to the Forbes manor in London, where Sir James (Andre Morell) receives a letter from his prized medical student Peter (Brook Williams). It seems his practice in the same small Cornish village that he and his betrothed Alice (see above) reside has hit some snags—an apparent blood disorder has killed off a dozen people and he doesn't know why. This gives Sir James, his trusty doctor's kit, and daughter Sylvia (Diane Clare) an excuse for him to visit his former pupil, and for her to see her old high school chum Alice.

After a run-in with a gaggle of lascivious aristocratic fox hunters near the village, James and Sylvia head to Peter and Alice's; he's out, and she looks ... peaked. James finds his protégé at the local pub, where he's being harassed by the villagers for not stopping their ongoing population depletion. The problem is that Peter isn't allowed to do any autopsies because the village overlord, Squire Hamilton (John Carson), denies him access to the dead. Sir James and Peter decide to dig up the graves of the death-filled dozen, and find the sites ... lacking. All except for the formerly warmer Alice, who succumbed to the same sickness. She seems to rise without issue, if not more than a little gray around the everything. What is the deadly secret behind *The Plague of the Zombies*?

Well, if you're familiar with the story of *Dracula*, you know damn well what the secret is—a mere swapping out of archetypes conveys the tale in efficient fashion. So yes, Hamilton is Drac, Sir James is your Van Helsing, Peter assays the Harker role, and our Squire has a dozen or so zombies instead of vampires at his disposal. To do what, you may ask? Take over the world, perhaps? Seek revenge on those who have robbed him? Nope. He uses them as cheap labor in a tin mine beside the village.

So what we have then with *The Plague of the Zombies* is a cheeky takedown on elitism and class structure; Hamilton and his rogue band of highway dandymen rule the village with a pompous and toxic flair (they corral Sylvia with the intent of raping her) before Sir James puts an end to their insidious chicanery. (See? Not all rich people are bad!) The fact that someone of similar stature is needed to save the poor, uneducated folk undercuts the commentary, but the seed is still there.

As is the one that would bloom two years later with George Romero's *Night of the Living Dead*; which isn't to say *Plague* paved the way for *Night* with a scathing mirror held up to a racist society. Rather, it's the aesthetic that forecasts the evolution in zombie history—these undead *appear* undead, wearing the muddied and caked disgrace of entombment with nothing but vacant, milky-white eyes to guide them above ground in obedience to their master. Not quite there yet—the arms are still raised in a stiff salute to their horrific forefathers—Romero made them *truly* chilling by having them be a slave to nothing but their unending bloodlust (well that and the graphic cannibalism certainly dotted every "i"). But this was definitely the bridge between wide-eyed somnambulism and rotted perversion.

Director John Gilling (*The Reptile*) and writer Peter Bryan (*The Brides of Dracula*) have fun upending the normal Hammer tropes of the day. While it is set in the 1860s, the film isn't reliant on a lack of modern convenience to put the protagonists in peril, but rather has them using science (however cockeyed it may be) and common sense to solve the mystery. Helping them are a solid cast, with Morell especially bringing that Cushing heat with an extra dash of wit. I could have seen ten more films with Sir James leading the charge against the Monster of the Day.

But it was not to be. Hammer was soon back to its normal ways before slowly fading away the next decade. *The Plague of the Zombies* is worth a look alone for the fresh paint it splashed on the canvas; that some bled off onto the next artist's easel may be its greatest victory.

═══════════════════

From pre–Romero to post, European filmmakers continued to play in the Gothic graveyard while embracing the modern bloodshed. If you know what's good for you, you'll stay away from the...

Tombs of the Blind Dead (1972)

Tombs of the Blind Dead dares to ask the question: Should one camp out in an abandoned, ancient monastery while evil and resurrected Knights Templar ride around on horseback and slay everyone in sight? I'm fairly certain you know the answer; if you didn't, it would be a much shorter film.

Also known as *La Noche del Terror Ciego,* this Spain/Portugal co-production was actually a big hit worldwide—so much so that it spawned three sequels, and all four were made by the same Spanish filmmaker Amando de Ossorio. I cannot speak to the sequels at this point, but *Tombs of the Blind Dead* offers an interesting twist on Romero's nascent meat munchers.

Once upon a time, through century and sea, there was a cult/squad/tribe called The Knights Templar, a heretical group of fellows who practiced the occult in their quest for eternal life. (They were real! Look them up.) Killed for their transgressions by the Catholic Church—with their eyes plucked from their very heads—the sightless undead Knights

haunt their abandoned monastery on horseback, and lay waste to any interlopers.

A trip to the countryside is in store for best friends Betty (Lone Fleming) and Roger (César Burner), before they run into Betty's old private school chum Virginia (María Elena Arpón). The two were closer than friends at the time: a literally steamy flashback shows us their sapphic activities. But Betty has now moved on while Virginia still clearly carries a torch for her.

It's natural grist for the drama mill, and a good reason for Virginia to tag along for the ride. Apparently we need to bring the people to the Templars to get this party started, and soon she's jumped off the train to camp by herself, leaving Betty and Roger semi-concerned about her old friend.

The next act brings about the rise of the Templars, no doubt awakened by Virginia's transistor radio blasting and bonfire crackling on their sacred grounds. She manages to escape the painfully slow grasp of the Templars and heads off on horseback … which happens to be their specialty.

Meanwhile, Betty and Roger start to genuinely worry about her friend, and they set off for the ruins of Berzano—the Knights' home base—to track her down. But once the sun sets, the dead shall rise and ride again….

Tombs of the Blind Dead won me over completely during an extended sequence of the Templars rising from the grave. Plastic skeleton hands clawing at coffins—and honestly every crypt climber in every B-flick will do—always receive an automatic seal of approval. It's simple to me: if you have a graveyard, someone had best be rising dead, undead, or near dead. Otherwise you may as well set your story on a golf course. (Hmm…)

With no obvious social targets on display—not that it has to have any—*TOTBD* plays as straight horror then, with only occasional exploitive elements. I could actually see the word "artsy" being thrown around as much as "aimless" when expressing how the film plays. De Ossorio's use of slow motion sounds cheap and easy—because it is—but is no less effective for it. The horsemen's glacial gallop has a dreamlike quality that enhances the film. It's his regular-speed moments that drag it down—a lot of talk between Roger and Betty; then Roger and Betty and a doctor; then Roger and Betty and the authorities, and *then* an intro to a local smuggler who decides to help them look through the ruins for Virginia at night.

Who cares? When it works it really works, and if you don't like the daytime pace, enjoy the beautiful scenery while you wait.

(A quick sidebar: For those diving into much older films for the first time, you have to adapt to an era where films weren't edited by coke fiends with the attention spans of goldfish. Scenes get a chance to breathe in these films—sometimes, even a little too much. Okay, back to the show!)

There has been some debate through the ages as to the specificity of the Templars' malady. De Ossorio himself has likened them more to vampires, and I can see his point—they only come out at night and prefer sucking blood to eating flesh. The title does makes me think of zombies though. So, I'm listing them as zombies for a couple of reasons: one, the title leads us there; and two, for vampires they don't look so hot—or even presentable, really. (Time to upgrade those tattered robes, guys.)

It's all semantics though. What matters is the eerie site of the Templars riding through the mist, offering a strange but wonderful concoction of Gothic and the almost-gross (a lot of fake blood and skin nibbling—and I do mean nibbling) that stays with the viewer long after the final train pulls into the station.

=====

Let's keep it scenic, yes?
Off we go to England,
with its lush green hills, fog, and...

The Living Dead at Manchester Morgue (1974)

Zombies. The damn things are everywhere now, for about the last twenty years filling the screens big and small, carried on the rotting backs of *Shaun of the Dead* and the *Dawn of the Dead* remake (both 2004). *The Walking Dead* is one of the biggest shows on TV, and films ranging in quality from great to Netflix saturate the market. But let's go back to a time when the zombie film as we know it (the Age of Romero) was in its infancy. Jorge Grau's *The Living Dead at Manchester Morgue* (1974) acts as a bridge between two seminal George Romero films, *Night of the Living Dead* (1968) and *Dawn of the Dead* (1978), and rightly stands as one of the finer Euro horrors. If you haven't seen it, it's definitely worth the trip.

Released in 1975 in North America as *Don't Open the Window*, this Spanish/Italian co-production was frequently paired up with *The Last House on the Left* at drive-ins. In other parts of the world, the film was also known as *Let Sleeping Corpses Lie*. Whatever you wish to call it, they're all terrible titles, but that in no way distracts from the low-key dread, picturesque flavor that Grau brings to the subgenre.

Manchester, England. Edna (Christine Galbo) is off to visit her drug-addled sister in the countryside. George (Ray Lovelock) is an antiques dealer heading to his house in the country for a getaway. The two

RAY LOVELOCK   CHRISTINE GALBO
ARTHUR KENNEDY

NON SI DEVE PROFANARE IL SONNO DEI MORTI

ALDO MASSASSO • VERA DRUDY • GIORGIO TRESTINI • GENGHER GATTI   REGIA DI JORGE GRAU
CROMOCOLOR   EASTMANCOLOR

The Living Dead at Manchester Morgue, Hallmark Releasing Corp., 1974

meet at a gas station as Edna rolls over George's motorcycle, causing any-thing but a meet-cute for our protagonists. Edna agrees to lend George her vehicle as long as he drops her at her sister's house first. Before they get there, Edna encounters a recently deceased gent by the river while George is off asking directions of a group of men from the Department of Agri-culture. These men are (important plot point!) trying out a piece of farm equipment that is supposed to kill the pests that are destroying the crops. Apparently the contraption uses radio waves that cause the insects to go homicidal and kill each other off. However, as we find out, it has the same effect on dead folk.

Soon George and Edna find themselves suspected of murder by a police inspector (Arthur Kennedy), as people linked to the two are found dead, but the real culprits, our zombies, are AWOL. Can our heroes stop the John Deere of Destruction before the whole countryside is infested with the undead?

Grau was approached by the producers to essentially make a color version of *NOTLD*, and there are similarities. Both films have protagonists that represent a specific social agenda—*Night* tackles race with its black hero, while this film emphasizes the generation gap, with our heroes rep-resenting, in the words of the elder inspector, "hippies"—not to mention Satan worshippers (the Devil was totally on brand in the 1970s). Of course, this get-off-my-lawn scenario is much less confrontational (and contro-versial) than Romero's full-force commentary on race relations. *Manches-ter Morgue*'s opening lays it out clearly—set in the middle of Manchester, it shows a naked young woman streaking through the streets, while older people in cars peer with a blasé look in their eyes. By this point in the 1970s, flower power was nothing but a 1960s hangover, so the young versus aged approach comes off as a little stilted, but it does provide a humorous *Tales from the Crypt* touch come the final denouement—leading us into the lighter, consumerism commentary of Romero's *Dawn*.

Grau also opens up the action, taking away the claustrophobic set-ting of Romero's farmhouse, and instead turns *Manchester Morgue* into a gorgeous travelog of the countryside in England (specifically Derbyshire, Cheshire, Manchester itself and other locations). Beautifully filmed by DP Francisco Sempere, this actually creates more suspense—freed from the confines of an enclosed space, our undead friends could (and do) show up anywhere. It should be noted that if you're expecting hordes of zombies, keep on walking—Grau and crew pare it down to three or four tops at a time, but don't worry, they still manage to bring the carnage.

This film was a calling card and a sign of things to come for makeup wizard Gianetto de Rossi (*Zombie*). The zombie makeup itself is under-stated, as we assume these are deceased of a more recent vintage. However, he has some stunning set pieces including a disembowelment and a breast breach that still pack a punch—delectable and dripping in glorious East-mancolor. De Rossi's subsequent work with Lucio Fulci stands as some of the most visceral effects work of any era, and this is another great example of his artistry.

As for our living characters, Lovelock and Galbo are good, with Love-lock successfully pulling off his arc from braying asshole to likable protag-onist in a tidy 95 minutes. A special mention for our third corner of the triangle—Kennedy ably displays the caustic determination of the inspec-tor, with a gratuitous Irish accent, no less.

Grau also carries over Romero's theme of the enemy within—the zombies are a threat, sure—but the inspector is *really* out for blood. While the undead are governed by instinct and a need to feed, the inspector is ruled by a blind hatred and prejudice toward the younger generation. In his mind, it's not a far leap from wearing flowers in your hair to satanic evisceration. (I think enjoying *Godspell* is the missing link.)

The Living Dead at Manchester Morgue was meant to be a color rehash of *NOTLD*, but instead manages to add its own quirky touches to Rome-ro's vision, expanding the palette and scope of this relatively new subge-nre. Whether Romero looked back and was inspired by Grau's work is up for debate, but for horror fans, a stop at the *Morgue* should be more than a curiosity—it is an essential destination.

A lot of fans have heard of this film and many have seen.
But there are those who have yet to feast. Read this and get your ass watching.
Frightening, gross, epic. Zombies fighting sharks. It can only be…

Zombie (1979)

"The boat can leave now. Tell the crew." With these words, a horror classic was born. *Zombie* (1979) was the first Lucio Fulci film that assaulted my eyeballs, AND it was the first zombie flick I ever saw. Heady stuff for a quivering ten-year-old but it proved to be the perfect gateway to the splat-tery splendors of Italian terror, a door that will forever remain ajar.

Let me be as straightforward as I can: if you're a fan of Fulci but hav-en't caught this yet, you can forget about the surrealism of *The Beyond* (1981) or the Lovecraftian flourishes of *City of the Living Dead* (1980). This is Fulci driving a simple narrative right through the hearts of hor-ror lovers everywhere—coming out the back bloodied and unbound,

Zombie, Variety Distribution, 1979

unapologetic in its mission statement to horrify and repulse. Mission accomplished.

Zombie was released in Italy in August 1979 as *Zombi 2*, titled so as to capitalize on *Dawn of the Dead* (1978), George Romero's trenchant parable on consumerism that was called *Zombi* for discerning Italian audiences. (In the UK, *Zombie* is known as *Zombie Flesh Eaters*, which is a little redundant—like calling a film *Accountant Number Crunchers*.) *Dawn of the Dead* did big business in Italy, and believe it or not, Italian law allows filmmakers to throw digits and words behind their movies to piggyback on previous properties, even if they have no connection at all. (See: *Patrick Still Lives* as an example, or *Ghosthouse*, aka *La Casa 3*, aka *Evil Dead 3*, aka *Thatsa Spicy Raimi*.) *Zombie* was rolled out to the rest of the world in 1980, washing up on North American shores in the summer, infecting grindhouses and drive-ins across the nation.

It certainly infected my friends and me when we witnessed it on home video back in 1981. This was the Wizard Video edition, with the iconic "smiling" zombie on the front, with the tag above the picture reading, "WE ARE GOING TO EAT YOU!," and the tag below the picture and title exclaiming, "...THE DEAD ARE AMONG US!" Well, this was a cinematic challenge for impressionable youth; it seemed more vicious than *Halloween* and *Friday the 13th* combined. It turns out it was *way* more vicious, in fact, and left an eternal impact. (I believe they call it *scarring*).

But before we check in on the frazzled nerves of the young, let's take a trip to the Caribbean, shall we? Our opening quote is uttered by Dr. Menard (Richard Johnson), right after he plugs a bullet into the head of an islander wrapped and tied in a bed sheet who tried to go for a post-mortem stroll. Menard is dealing with an epidemic on the island of Matul. It's an infectious disease that consumes the living and reanimates them faster than the doctor can handle. So Menard sends a boat to New York in hopes of getting help, and we see it adrift in New York Harbor, where it catches the attention of the NYPD *and* the Tor Johnson lookalike zombie on board, who is quite keen to take a bite out of law enforcement.

This, of course, makes headlines. Enter Peter West (Ian McCulloch), ace reporter who discovers the boat belongs to the (missing) scientist father of Anne Bowles (Tisa Farrow). They "meet cute" on the boat, decide to team up, and head off for the last place her father was seen: Matul. They catch a charter with Brian (Al Cliver) and Susan (Auretta Gay), an entomologist and diving enthusiast, respectively, and cast off. Not only does Anne find out what happened to her father, they discover that island life isn't all it's cracked up to be...

Romero's *Dawn* ushered in a new age of full-carnal disclosure—this time with the latest tools for maximum impact. Spearheaded by effects guru Tom Savini (*Friday the 13th*), *Dawn* upgraded the hardware laid out by Romero in his landmark *Night of the Living Dead* (1968), shocking audiences with heart-stopping, ultra-realistic grue that spilled off the screen and clogged up VCRs. But my comrades and I hadn't taken that trip to the Monroeville Mall yet, so *Zombie* was our first foray into the *really* gory undead. And somehow we just knew that because it was foreign, they could get away with more than most American films. It seemed like another world where the filmmaking mores we had previously witnessed didn't apply. Not that we were cineastes lamenting the decay of modern civilization; not even close—we were kids. But the first time you see someone's neck fileted with rotted teeth and dead eyes, arterial spray reaching for the sky in a desperate bid for freedom, you tend to notice; little nose pickers like ourselves certainly did.

So what *do* you get in a Fulci zombie flick? You get spoiled, that's what. Spoiled flesh, spoiled food, spoiled soil, mixed with the excitement that *anything* can happen and probably will. Even those who haven't seen *Zombie* have heard of the underwater battle between a hungry shark and an even more ravenous zombie. (Frankly, it's amazing to even type those words all these years later.) Of course, there's the eye vs. splinter gag (guess who wins!), and many moments for flesh fiends to feast on. Fulci *delivers*, is what I'm trying to say. And he does it in a very accessible way—no subscription to *Eibon Weekly* is required, nor any psychic ability needed. It's an adventure tale, really, a simple search and rescue. The only difference being, you can't rescue the dead, and you really should search for a place to hide.

But the action alone doesn't cover the film's myriad strengths. The film is oppressive from the start—we open facing the barrel of a gun; Menard shoots, utters the portentous phrase, and the screen cuts to black. Cue Fabio Frizzi (*The Beyond*), composer extraordinaire, as he unleashes one of the greatest themes in all of horror, "The Marching Zombie Lament" (that's what I called it then, and I'm sticking with it). A steady bass drum is followed by a synthesizer statement, sad and slow, that tells the viewer that things are not going to start, proceed, or end well. At all. It lends a pall of gloom, and sets a tone familiar with many a horror freak: ITALIAN HORROR IS SERIOUS BUSINESS.

This is where my education begins—things do not go well for our protagonists, and the ending suggests an impending *corpse de resistance*. Downbeat horror didn't sit well with me as a kid. It really bummed me out, and, other than my lack of willpower to stop watching this hypnotic gem, it kept me away until I could give it the proper distance as a semi-well-adjusted adult. And listen, most '70s horror films end on a bum note—you can't escape death, so why try? But the Italians caked it with an extra layer of *meanness,* offering a boot to the head *and* the stomach for extra impact. And when you have renowned makeup artist Giannetto De Rossi (*The Beyond*) splashing in the plasma, it hurts even *more.*

There's a lot of impact (and style) to be found in the cinematography of Sergio Salvati. He would shepherd Fulci's vision for this and his subsequent "Gates of Hell" Trilogy (*City of the Living Dead, The Beyond,* and *The House by the Cemetery*), showing a world two or three blocks over from reality. *Zombie* is their most grounded collaboration, and yet they achieve not necessarily a *different* reality, but rather one that has come before— the island scenes evoke zombie films of yore, such as *White Zombie* (1932) and *I Walked with a Zombie* (1943). (This was Fulci's intent—the New York angle was added to the screenplay to tenuously link the property to Romero's popular work.) As an adult, I can stand back and admire the sheer craft of the piece without the feeling of dread that permeated our souls all those years ago. It's a gorgeously shot film with strong intent. That can't be said for all of Fulci's films; *Zombie* has a refined power that's still hard to shake.

What isn't so hard to shake? The overwrought performances (save Johnson and McCulloch), or mostly atrocious dialogue, with the exception of Menard's delicious opening salvo. But hey, this is the tradeoff for such visual splendor and visceral fortitude. We knew back then that certain parts of the film were laughable; but when the next entrails buffet, or cemetery uprising, or lunge from the darkness occurred, the smiles were quickly erased and the fear emerged.

Most detractors of *Zombie* point to a lack of social commentary in the shadow of Romero's classic 1978 opus, acting as if a movie without something important to say is somehow a lesser beast. That's just plain old snobbery. Horror hits in many ways, each valid in its own right. If you're new to the genre, or new to Fulci (or maybe just looking to expand your undead palette beyond AMC), may I recommend your voyage start here? Climb aboard. I'll tell the crew.

It only seems right to end this festival with a film that tries to one-up the previous on the outrageousness—and nearly succeeds. It's all about that touching mother-son relationship, believe me. Are you prepared to enter the...

Burial Ground (1981)

It is truly amazing how crowded the zombie market was in the early 1980s, at least in Europe. After the success of George Romero's *Dawn of the Dead* (1978) begat Lucio Fulci's unofficial "sequel" *Zombie* (1979), the floodgates were opened and the undead made their (slow and shuffling) move at the box office. Amidst the barrage was one *Burial Ground* (1981), a film that boils down a zombie flick to its very essence: people get munched, and they get munched *good*. Forget social subtext; *Burial Ground* barely has *text*.

Also known as *The Night of Terrors*, *Burial Ground* was released on its home turf of Italy in the summer, with the U.S. not receiving a release until late 1985 before dropping on video in early 1986. There's really no need to mention reviews from the mainstream; what do you think they would say that would in any way add to the discourse beyond "cheapjack Romero rip off"? But *Burial Ground* even missed most of the diehard gore hounds when it originally came out—a real pity because this one is something special, even in such a crowded field.

We should talk about the plot, or lack thereof. A well-to-do professor (Raimondo Barbieri), holed up in his sprawling manor comes across an underground cavern of the undead—apparently some secret cult that figured out how to beat death. After they snack on him, his friends, acquaintances, and disposable eye candy roll up to the manor as the prof had news to share of his discovery with them all.

The zombies attack everyone in the mansion. So. What's new with you?

That's all you get with the story, I'm afraid; anyone who can make Fulci look like a Swiss-timed plot meister deserves a shout-out—so director Andrea Bianchi (*Strip Nude for Your Killer*) and screenwriter Piero Regnoli (*Nightmare City*) please take a bow for creating a gut muncher that has gut-munching and *only* that on the mind. The zombies are the only characters who get a story arc; they're hungry at the start and full by the end.

Okay, you could say the humans are alive at the start and dead by the end, but you get the point. There is no reading of the scrolls to try and stop the outbreak, no mediums contacting the afterlife looking for an impasse, and no heroic stand by one individual clearly designed to be the hero (or heroine). With the exception of two people (who we'll get to later on I promise), the characters are forgettable to the point of being amusing.

There's a blond girl, a blond guy; two (or three) bearded guys, two brunettes. Did I mention a blond guy? Okay. I'm probably even off on this count, as the cast sort of floats by you on their way to the slaughterhouse, leaving nary an impression as they do.

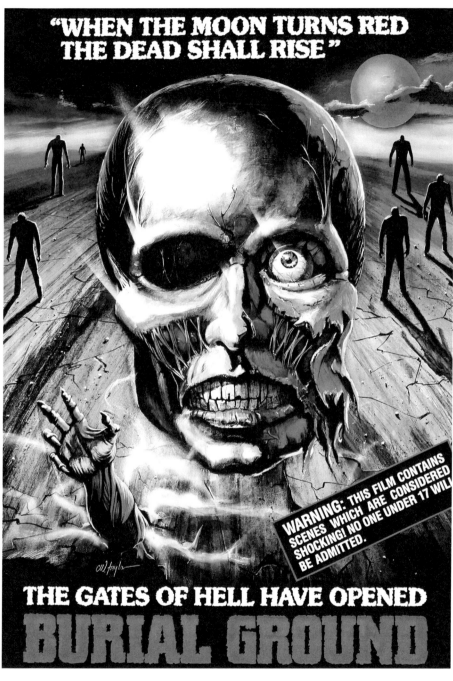

I think this blanching of any personality traits is intentional however. I mean when you have two people such as Evelyn (Mariangela Giordano) and her son Michael (Peter Bark) in the mix, why bother fleshing out the rest? (They wouldn't stand a chance anyway.) Because if you're wondering where the perversity of Italian cinema is located, look no further than these two.

Michael is a very clingy 12-year-old. Most of his on-screen time is spent clutching at his mother's waist, his white belt and mom jeans setting him apart from the fashion of the day. Now, that's a funny enough scenario as is, but in case you hadn't noticed, Michael is an unusual looking boy—he's about the height of an average 12-year-old, but his facial features belie that fact, as he seems … mature. The fact that a man in his mid–20s was hired for the part has always been *Burial Ground*'s biggest selling point, especially to those who've never viewed it before; what's really trippy is what Bark does with the role.

First of all, he's dubbed by another grown-up actor, which never seems to jive with the bug-eyed expression constantly plastered across Bark's face. And secondly—well, actually that's it—Bark's befuddled visage is the only trick in his bag, and his reactions to the events unfolding are priceless in their inertness. And if you haven't seen it yet, you'll soon find out why they had to hire an adult for the part. Just watch it. Please, I incest.

I don't blame him, really. The entire running time of *Burial Ground* is filled with zombies marching, marching, marching and then munching, munching, munching. The repetitiveness becomes hypnotizing—as viewers we're usually so attuned to the ebb and flow of plot turns and contrivances that we are transfixed by this film's resistance to structure.

So if the film is nothing but a barf-bag buffet, how are all the fixings, anyway? Well, in the hands of special effects director Gino De Rossi (*City of the Living Dead*) they're pretty tasty. It's not his best work (painting a nose black to make it disappear doesn't really work if you still see the nose), but innards fly and heads do roll for the majority of the film. Effects are plenty, and plenty outrageous. Bring an umbrella.

Burial Ground has no time for trivial concerns such as plot or circumstance; it plays like the first draft of a video game where all they have so far is a location, monsters, and victims. But as in video games, some movies are best enjoyed in "simple" mode—especially when the screen is littered with such perverse delights to see—you won't even miss the story. If you're so hung up on cohesion, go watch a Fulci, will ya?

Festival Nine:
What the Film

I think everyone who really digs horror films has a What the Film—
or WTF—in their pocket to share with like-minded individuals; a passion
that says "Why yes, I like films about man-babies and ones about ancient
Native American shaman hanging out in a cyst on Susan Strasberg's back,
as well, thanks for asking!"

Us horror fans *do* love some weird shit, don't we? But weird is rela-
tive, and subjective, and maybe overused. But for mainstream viewers, the
films in this festival would indeed be classified as such. At the very least.

For instance, our first film, *The Baby* (1973), is about a social worker
who has to tend with a family that has kept their grown son in infancy: diapers, giant crib, the whole nine. Is this "weird"? Well actually, it's incredibly strange, more than a little perverted, with the whole point being some
people are very fucked up. Okay, file under "bizarre."

But our next film isn't that odd, is it? *Phantom of the Paradise* (1974) is
a Brian De Palma film in which a composer has his music stolen by a Svengali who sold his soul to the Devil. Does a mix of *Faust* and *Phantom of
the Opera* sound reasonably within the realm of normal? Hmm? You say
the Svengali is played by 1970s soft-rock icon Paul Williams and he writes
all the music, across different styles? Maybe that is sort of "odd," come to
think of it.

Okay, but the late Tobe Hooper's follow-up to *The Texas Chain Saw
Massacre*, *Eaten Alive* (1976), has Neville Brand flailing and screaming
through the Florida Everglades in a psychotic stagebound version of Tennessee Williams' *Psycho*. Well, shit. That definitely reads "crazy," doesn't
it?

Right. So they're *all* nutters here, and there's no discrimination—
Hollywood Meatcleaver Massacre's (1976) minuscule budget adds to the
baked-in, grimy weirdness of the story instead of handicapping it. And *The
Manitou* (1978)—Director William Girdler's final film before perishing in

143

a helicopter crash—has a big budget feel at a fraction of the price, with its touching tale of tumors, Susan Strasberg's sac shaman, laser shootouts in outer space and Tony Curtis as a fake psychic. (He's the normal part of the film.)

Horror is a great reminder of perspective: my treasure may be your trash, and vice versa. But there's no other genre that inspires hearty, healthy debate, with room for all at the table. I've certainly seen enough trash to fill up a landfill, but I wouldn't have it any other way; feel free to rummage through my pile anytime you like.

What these films represent is the true wonder of cinema—that someone could think up the wildest scenarios, be given money, and have their vision displayed for all (okay, some) to see. Yes, every film is a miracle. That these were greenlit should act as a litmus test for insanity, and serve as calling cards for the odd and disenfranchised.

All of these titles were essentially misunderstood upon release, or straight-up hated. I prefer to think they were just unloved; but time has a way of settling the weird into the world like it always belonged here. And as horror fans, we know it does.

====

Let's rip this band-aid right off the skin, shall we?
No one was—some still aren't—
prepared to deal with...

The Baby (1973)

Only in the 1970s, man, only in the 1970s. Long before PC culture invaded popular entertainment, movies were the haven of the taboo, a safe house for ideas two steps from the norm. Now, many of these films of perversion were relegated to grindhouse theaters and the third feature of a "Dusk Til Dawn" showing at your local Drive-In. But occasionally a film will crawl towards the mainstream and plop itself down, bawling for attention. *The Baby* (1973) is one such film, so twisted in conception that it's hard to believe it would be released in *any* decade. Except the 1970s of course, where you could even get the director of a *Dirty Harry* and a *Planet of the Apes* flick to helm it.

Distributed by Scotia International in March, *The Baby* was given a limited theatrical release—and that's really for the best—as much as the film *tries* to position itself aesthetically as mainstream, the subject matter is so far off the charts that the margins are where the film deserves

to reside. (Of course that's where you'll often find many of us genre fans. We're margin munchers.) A curiosity of *any* time, *The Baby* simply refuses to be forgotten. Because once you've seen it, there's no turning back, Jack.

Our film opens as social worker Ann Gentry (Anjanette Comer) pores over her new assignment, while her mother-in-law Judith (Beatrice Manley Blau) watches with great intent. We see pictures of an infant boy, and then more as the boy ages but his status doesn't—he grows and yet is still seen and kept as an infant, diapers and all. Ann arrives the next day at the home of Mrs. Wadsworth (Ruth Roman), her two grown daughters Germaine (Marianna Hill) and Alba (Suzanne Zenor), and her now adult son, aptly named Baby (David Manzy).

Ann is the latest in a long line of workers sent to deal with Baby. Naturally, Mrs. W. and the sisters are leery of anyone messing with their tight-knit clan, but reluctantly go along with Ann's plan to help poor old Baby develop mentally and physically. That is until they see her making progress. This leads to an all-out battle for custody for the man-child, culminating in a siege-like standoff and a doozy of an ending. Will Baby find the proper healthcare before it's too late? Depends.

Now, using just the description above as the basis for a movie (or more appropriately, a "social issue" telefilm), you could deliver an earnest, yet unusual drama about overcoming obstacles and championing the underdog. I mean, the 1970s did give us *The Boy in the Bubble*, after all. But co-producer and writer Abe Polsky (*The Rebel Rousers*) has no real interest in grounding *The Baby* in reality; he plays the exploitation card from the start. There's no way in hell Baby would still be living with that family in the state he's in, diaper bound and cooing. (My wife's in social services; I think if I showed her this movie she'd start throwing chairs around the room.) But the truly weird is lathered on when: (a) Baby is left in the care of a sitter who breastfeeds him when he cries (and she gets off on it), and (b) The sisters' idea of looking after their brother involves using a cattle prod to keep him in line, as well as slipping naked into his oversized crib for some cuddle time. Add to that some insidious motives and we're a far cry away from the *ABC Afterschool Special*.

Ted Post was a TV vet who was given the occasional big screen project (such as *Magnum Force*) because he worked well with actors and knew how to finesse a budget. *The Baby* still holds much of its fascination because Post betrays his material in a sense; he shoots the film in a mundane style that doesn't cater to the L.A. Gothic aesthetic on display (that *house*). Instead he allows it to (almost) pass by undetected—until the babysitter scene, when all bets become null and void. There's also no moral mast to latch onto in *The Baby*. Everyone has an agenda (even Ann—it's heavily implied in the opening shots), leaving Manzy's sympathetic portrayal of Baby the only one to root for until the bloody finish.

Post, however, lets his cast find the high drama and run with it; Comer plays it straight, leaving Roman, Hill, and Zenor with more scenery to gobble up as the Wadsworth women. The sisters' baby doll act is a gas (keep an eye on Germaine's amazing hairdo—it gets bigger as the film progresses like some demented gag from *Airplane!*). Roman rules as the matriarch, her silken-ashtray voice and wide-eyed weirdness leading the charge like the old pro she was. And don't worry, there's bloodshed to be had, providing the bonafides for the B-crowd. All this, in an unbelievable *PG* package! (Apparently, the MPAA had no issues with the film's intent. Yikes.)

Now as fascinating and enjoyably psychotic as *The Baby* is, the only hiccup in Polsky's script is an antifeminist stance that's hard to absorb. I mean he certainly tries; he seems to be saying that women suppress men (uh-huh), and seek to dominate and ultimately control them through any means necessary (double uh-huh). It's the type of tract one would expect from a first-time playwright with mommy issues. Besides, it's kind of hard to get your message across when your hero is a diapered man with rubbery legs. But hey, it's just another incident logged in a very specific case file, filled as it is with sordid behavior and misguided clients. And while the pile of B-movie folders almost touches the ceiling, *The Baby* sits next to it as a singular document, waiting for the next unsuspecting case worker to take it on. Are you up to the task?

From the crib to the concert hall we go, for a deliciously different morality tale dipped in decadence and backstage smarts. Salutations from the...

Phantom of the Paradise (1974)

Fighting off a 1960s sugar hangover of Disney singalongs and reluctant nannies, musicals took turns being either idealistic (*Hair*) or Good Book Wavin' morality plays (*Godspell, Jesus Christ Superstar*). We called them rock musicals—the music (slightly more) hard-hitting, the lyrics speaking to the issues of the day—spirituality, war—heady stuff (on paper). But who was giving the Devil his due? Where was a musical about the fun side of sin, temptation, sacrifice, and ill-gained ecstasy? Where was the rock musical ABOUT rock and roll? And then, yay and verily, it did arrive on the world's

Phantom of the Paradise, 20th Century-Fox, 1974

doorstep in a black bassinet, cackling and screaming, eager to please and ready to reign. Welcome to *Phantom of the Paradise* (1974). As a wise old glam queen once said, "Life at last! Salutations from the other side!" Released on Halloween by 20th Century–Fox, *POTP* did not reign. At all. Critics were not kind, and audiences were left confused by this cross-stitched amalgamation of *Faust*, *Phantom of the Opera*, *Dorian Gray*, and *Billboard* magazine. *Phantom* was beloved in exactly two locations—Paris, France, and Winnipeg, Canada, where it played for months in theaters and garnered Gold record certification for the soundtrack. I can't vouch for France, but I grew up around that part of Canada and my older brother played the album all the time—I knew the songs *way* before I saw the film. Regardless, long after the smoke machines cleared and the California snow blew away, fans of the delightfully macabre have come to embrace this weird, hilarious, kaleidoscopic candy coated manifesto. Take your seats, the show is about to begin....

Singer-songwriter Winslow Leach (William Finley) is duped into turning over his magnum opus, a cantata based on *Faust*, to malevolent music impresario Swan (played with a sublime showbiz lacquer by Paul Williams). Realizing Swan is instead using his music for his tacky novelty 1950s act The Juicy Fruits, Winslow confronts Swan and is promptly framed and sent to prison for life. After he escapes, Winslow is disfigured by a malfunctioning record press while trying to put an end to Swan's desecration of his music. During rehearsals for the grand opening of Swan's new theater, The Paradise, Winslow sabotages Swan's other nostalgia act (this time taking on the 1960s), The Beach Bums. Realizing Winslow is not going to go away, Swan signs him to a lifetime (and beyond) contract to rewrite his cantata for Phoenix (Jessica Harper), a young ingénue who Winslow feels should be his voice (record presses are a bitch on vocal cords). Tricked once again by Swan, and left for dead—with glam rocker Beef brought in to sing in Phoenix's place—Winslow wreaks havoc on the Paradise and all who stand in his way from saving Phoenix.

I really had to work to simplify the plot description, because there is just so much going on in this film. It truly is a potpourri of literary influences, cinematic homages, and inside jokes. The thread that ties it all together is a loving satire of the music business—the obsession with fame at any cost, the decadence that envelopes it, and the regurgitation of old ideas covered in new upholstery. The Juicy Fruits, The Beach Bums, and The Undead (the glam band that precedes Beef at the Paradise opening) are all played by the same characters, emphasizing Swan's knack for savvy marketing over originality. Everything from contracts the size of phone books to seedy "auditions" to macho artifice (oh, Beef) is covered, not so much damning as pushing it to the front of the stage for a closer look.

Working the curtains for this murderous matinee is none other than writer/director Brian De Palma. Fresh off the sly thriller *Sisters* (1973), he comes into full bloom here, displaying a masterful and light touch, very much playing up the comedic, colorful aspects of the film without sacrificing the gothic gestures throughout. There's always something interesting going on in the frame with De Palma, whether it's forced perspective or visual metaphors (the narcissistic barrage of mirrors comes to mind), stuffing the screen for all to see. A feast for the eyes…

… And the ears. At the time of *POTP*, Paul Williams was one of the hottest singer/songwriters around. Responsible for co-writing some of the biggest hits of the day for the likes of The Carpenters and Three Dog Night, he specialized in catchy, melodramatic soft rock, often romantic, but also often dark and brooding. His music in *POTP* is a revelation. I'm sure people at the time were concerned that Williams would be a bad fit to compose a soundtrack of rock and roll. Except it's not that, it's a soundtrack *about* rock and roll—and he covers every era from the 1950s doo-wop of "Goodbye, Eddie, Goodbye" through the faux Beach Boys of "Upholstery" to the wave of glam rock starting to swell on these shores on "Somebody Super Like You" and "Life at Last." These are facsimiles, tributes really, played and sung affectionately and without cynicism. So while the film lampoons the machinations of the music industry, the songs themselves act as a reminder of why people fall in love with music in the first place. The remainder of the songs are more in keeping with Williams' regular milieu, but tied to the story thematically. Every good Phantom should have his own theme. Finley does, and it's beautiful.

The casting of Finley in the lead is an unusual choice, except De Palma used him before in *Sisters*. Tall, gangly, and devoid of standard leading-man looks, he portrays the sadness and rage inherent in Winslow. By the time he dons his Phantom costume, we are firmly entrenched in his corner, having watched him go through every obstacle just to be heard and seen for who he is. This is a heartbreaking performance in and out of the mask. Harper brings the right amount of naiveté and street smarts to the girl with scruples, who still can't resist the dark lure of fame. Gerritt Graham has a star-making, hilarious turn as Beef, proving how much of Hollywood is built on illusion. Williams' natural likeability dovetails perfectly into his role as Swan. Part Phil Spector, part snake oil salesman, *all* satanic snake, he simply oozes smarm as a vain, talented man who sold his soul (at one point he intones to Winslow "I'm under contract too") for the chance to stay young (and talented) forever. But when the talent dries up, he resents the new blood he's brought aboard to keep the charade alive. It's a mesmerizing performance—if you're going to play a devil, you might as well have a helluva time.

Why didn't audiences respond to *POTP* when it came out? I think they were too far culturally *in it* to see what it was—it needed a generational distance to appreciate the satire. As well, music fans had a hard time calibrating the horror with the tunes—a measure that was slowly remedied as *The Rocky Horror Picture Show* (1975) began its slow, bizarre climb up the ladder of success. Hard to fathom, but the very industry it was lambasting appreciated it—*POTP* was nominated for an Oscar and a Golden Globe for the music, and a Writer's Guild of America nomination for De Palma. Unlike *Rocky Horror*, *Phantom of the Paradise* never got the "midnight movie" love. But while *Rocky Horror* wore itself ragged, *Phantom* waited patiently for the curtain to rise and bask in the spotlight. That time is now. Life at last.

═══════════════

Sweep the confetti and raise the curtain; here's a film that looks
and feels like a play—a very twisted one, mind you.
Be prepared to be…

Eaten Alive (1976)

For me, the most interesting thing about the late horror maestro Tobe Hooper's storied career was he took chances. He always swung big. From his landmark second feature *The Texas Chain Saw Massacre* (1974),* to *Lifeforce* (1985), to even *The Mangler* (1995), he pushed the genre into the absurd through concept and execution, audiences be damned. It's an admirable trait in a filmmaker, and one that's on full display with *Eaten Alive* (1976), probably his most bizarre film. (Which is saying a *lot*.)

After a limited stateside release in October 1976, *Eaten Alive* was given a wide release in May of the following year by Virgo International Pictures to theaters and drive-ins across the land. This start of the ever-undulating arc of Hooper's career was met with a resounding "WHAAAAT?" by the public and critics alike. This was not the follow-up to the cultural explosion that *Chain Saw* people were expecting. And to be honest, this may be a film that you need a couple of views to warm up to; it certainly was for me. And so it goes when you're a member of the Cult of Hooper— our Leader's message doesn't always hit you at first, but stay with him and his intentions will eventually ring true.

---

* The original film title has two words, *Chain Saw*; the rest of the films have it as one word (thus *TCM* below). If I don't do it right, they'll run me out of horror town with pitchforks and torches.

How about the story (or lack thereof)? Set at the Starlight Hotel, *Eaten Alive* follows the escapades of proprietor Judd (Neville Brand) as he gets into all kinds of hijinks with his pet alligator that haunts the swamp surrounding his stilt-propped abode. Lodgers come but never leave, meeting their demise either by gator or Judd's trusty, rusty scythe. And that's it really.

There is a bit of a throughline with the father (Mel Ferrer) and sister (Crystin Sinclaire) investigating the whereabouts of a missing girl (Roberta Collins), but beyond that, it's slim pickings. The other guests include a bizarre family consisting of William Finley, Marilyn Burns, and Kyle Richards, who spend most of the film under the hotel to avoid spending time with Uncle Judd. Throw in visits from good old boy Buck (a wonderfully scuzzy Robert Englund), a laid-back sheriff (played by the laid-back Stuart Whitman), and a trip to Madam Hattie's (a practically unrecognizable Carolyn Jones from *The Addams Family*) house of ill repute. Mix 'em all up, and away you go. The narrative follows Judd mumbling incoherently about "directives" and "lists" and mowing his guest list down to zero.

But *TCM* wasn't exactly brimming with plot either, so why the cold shoulder? Well, *EA* doesn't possess the same drive as *TCM*, with its sense of relentless psychosis that permeates the latter half of the film. But *EA* wasn't designed that way; it's Southern Gothic with all the trimmings—sex, sleaze, and enough drama to fill three Tennessee Williams plays. *This* is a large part of what kept people away—some of the characters are over the top and arch (especially Finley, who even barks at one point, although he's a mentally-fragile husband). This style comes across as grating if you're not on Hooper's wavelength. Aiding immeasurably in this "Psycho on a Hot Tin Roof" vibe is the way it's filmed. Shot completely on sound stages in L.A. with red lighting that permeates every wooden slat of the Starlight Hotel, *EA* plays like an Off Broadway musical without the music. Characters come and go from the hotel, with Judd's anguished antics always pushed to the front of the stage. Nothing about the film feels *real*, and as it follows *The Texas Chain Saw Massacre*, one of the most visceral horror films of all time, *Eaten Alive* seems all the more heightened in comparison.

So these are some of the reasons people stayed away from *Eaten Alive* (or left a screening disappointed and/or annoyed) and they're all valid points—if you were expecting *The Texas Chainsaw Massacre 2*. (Sorry, there was still a ten-year wait on that one.) But that's not fair game I say. Why must the yardstick of merit be wielded, especially for a then-burgeoning talent like Hooper? Some of the themes of *TCM* are present in *Eaten Alive*—Hooper taps into that fear of the South better than anyone, and the film is even seedier than its predecessor. But here these themes are reconfigured into an experimental drama that just happens to prominently feature a disturbed war vet, a farming implement, and a ferocious (albeit, very phony looking) reptile. It's very much its own thing while sitting alongside *TCM* as a travelogue to places you do not want to ever visit.

Watching *Eaten Alive* is like spending a couple of hours inside a flickering neon sign, full of buzz and pop, unyielding to outside elements like time and taste. Credit writers/producers Alvin L. Fast (*Satan's Cheerleaders*) and Mardi Rustam (*Evils of the Night*), as well as Kim Henkel (*TCM*) for his "screen adaptation." (Hmm ... maybe it *was* a play?) The film plays much better when seen as an experience and not a series of seemingly unconnected, episodic scenes. Hooper and his writers want you to smell the swamp gas and the musty upholstery, and cower at Brand's unhinged performance as Judd. He's never more terrifying than when his towering frame blocks out the camera, scythe at the ready, screams bouncing off the plastered walls. *Eaten Alive* is such an immersive experience it should come with 3-D glasses. (Or at least Odorama scratch and sniff cards.)

Time has been very kind to *Eaten Alive*. Charter members of the Cult of Hooper (I can get you in, I know the president!) understand that membership requires embracing the weird. But the funny thing is, the films of our Leader only seem strange from the outside looking in. Do yourself a favor and join us, won't you? The snacks are great, and soon we'll be mounting a production of my new musical, Starlight Hotel Memories. Should be a scream.

═══════════

Here's one that's been tossed around and mishandled its whole shelf life— different names at every turn as if it's in the Witness Protection Program. Just be careful what you look for—you might just find yourself in a...

Hollywood Meatcleaver Massacre (1976)

If I had a dollar for every horror film that went by several names, I would be writing this from my villa in Jamaica. (I do not currently have a villa in Jamaica.) The interesting thing is that instead of massaging life back into a film that already made the rounds under a different title, it ends up diluting the reputation—if it even had one—of the original film. Kind of a "damaged goods" scenario, if you will.

But this was certainly business as usual during the drive-in era; distributors would often send a film out, wait a year, rename it, and send it

back out again as the second feature for another film making its first run. Lather, rinse, repeat.

Such is the case with *Hollywood Meatcleaver Massacre* (1976). Or do I mean *Meatcleaver Massacre* (1977), which has bookended footage of one Christopher Lee in some wood-paneled office, offering ominous intonations unrelated to the events about to unfold? (The producers bought the unused Lee footage off another producer.) Perhaps you watched a video called *Morak*, or *Revenge of the Dead*? All the same film, folks—so I'm sticking with the original title for this discussion.

Beyond a couple of local premieres, *HMM* didn't even get a chance to strut its stuff until home video several years later and under the proliferation of alternate titles. A pity to be sure, if only for pride's sake—having a theatrical and drive-in run was standard for even the *worst* films. And some would happily throw this one on that pile. But *HMM* is worth the film stock it's printed on: it's ambitious, interesting, and doesn't wear out its welcome at a tidy 77 minutes. (Watch the one with Mr. Lee for eight additional minutes of wood paneling. *The horror.*) And as per this festival, it's very weird.

Before the story unfolds, it should be noted that there is no meat cleaver used in the proceedings—merely an ancient demon summoned by a professor of the occult to avenge the death of his family. You know, that old chestnut.

We open at a Southern California university, where Professor Cantrell (James Habif) is lecturing his students on the Gaelic demon Morak, even while some dismiss his class as a big load of bullshit. The ringleader of the naysayers is Mason (Larry Justin), who confronts the professor after class. When Cantrell puts Mason down in front of his friends, Mason decides to head to the professor's house and scare him and his family.

Mason and his three cronies—Sean, Dirk, and Phil, smooth brains one and all—start by killing the family dog Poopers, and then descend on the rest of the clan. Their plan to just scare is tossed out the window with adrenaline and booze leading the way; they feel they haven't any choice but to leave no witnesses. The only problem is the professor isn't *quite* dead and lies in a coma. And when that happens, one tends to conjure ancient demons and sic them after the thugs who killed your family. It's certainly what I would do.

In natural psycho fashion, Mason is very comfortable with the murders. His chums, however, have a feeling that "something" is after them, and they are very much right. One by one, Cantrell conjures Morak to dispose of his wrongdoers, until only Mason is left. He's heard of a way to reverse the curse—but will it be too little, too late?

Hollywood Meatcleaver Massacre: let's start with that title. Meant to invoke a tender love story between a Texan boy and his chainsaw from a couple of years prior, it is a title chosen to provoke a response, and I fully endorse it. Showmanship (or hucksterism—and I mean that term with full affection) will always have a place in B-cinema. Sure the paint may not yet be dry, but the car is a real beaut and not a lemon at all, I promise.

This is kind of a frustrating statement, because *HMM*, aside from its obvious limitations—no budget in front of and behind the camera—is more imaginative than a lot of drive-in filler being released at the time. But I can see why it wouldn't play for the masses at the time, or even the midnight movie crowd; it's simply too messy, and without any kind of societal commentary or satire to give it weight. *HMM* floats by on imagination while using its resources in effective ways.

I'm personally a sucker for any film that features Los Angeles as a character unto itself, and *HMM* uses it to reflect the dead-end outlook from Mason and his pals; there's no glamour or tinsel in their life. It's rundown, seedy apartments and cheap beer.

Make no mistake, Mason et al. are not displayed in a favorable light nor do they appear sympathetic; instead they are seen as mere runoff of a downward spiraling society. A lot of 1970s fare has that nihilistic glow that just depresses some people. To that, I say (a) cheer up! I can tell you as a kid it was a fun—and fascinating—decade to grow up in, and (b) keep telling yourself it's only a movie…

It's just the way it was, especially with horror. But while *HMM* really has nothing on its mind besides vengeance, the rickety surrealism—dream sequences abound—carries it through. As does a terrifically unhinged performance by Larry Justin as Mason, by far the best in a film filled with one-and-done actors, not to mention director Evan Lee (no relation to Christopher).

With its brief running time, *Hollywood Meatcleaver Massacre* not only doesn't overstay its welcome, it crams a lot of inspiration (or information, I guess) into that time. Think *Death Wish* meets *Patrick* on a really tight budget and you're halfway there. Even in its brevity, *HMM* challenges the audience to sort through it all. I'd rather watch a film that shoots for the stars and scrapes the dirt than one that aims for the obvious tree. It's that kind of film.

Just when you thought it was safe …
to ride your bed … in outer space …
along comes…

The Manitou (1978)

When I think of some of my favorite B films of the 1970s, my mind tends to drift towards the works of the late filmmaker William Girdler. This man made nine movies in six years before his tragic death in 1978 at the age of thirty; chief among them were *Abby*, *Grizzly*, and *Day of the Animals*. Now, quantity obviously doesn't equal quality, and he made a few outright stinkers. But he was exciting to me because he became a better, more confident filmmaker with each film. This is especially evident with his final release, *The Manitou* (1978), your typical ancient Native American little person demon growing out of the back of a woman's neck who fights the heroes in space with laser beams kind of flick. You know the type.

Independently produced, *The Manitou* was released by Avco Embassy in late April, with a June rollout across North America, and worldwide the following year. With a budget of only $3 million U.S., the film certainly gained more favor from audiences than critics, but that's nothing new. Girdler was a low-budget guru whose only aim was to make viewers happy; there's a joy and energy in his films and a clear lack of cynicism that shines on the screen. He's often derided for hopping on the latest fads. *Abby* was considered a Blaxploitation rip-off of *The Exorcist*, and *Grizzly* was dubbed "*Jaws* with claws." And while those films do wear those influences on their tattered sleeves, they don't come across as cash-ins but rather, earnest extensions of that particular vein. There's a reason *Grizzly* is the first film that pops into people's heads when they talk about killer bear movies: it's so much damn fun.

The Manitou would have no such issue defending itself against charges of plagiarism. Based on the best-selling novel by Graham Masterton (who would go on to pen six more novels in *The Manitou* line—I think I may have some reading ahead of me), it is at once his most assured effort and easily his craziest. How crazy? Well, grab a bowl of popcorn (or pack a bowl—hey, you do you), sit back, and I'll tell you a tale of ancient medicine men, vengeful spirits, psychic charlatans, and galactic hospital battles.

Our film opens at a San Francisco hospital, where Dr. Hughes (Jon Cedar) and a colleague are looking at X-rays of growth on a woman's neck. The neck belongs to Karen Tandy (Susan Strasberg), and the growth is more of a hump. A hump that the doctors figure is not cancerous, but is filled with bones and tissue, not unlike … a fetus. They schedule surgery for the following day to remove the growth.

Scared, Karen seeks comfort in the arms of her ex-boyfriend, Harry Erskine (Tony Curtis), a phony Tarot card reader who bilks little old ladies out of their retirement money with predictions of romance and wealth. They reconnect, and Harry witnesses the procedure, which doesn't go so

EVIL DOES NOT DIE...
IT WAITS...
TO BE RE-BORN...

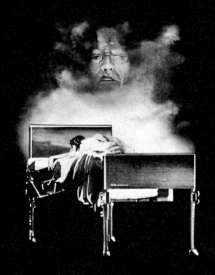

THE **MANITOU**

HERMAN WEIST and MELVIN SIMON Present · A Film by WILLIAM GIRDLER "THE MANITOU"
Starring TONY CURTIS
MICHAEL ANSARA · SUSAN STRASBERG · STELLA STEVENS · JON CEDAR · ANN SOTHERN Special Appearance by BURGESS MEREDITH
Screenplay by WILLIAM GIRDLER and JON CEDAR & THOMAS POPE · Based upon the Novel "THE MANITOU" by GRAHAM MASTERTON" a Pinnacle Book
Music by LALO SCHIFRIN · Executive Producer, MELVIN G. GORDY · Produced and Directed by WILLIAM GIRDLER Filmed in Panavision® Color by CFI

AVCO EMBASSY PICTURES Release   PG PARENTAL GUIDANCE SUGGESTED

well, as the hump is having none of this eviction notice and makes Dr. Hughes cut into his wrist. Later on at his apartment, Harry witnesses one of his clients flop about in a trance, yell apparent gibberish, and throw herself down a staircase to her death (after levitating down the hallway, mind you). He seeks assistance from his mentor, Amelie Crusoe (Stella Stevens). Why, you ask? Because the gibberish his deceased client was spouting, "panna wichi salitu" is the same gobbledygook Karen uttered in her sleep the night before.

One botched séance later, Harry and Amelie are off to see Dr. Snow (Burgess Meredith), an anthropologist who can translate the seemingly non-speak as Native American from a decimated 400-year-old tribe, and would only be spoken by a medicine man. The translation roughly reads as "I'm coming back, beyotches." Snow informs them that if they choose to believe that a 400-year-old medicine man could be reborn through a growth (which has now engulfed Karen's back), the only way to fight him would be with *another* medicine man. So Harry takes off for South Dakota, enlists the help of modern-day warrior (mean, mean stride) John Singing Rock (Michael Ansara), and somehow convinces Dr. Hughes to allow John to set up shop and try to cleanse Karen of her elderly shaman backpack. This brings us to the final showdown in the hospital, which I won't describe in detail because (a) I'm running low on ink, and (b) it has to be seen to be believed.

The Manitou starts as a believable thriller for, I don't know, a good fifteen minutes before it takes flight beyond the stars. Palpable fear of our own bodies' failings gives way to: laser tag seemingly out of *Logan's Run*, high flying grannies, our villain rising out of the séance table (call him the Balsawood Baddie), decapitations and skin fileting, snowstorms in the ward, and an incredible space battle between a bedded, topless Strasberg and Misquamacus (our wee, evil ancient chief) that surely had *Starcrash* looking over its shoulder. This train is so far off the track it's hard to tell when they ran out of rail.

This is what saddens me about Girdler's early shuffle off this mortal coil in a freak helicopter accident—I think he was just getting warmed up. He was very ambitious, and of course, *The Manitou* is nothing but ridiculous. But it plays that way because of the premise, not the execution. Some people snicker at the protracted battle at the end, and I will agree the effects are not A1. But of those folk, I ask this: Would it work any better if ILM did the effects? Regardless of the quality, it would still be Susan Strasberg, topless on a bed, shooting lasers at a little person in grotesque makeup. You're either on board with Girdler's vision or you're not. He was *not* a half-asser, that much is certain.

As for the makeup, Tom Burman (*Happy Birthday to Me*) provides some very effective moments strewn throughout the picture. The Big M's birth scene is impressive, as is the skinnin', cuttin', and decapitation. In addition, Lalo Schifrin (*The Amityville Horror*) provides a lush soundtrack that slyly sidesteps any jump cues, instead relying on the mood to give the film an epic feel belying the low budget. And that's what Girdler was so good at—he loved to film in Panavision, and the wide-open scope grants some impressive scenery of San Francisco but makes the picture seem grander than it really is. If you're going to watch goofy, you might as well enjoy the view.

Speaking of goofy, Curtis has a bit of fun as Erskine, playing his fakery for laughs at the beginning, and then dialing back the snickering as the events escalate. It's a wise move—otherwise, he'd have to go *really* over the top to compete. Strasberg does well with what she's given, however, there's a good chance this type of scenario was not covered at The Lee Strasberg Theatre & Film Institute. (Although I like to dream that it's been added since.) The real standout is Ansara, who brings a level of dignity and earnestness to John. While the role is written that way (thank the god of your choosing), it's a role that in the wrong hands could easily turn into parody. Some would say it was in the wrong hands anyway; Ansara was not Native American but rather of Lebanese descent. (However, he did play Cochise in *Broken Arrow* on TV.) Despite the unfortunate regressive casting of that time, he's very good and imbues John Singing Rock with a nobility that the character deserves.

The sad death of William Girdler extinguished a very promising, exciting, genre talent. But cinema projects immortal shadows in the sky; Marlowe, Kane, O'Hara, Bickle, et al. are tangled and swirling in the night winds, looming over the viewer wise enough to cast an upward gaze. But when I look to the heavens, I'd like to believe that tucked away in a far corner of the universe *The Manitou* is playing, with beams of light careening from the bedpost to the beyond and back. Ambition always deserves a place amongst the stars.

Festival Ten:
Duct Tape and Stardust

Any filmmaker will tell you: every movie that gets made and released is a miracle in and of itself, and that's completely sidestepping the issue of quality. The damn thing has to be made somehow, distributed, and released to the public in a bid for affection and profits. But it's a long ladder to climb, filled as it is with shysters and lower-middle, mid-middle, and upper-middle studio folks with opinions, notes, and more opinions. And why do they have so much say? Because they hold the purse strings, of course.

Shocking as it is to believe, making a film costs a lot of money. Well, most films anyway. This festival is dedicated to films that end up being celebrations of the medium itself, getting by on little more than imagination and determination.

Grit. A steely resolve. Rocks in your head. All the things necessary to set out on the filmmaking journey; talent is optional, although encouraged. Every film is released to make money, although that may not be why it was made (artistic pursuits and all) but once it is, those investors are hoping for some kind of return—maybe even a hit?

The films in this festival reach beyond their grasp because that's where the inspiration is; also, they have no choice—the tools given may be insufficient, but they can make special, accidental magic. This festival is about dreaming and perseverance. Let's look at the films ahead:

The first film, *Invaders from Mars* (1953), is more expensive than the other four put together, and its budget is still less than a quarter of a million dollars—and yet the ambition and ingenuity on display make it feel like ten times that amount.

And what of the legendary *Plan 9 from Outer Space* (1957)? Regardless of its flying saucer model kits and cardboard headstones, Ed Wood's masterpiece is brimming with childlike energy … and logic.

The 1958 *Fiend Without a Face* goes the shy boy route at first to hide its lack of resources, leaving the filmmakers the funds to trot out spectacular stop-motion creatures in the back half and make the whole venture worthwhile. I guess taking lemons and making lemonade didn't start with *Jaws*; the curiosity to see the creatures actually builds and pays off with the charmingly eerie Harryhausen-like effects.

Do you have the time to listen to me whine about *Basket Case* (1982), Frank Henenlotter's gloriously seedy tribute to Times Square and those who live within it? (I hope you read that sentence with Gene Shalit prancing in your head.) Micro-budgets can't suppress ideas, only actualizations, and if you have Henenlotter's talent and humor, you work your way around the spreadsheet to arrive at a coherent and wry take on brotherly love and wicker baskets.

Oh boy howdy, let's chat about *Things* (1989), shall we? This one's a bit of a cheat, I'll admit—it was straight-to-video, shot on 8 and 16mm, and it sat on Canadian video store shelves for years before word of mouth gave it the reputation as horror's answer to *The Room*.

As I type this I still haven't seen *The Room*; I am confident however, that it is nothing like *Things*—few films are. Fellow Daily Dead scribe Bryan Christopher and our Corpse Club podcast joined me for a commentary track with co-star/producer/writer Barry J. Gillis, and with full confidence I can attest: he is one of the most Canadian Canadians you will ever meet, and very nice to boot. He's also affectionately nicknamed King of Canuxploitation, a title I'm sure he proudly wears. It's a hundred times too long; it's impenetrable; it's really goofy; it is greatly weird, and great in spite of itself. It is *Things*.

"Endearment" is certainly a word that comes to mind when I think of the super-low budget; the blood and sweat are given freely—and literally—to entertain, and so the commitment and intent seems genuine, which comes on like a comfort to a grizzled horror vet.

Each of these films are an inspiration in their own way; Tim Burton's excellent biopic *Ed Wood* (1994) captures the spirit of the artist with boundless optimism and occasional bursts of talent. Optimism is the more important part. This festival is about a true love of film. And the occasional monster.

═══════════════════

We open up with a film overflowing with imagination;
especially from a little boy, who swears
his town has been taken over by...

Invaders from Mars (1953)

Gee whiz, sci-fi sure was simple in the early 1950s, wasn't it? Slap a little Red Scare subtext here, a damsel in distress there, scientists, the military, and of course aliens round out the films that beamed from every drive-in on a Saturday night. One of the earliest (and best) of the bunch is *Invaders from Mars* (1953), which sets itself apart by employing a unique viewpoint and having spectacular and surreal production design. Don't write this off as a cheap time-waster, you whippersnappers.

Distributed by 20th Century–Fox near the end of April, this independent production received some favorable notices and made a swift return on its $290,000 budget, for good reason. Seen through a child's eyes, it captures that imagination and runs with it for 78 minutes, shoddy playthings and all. *Invaders from Mars* is told with the fervor of an excited youth playing catch-up with an exploding imagination.

Little David MacLean (Jimmy Hunt) is a burgeoning astrologer. At night he peers out his bedroom window through his telescope to peruse the stars in all their mysterious wonder, much to the amusement of scientist dad George (Leif Erickson) and mom Mary (Hillary Brooke). One night he awakens to the sound of thunder and sees a luminescent saucer land in the sand dunes beyond the backyard forest. Frightened, he wakes up Pop, who investigates—as he should, for his top secret government project is held within the area. George doesn't return until morning, however, and when he does, he's distant and *very* belligerent toward David. He's also the proud new owner of a surgically implanted device on the back of his neck which doesn't escape David's view.

After witnessing a little girl get sucked into the sand pit and coming back looking wan and pale and acting mean, he turns to the police for help; but alas, even the chief has succumbed. Who can poor Davey turn to for help? Who will believe him? Why, more scientists, of course—this time from the observatory: Dr. Stuart Kelston (Arthur Franz) and Dr. Pat Blake (Helena Carter) make their way to David and lo and behold, they believe him! Before long the Pentagon is contacted, tanks are paraded while providing gratuitous explosions, and everyone heads underground to smoke out the aliens. Can the earthlings defeat the felt-green monsters and their *checks notes* disembodied-in-a-fishbowl-with-tentacles leader? Only the stars can say....

Imagine an 11-year-old using every toy and craft at his or her disposal to create this narrow and limited landscape and you'll get an idea of *Invaders from Mars'* charm; a lot of the early sci-fiers use simplespeak, but *Invaders* actually feels like it came pouring from the brain of an adolescent. The film starts off as an intriguing The-Boy-Who-Cried-Wolf

scenario (the unmovable trope of body snatching stories) before turning into The Boy Who Is Right, and quite early in the picture to boot.

It's an unusual yet effective move that transitions all sympathies toward David, who up to this point is mired in fear, anxiety, and terror. One of childhood's biggest fears is not being believed by grownups and being called dishonest—especially in the eyes of your parents and authorities. The film leans into that fear until it can't use it anymore—once David is believed, the paranoia dissipates and we're left to focus on the spectacular.

This is where director William Cameron Menzies really shines. Coming from a background in production and set design (see Gone with the Wind; not to mention helming 1936's terrific Things to Come), he shoots through David's POV for maximum effect. For instance, the police station that David visits appears cold and blanketed in oppressive white with walls that never seem to find a ceiling and a desk that feels ten feet too tall for a boy to approach. Or the observatory, which seems exactly as a child would envision it: sparse, except for the telescope and another unseen closure beckoning David to be engulfed in its wonders. Menzies has control of Richard Blake's barebones script right from the start (Blake also wrote the screenplay for Counterplot); it's really the aesthetic and palpable unease that sells the story, not the conventional dialogue. Again, if a kid was making this, it wouldn't be the words highlighted, it would be the actions.

Which works out well for our cast of good-looking folks, led by Carter as Dr. Pat, and she commands every scene she's in with her breathtaking visage and level-headed approach to the events at hand. Erikson leans into the Bad Daddy routine with relish and little Hunt makes a likable and smart protagonist. The rest are pro forma 1950s stick figures, although Morris Ankrum's eyebrows lead the charge any chance they get.

The Red Scare subtext is there like every other sci-fi film of the day— them Russkies are trying to take over! Again!—but Invaders from Mars chooses to focus on the fears of the young, right through to the eye-popping underground finale. And for those youngsters in the audience, it offers an upbeat ending (before a rug-pulling coda) that vindicates the fear with the only means necessary for an 11-year-old: a ray-gun. The next time your kid says there's a monster in the closet or an ogre under the bed, don't be so quick to scoff; instead maybe grab a ray gun of your own and help them out.

===

Our next film is legendary, but it should be for the joy of film,
not for some lame title given it decades ago.
Sure, Plans 1 through 8 were stinkers, but it's all systems go for...

Plan 9 from Outer Space (1957)

Yes, there is such a thing as filmic injustice: you have to blame the Medved brothers, film critic Michael and his brother Harry, for their 1980 book *The Golden Turkey Awards*. In it they proclaim *Plan 9 from Outer Space* (1957) as the Worst Film of All Time.

Or better yet, you really should thank them for shining a spotlight on it, even if the opinion is horrifically off-base and narrow-minded. This albatross has guaranteed that any horror, cult, or sci-fi fanatic will, or has, at some point checked to see what that fuss was about.

For yours truly, that time was now. When a film has been in the public consciousness for that long, you feel like you've seen it all—even when you haven't. There have been so many clips and scenes, shown time and again, over decades creating the illusion of a more complete viewing. So I sat and watched what for me was a stitched-together-Frankenstein's monster-of-a viewing; and it's a fully, completely bonkers affair—a love affair with the film itself.

No, *Plan 9* was not a hit. Ed Wood never experienced one of those in his lifetime. It would take that negative press decades to turn around, but as a result, this title has stayed in the cult consciousness long past what he could have imagined, without a doubt.

Let's dig into the story, Medveds be damned: We open on psychic-to-the-people Criswell, as he speaks in cryptic, confusing, and delightful sentences crafted by Wood himself.

> Greetings, my friend. We are all interested in the future, for that is where you and I are going to spend the rest of our lives. And remember my friend, future events such as these will affect you in the future. You are interested in the unknown, the mysterious, the unexplainable. That is why you are here. And now, for the first time, we are bringing to you the full story of what happened on that fateful day. We are bringing you all the evidence, based only on the secret testimony of the miserable souls who survived this terrifying ordeal. The incidents, the places. My friend, we cannot keep this a secret any longer. Let us punish the guilty. Let us reward the innocent. My friend, can your heart stand the shocking facts about grave robbers from outer space?

(Wow. I simply love this dialog; it's weird, florid, and comes across as completely sincere—sell me those goods, Eddie.)

So Criswell carries on with his narration and shows us a saddened man (the already-deceased Bela Lugosi, in a few scenes that Wood shot for another film) attending his wife's funeral. As he mourns, an airplane flies above, and the pilots are almost blinded by the light from a flying saucer! Yes, a flying saucer! The saucer lands in the nearby cemetery, Bela's wife (horror TV host Vampira) is resurrected from the dead, and she kills the

gravediggers. Bela mopes around for a few minutes and is then struck dead by an automobile. Guess where he ends up, and quick?

At this point, the police and the government step in—the police go to the graveyard, and the government visits the home of the pilot Jeff Trent (Gregory Walcott), to glean more information on what he and his co-pilot saw in the sky. Meanwhile at the graveyard, Inspector Clay (Tor Johnson) is killed by the undead Mr. and Mrs. Lugosi, and then resurrected by the aliens to carry out their nefarious plan. Which is what, exactly?

As the commander of the saucer, Eros (Dudley Manlove), and his alien wife Tanna (Joanna Lee) are told by the Ruler (John Breckinridge) that Plans 1 through 8 were a flop, but Plan 9 ... well, that's the chicken dinner winner. It involves bringing the recently dead back to life to destroy mankind. (For the usual reasons: human hubris, etc.) So back we go stomping through the graveyard, and now we have our trio of ghouls— Vampira, Lugosi (or rather, Wood's chiropractor with a cape draped across his face), and Tor Johnson, all ready to do the bidding of the Ruler.

I suppose my only question is: are three ghouls enough to eradicate the population of Earth with *Plan 9 from Outer Space*? Not on your life, but with peanuts, you get three ghouls and you'll like it, mister. But the paucity of funds is exceeded by the ingenuity and enthusiasm on display— with Wood you get a writer/director with a vision. Now, you may not like his vision, or that he has seen it out properly; but it is his own, from beginning to end.

How does one judge *Plan 9* (or as it was originally shown, *Grave Robbers from Outer Space*)? As a horror film, it isn't scary; as sci-fi, it's even less effective. But as someone who has watched a lot of 1950s programmers, *Plan 9* is better than given credit for. The cardinal sin of any film is being boring; *Plan 9* uses different locations (okay, four) to keep things moving. Sure it drags here and there at 79 minutes, but so do quite a few that barely cross 60 minutes. It also has ambition; nine plans is a *lot*.

I think the only ways to judge it are on its sincerity and its entertainment value—both can be true. I have to believe that *Plan 9 from Outer Space*'s enduring popularity is not only a tribute to a fun popcorn film, but also to Wood himself. He gave his all for his films, with a refreshing lack of cynicism. If more filmmakers had half of Wood's passion, we wouldn't need books to needlessly rank the worst.

Off to Britain, we go—"pounds" might sound like more money, but aren't. This film is proof that ingenuity blooms in all the corners of the film world. Beware of the...

Fiend Without a Face (1958)

In the 1950s, independent film was just as keen to stick its nose in the atomic blender as the Hollywood big boys. Of course, budget restrictions frequently left most of the monsters wanting, be they big or small. But sometimes a shot of quirk was enough to stand apart from the Tinseltown terrors. I give you *Fiend Without a Face* (1958), a low-budget romp which shows less until it has to show it all, with giddy results.

Produced by British company Amalgamated Productions and distributed by MGM (in the States), *FWAF* was sent out on a double bill with *The Haunted Strangler*, a Boris Karloff vehicle. With a combined budget of 130,000 pounds, the double feature brought in domestic and international receipts of over $650,000—film diplomacy at its finest.

Filmed in Britain but taking place in Winthrop (?), Manitoba, Canada (never heard of the town, and if I haven't drunk in it, it doesn't exist), *FWAF* posits, as all sci-fi of its time did, that atomic power is bad news and an abomination against natural order (what's the rush, I say—let Mother Nature sort it out).

So the military is based in Winthrop, and they're using atomic energy via aircraft as a form of advanced radar (I think—there's a lot of heavy science going on here; some of it may even be touched by reality, but that's highly doubtful). Major Cummings (Marshall Thompson) is sent to investigate the sudden death of a soldier who drops dead screaming in a field near the base, clutching the back of his neck. He meets the soldier's sister Barbara (Kim Parker), who works as a secretary in town (what else could she do? She's just a gal!), and tries to get to the bottom of the mystery—why are people dropping dead, screaming? Why does the cows' milk taste funny? Is the budget so small that we're never allowed to see the creatures?

The clues lead to a prominent author and scientist, Professor Walgate (Kynaston Reeves), who, while researching mind control inadvertently pulls a Frankenstein, in which lightning and atomic energy mix to create an invisible creature that lives off of brain fluid and spinal columns. (Writers in the 1950s had the best reefer.) As the atomic power is increased, it causes the creatures to become visible, and our heroes must defend themselves siege-like in a house against the hordes of fiends without faces. Will they survive? If only Major Cummings can get to that shack filled with dynamite (located between the house and the atomic power plant, natch) before the fiends take over the town...

The MVPs of *Fiend Without a Face* are, without question, the titular creatures—once we get to see them. A British £50,000 budget doesn't score you a lot of effects, so for almost the first hour, the fiends are invisible—a

chair moves here, hay in a barn moves there. It's an effective way to convey a lack of funds, but when they get their chance to shine, it's glorious. Each is basically a brain fused to a spinal column, with antennae sprouting from its thought ball, and it moves by pushing the spine along the ground like a Disney cartoon snake. Leaping through the air, it attaches itself to its victims at the back of the neck and wraps the spinal column around the person's head. (Sounds familiar? We'll come back to that, I promise.)

And how do the filmmakers pull it off? Stop-motion animation, and quite well-done to boot. Once the siege takes place, these suckers crowd the screen in a relentless attack on our cardboard protagonists. (They're all here—Hapless Cop! Prof. Exposition! Powerless Damsel! Barking Colonel!)

Blame screenwriter Herbert J. Leder if you must. He would go on to direct *It!* (1967) with Roddy McDowall, and if you've seen that one, you know he clearly has a fondness for telepathy and weirdness (a great combo in my estimation). The siege on the house, right down to boarding up the windows with planks from the basement, would be used later in George Romero's *Night of the Living Dead* (1968). (I always love how characters practically have a Home Depot in their basement; I can't even find a hammer.) I don't know if Romero got the idea from *FWAF*, but it makes for a great "building blocks of horror" story, as does the design of the creatures. *Alien*'s (1979) facehuggers, if they could bow, probably should, in the direction of our cerebellum snakes. When they jump up and wrap their spines around the necks of the victims, visions of John Hurt danced through my head. Again, was this intentional on *Alien*'s behalf? Who knows? I don't think there's anyone alive to complain about it; it's just some cool connective tissue (or wishful thinking on my part).

There is a longstanding rumor that director Arthur Crabtree (*The Strange Case of Dr. Manning*) hated the script so much he left the production, and star Thompson took over directing chores. Regardless of who held the reins, *Fiend Without a Face* has a back half well worth sticking around for. If I was a savvy business fella and had the rights to this (Criterion [!] beat me to it), I would re-release it as "Night of the Living Aliens"— and make the possibly accidental inspiration look intentional.

Fast forward to New York in the early 1980s;
it's rough, colorful, and if you're none too careful,
you may end up a...

Basket Case (1982)

1982. What a year. From *The Beast Within* to *Creepshow* to *Friday the 13th Part III* to *Q*, it displayed a smorgasbord of fantastical delights for terror consumers. Standing heads (two, to be exact) and shoulders apart from the crowd was Frank Henenlotter's grimeball debut, *Basket Case* (1982), a lovely tale of a boy and his twin brother. Who happens to be a monstrous blob. And lives in a basket.

Shot on 16mm for a reported US$35,000, *Basket Case* premiered in Henenlotter's beloved Times Square and became a big hit on the grindhouse circuit. This shouldn't be surprising, as the film is a big, fat, wet kiss to the pre–cleaned-up New York City of the 1980s (think diseases, not Disney). Critics at the time acknowledged its uniqueness, but most could not overlook the technical deficiencies or the broad range of performances on display. No matter. Horror fans who have had the chance to put a quarter in the slot for the peepshow walk away with a giddy lilt. Step right up folks, have we got a show for *you*…

For the uninitiated, a story (which I'll tell chronologically, and not as presented in the film): meet Duane and Belial. Conjoined at birth, Duane is a normal, healthy boy. Belial is less so. He is a gelatinous looking protrusion (Mr. Potato Head if sculpted by Tom Savini) with razor sharp teeth, eyes like coal, and two arms made for clawing. Not happy with his lot in life, Duane's father (Mom died giving birth) has three unscrupulous doctors separate the boys in adolescence, and has Belial disposed of and left for dead in the trash. Because of their psychic link, Duane finds Belial and rescues him.

After the boys do away with dad, the boys go and live with their aunt, who raises them with unconditional love (in one tender moment, she reads them Caliban's speech from Shakespeare's *The Tempest*—fitting, as Caliban is deformed, and speaks of the island as a safe haven). As adults, their next stop is New York City, to track down the doctors who would dare tear them asunder.

This is the meat of the film, as Duane (and basket-bound Belial) checks into the Hotel Broslin: a fleabag paradise, and site for many of the film's colorful supporting characters, including proverbial hooker with the heart of gold Casey. Also on hand: a love interest for Duane in the form of receptionist Sharon, who works for one of the doctors the boys are pursuing. As they cross the docs off their list one at a time (and Belial does some side work—he's very touchy), love begins to bloom between Duane and Sharon, leaving Belial none too pleased. Will our star-crossed lovers find true happiness? Maybe … if Belial goes to counseling for his separation anxiety. Like I said, he's touchy.

Even today, *Basket Case* is a micro-budget miracle. One of a kind (even though there are two later sequels), the story alone sets the film miles apart not only from the release year, but the decade. Henenlotter dedicates the film to Herschell Gordon Lewis, the Godfather of Gore, and it certainly has the uncluttered look of Lewis—except he surpasses his idol. *Basket Case* is much faster-paced than any of Lewis' vehicles, and careens from kills to quirks and back again, all wrapped up in a candy-apple-red quilt of slaughter that checks out at a tidy 91 minutes. But Henenlotter has more on his mind than just mayhem, making sly comments on familial ties and jealousy (Belial's feelings are expressed through rage, and ... more rage, actually).

Henenlotter also toys with the audience, never fully showing Belial until the halfway mark, leaving many characters (as well as the audience) curious as to the contents of the wicker abode. When we get the full reveal, well, some will gasp and some will laugh. But I guarantee you've never seen anything like Belial. A wonder of filmic economy and invention, he's really the star of the show, and Henenlotter lets him shine. Whether he's throwing a hissy fit up in Room 7, or performing scalpel acupuncture, Belial is a unique creature—terrifying and yet sympathetic. His relationship with Duane is laid out sincerely by Henenlotter. And while goofy hotel managers and drunks circle around our main characters, their bond is integral to the tragedy that unfolds.

Too arthouse, you say? Let's keep in mind we're one step out of the gutter on 42nd Street and check off some grindhouse goodies: table saws, bisections, claw marks, toilet travails, and other assorted (and sordid) delights. Henenlotter came to play, and his can-do enthusiasm, innate humor, and love of the askew dwarf any and all budgetary concerns. Talent is talent, no matter how big or small the bankroll.

In front of the camera, there aren't a lot of names that set IMDB on fire. And that's okay, as none of the cast is boring, and some give fascinating performances. Kevin Van Hentenryck, who looks like a cross between Tom Hulce and Tom Hanks (Tom Hulks?), brings a bright-eyed naïveté to Duane that plays brilliantly against his feral brother. Terri Susan Smith has a goofy charm as his love interest, which is good as it distracts the viewer from a rug that would give Burt Reynolds pause (as part of a punk band at the time, she had a shaved head). Beverly Bonner also has some nice scenes as our lady of the night Casey, helping Duane navigate his way through The Big Apple. The batshit crazy appeal of the story is so strong that the entire cast gets whisked along for the ride.

Frank Henenlotter has stayed on this path for his entire career. Whether curating for Something Weird Video, or bestowing further epics of the funny and profane on us, such as *Brain Damage* (1988) and

Frankenhooker (1990), he has always shown an affinity for the seedy side of the street. Do yourself a favor—cross on over (check both ways), grab a ticket for *Basket Case*, and plunk yourself down. The floors may be sticky (don't ask), but sometimes the squalor holds the most glorious sights.

———————————————

Probably the strangest no-budget—hookers in weird masks,
slimy alien babies, interdimensional traveling, cheap beer,
and plastic chainsaws. Prepare to enter the world of...

Things (1989)

Well, I've stared at the unforgiving blankness of my computer screen long enough. I *must* proceed. There is nowhere to go but onwards, tackling (and trying to grasp) one of the most profound, odd, galaxy-brain takes in horror cinema: *Things* (1989). As nondescript as that title is, the film itself is anything but—there are a million things to discuss in *Things*, and I'll try my best to be at least as coherent as the film itself.

Made for around $30,000 Canadian and shot on 8mm and 16mm, *Things* skipped theatrical and caught the tail end of a DTV boom in the late 1980s. So yes, I am cheating a bit as it never played in theaters (let alone drive-ins), with patrons unwittingly taking home the box art with the mullet-maligned hoser holding a power drill (and believe it or not, it has something to do with the film).

Well, a *lot* has to do with this one, and often at the same time: mad labs and monsters, news broadcasts from a living room filled with TVs as a backdrop, beer drinking, boob-tube watching, cockroach-filled cheese sandwiches, Alastair Crowley and a pieced-together, cheap-ass Necromicon with tape recorder (demons sold separately), and so much more.

So much less as well; *Things* is bursting with oddities, some visual and others audio, yet moves without regard to pacing or editing from any sane corner of cinema. This is a horrific-looking iceberg that regardless of speed, is impossible to move away from: the only direction is forward, into the unfocused abyss of reds and blues.

No, it isn't *The Color Out of Space*; nor is it *The Evil Dead*, which it so desperately wants to be. And making those comparisons will only lead you down a path of disappointment, and/or possible disgust. *Things* finds a very unique wavelength and holds on for the whole running time, a mean feat for even a "good" film.

But where are my manners, eh? You may be wondering what *Things* is

about: Don (Barry J. Gillis—who also serves as co-writer, editor, producer, 2nd unit director, and probably got the beer) and Fred (Bruce Roach) head out to Don's brother Doug (Doug Bunston)'s cabin for some partying. Upon arrival, Doug's wife goes into labor and pops out giant ants instead of a human baby. Don, Fred, and Doug spend the rest of the film defending themselves from these, uh, creatures, demons, experiments, or whatever the hell they're supposed to be. Things, I guess. Beauty.

I'll go easy on the Canadian-centric attempts at humor, because *Things* does all the heavy lifting for you; even for someone from here. The accents are somewhere between Pierre Trudeau and Bob McKenzie (those references are for those abroad; at home I'll use Bruno Gerussi and Al Waxman). Gillis rocks a very era-appropriate mullet (still rocked in smaller villes where time has ceased), and I'm only assuming the beer is something truly unsettling like Labatt's or Club. (Brrr.)

Perhaps it is the particular Great White North vibe that gives *Things* its flavor, but I think that's only partly true; regardless of its cast, it's what they do and say that sticks with you. If you need a crash course in behavior that is especially unhuman, look no further—you're surrounded.

Ambushed, really—"assaulted" would work too. The bargain basement wedding video credits aren't necessarily an affront; those are standard for any SOV (Shot on Video) flick. No, the way the film is shot will pique cult interest though. In using a mixture of 8mm and 16mm (toggling back and forth all willy-nilly), cinematographer Dan Riggs not so much as failed to focus on story, structure, and framing, but rather he just tried to keep the camera in focus. I'm sorry to say that Dan lost that battle.

But the look of *Things* is important to the specific world created by director Andrew Jordan and Gillis. The viewer is left to search for standards to hold on to, as well as for rules applied to cinema throughout the ages. Scenes are cut off midway, and awkward camera placements emit a discombobulated take on the usual Monster-on-the-Loose flick. The Argento lighting would suggest a change in mood or plot development, if any of those metrics applied here.

"So Scott, it just seems like you're describing a shitty, no-budget, regional backyard flick. Big deal." I hear you. But … well, let's talk about what you hear, okay? Dubbed in after the fact, all of the actors (or rather, the people pushed in front of the camera) are afforded the opportunity to give voice to their actions, and perhaps inject a bit of gravitas to their roles. If that were true though, one would miss out on Doug's constant farting, or his Jerry Lewis cry of "WHAAAAAAA!!!" when one of the ants crawls up his neck. As an audience, we would also be deprived of Don's thick brogue and faux, teeth-gritted outrage at the attack and everything else, including lack of beer. (This last part rings true.)

No one, and I mean no one, acts remotely human in *Things*. Doug veers from angry to psychotic with side trips to ecstasy all within a span of moments; Don pours whiskey on his head for no reason, and Fred just shrugs and guffaws before he disappears half way through—to the "third, fourth, or fifth dimension," no less. He does return for the finale however, wielding a plastic chainsaw and laying waste, not to mention offering up the only loose plot thread to be resolved. Sort of.

But *Things* is a film robust with Sort Ofs: it's sort of like *The Evil Dead*; it's sort of an attempt by stilted third graders to make a grown up film; and it's sort of a "mainstream" calling card for adult star Lynn, were she able to convey emotion and not side-eye her cue cards the entire time.

Nothing works in *Things*—at least in the traditional sense. The acting is bizarre, the dialogue even more so, and the effects, while bountiful, are less than impressive. But within this vacuum of ideals and talent lies a heart beating with the love of horror, rooted in friends' sleepovers when the tape of *The Evil Dead* or *Equinox* (yeah, that's right) gets thrown in the player at two in the morning. The inspiration is borrowed, the talent is on furlough, but the sincerity somehow pulls the soupy phantasmagoria that is *Things* into its own orbit, alone yet supreme. And unfocused as all hell.

Festival Eleven:
Potluck of Horror

Welcome to Potluck of Horror; or, The Free-For-All Festival! Exciting for me, hopefully enjoyable for you, and themes be damned. Well, there is a theme, actually, and it's this: these are all films I've wanted to write about for a long time, but circumstances and timing threw them off course.

Ever since I began writing my weekly column, "Drive-In Dust Offs" for the Daily Dead website in 2015, the goal was to look at—and shine a spotlight on—films that I felt a new generation would like to know about, if they didn't already. That was the mission statement. It still is! While I haven't written the column in a minute, I will add to the over 330 pieces already there—someday. For now, let's take a look at what I have written about for this particular festival, and maybe dig into why these have missed the column.

First up is Jack Arnold's amazing *The Incredible Shrinking Man* (1957); why haven't I covered it before now? I thought it was too popular to write about for the column; I wanted to highlight lesser-known films through the era that could use a little more love—and this film was already universally loved in sci-fi and horror circles. So here it is now!

The Curse of the Werewolf (1961): I honestly have no idea why I haven't tackled it before now. I've written several Hammer pieces for the column before, and several Oliver Reed pieces too—perhaps I just wanted a Hammer break? (I think this may be the reason.) Regardless, it's here now, and needs to be discussed alongside other Hammer classics like *The Curse of Frankenstein* (1957), which I've covered before, and *Horror of Dracula* (1958).

Messiah of Evil (1973) was just a matter of timing; someone was always doing a great write-up on it, so it was just a waiting game, really. I always knew I would eventually get to this bizarre and creepy early 1970s entry. (Plus, I hadn't watched it in its entirety before. Don't tell anyone.)

The Bees (1978) is a late-in-the-game-winner for me. I recently viewed it for the first time since childhood, and it is a full-bore environmental Animal Killdom gem that could easily fit in our first festival, but works nicely here.

Finally, we end with John Carpenter's *Prince of Darkness* (1987). Even though he is one of my favorite directors, and very popular with horror fans, I have purposely stayed away from his work, with one film exception—I wrote about *Halloween* (1978) for my 100th Drive-In Dust Offs. Here I get to wax about a film that is becoming my second favorite Carpenter, after a long and slow climb up my ladder. So there you have it. Thank you for indulging my picks—one could fill volumes with films that deserve discussion, but I hope you enjoy these picks. They all kick ass and take names. And even in horror, it's better late than never. On with the festival!

We start off with a metaphysical—and metaphorical—trip with a man losing his religion, his belt, his manners, his shoes, and his best gal! Jeepers! Stay tuned for the downbeat story of...

The Incredible Shrinking Man (1957)

As the wise prophet and proprietor of balloon animals Steve Martin once said, "Let's get small"—but who am I to question such profound statements? If your name happens to be Scott Carey, you'll soon live it as *The Incredible Shrinking Man* (1957)—a terrifying concept, and one of the best sci-fi horror films ever.

Ironically, this is a film that has only grown in stature since its release. It was a success at the box office but shrugged off by critics of the day as another sci-fi programmer even though the sights on display—not to mention the existential bent to the whole enterprise—still hold up and look terrific.

Scott Carey (Grant Williams) and his wife Louise (Randy Stuart) are hanging out on the bow of his brother's yacht, a little vacation before he heads back to work as an ad executive. While Louise goes to get Scott a beer, a mysterious mist washes over the boat, leaving Scott's chest covered in some kind of viscous goo. Thinking nothing of it, the happy couple continue their vacation.

Six months of normal domesticity go by and then Scott starts to notice ... things. His shirts fit looser; he starts to swim in his pants; his doctor can explain the weight loss much easier than the height loss. (One can only blame it on mismeasurements for so long.) So with the

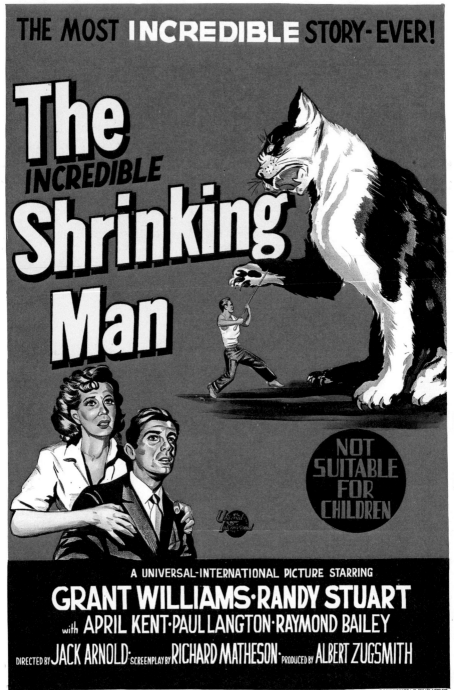

medical community's formal assessment that Scott is indeed shrinking and screwed, he and Louise do the only thing they can think of: go public with his story with the hopes of earning money off of its sensationalism. Which works for a while...

Louise makes accommodations for Scott; she sets him up in a doll-house and makes him clothes and has no choice but to treat him like a doll. After a run-in with the cat, inches-tall Scott falls into the basement to spend the rest of his days. Louise finds a bloody piece of clothing in the cat's mouth, leading her to believe that the cat got fat off of her hubby. (Don't blame the cat!) With Scott's brother's help, a devastated Louise plans to move out and sell the house.

Meanwhile in the basement, Scott has a whole new problem—there's a hairy spider that's hungry, and he's on the menu. Who will get Scott first: the spider, or the existential maw ever widening on *The Incredible Shrinking Man*?

The screenplay by Richard Matheson (his first, based on his debut novel *The Shrinking Man*) is literate and smart. While it is of course fantastical to believe any of the science hooey being flung at the screen, it's fun hooey and logical within its own realm. It doesn't have to be true—but a great writer like Matheson points out the dramatic irony surrounding the protagonist, showing the mental devastation caused by a slow-burn tragedy: Scott's wedding ring falling off while talking to Louise, or the humiliation he feels sleeping in a little girl's playbox. These are crucial pressure points because Scott comes across as ... abrupt and kind of a dick, actually. Shocking? Absolutely! Scotts throughout the world are considered the most laid back people and not assholes at all, actually. (I read it in a scientific journal.)

The hubris of man is often the cause of downfall in these old sci-fi horrors. Scott gets the double whammy of radiation on the boat and then gets accidentally sprayed with insecticide when he's home, triggering the shrinking of his molecular structure.

Speaking of structure, the film is set up to have us sympathize with Scott at every turn. It's a credit to Williams' performance that he doesn't play him as a happy-go-lucky fella beset by tragedy, but rather as an ordinary man with fears, paranoia, and an unsure grip on his masculinity. (Unlike every other Scott in the world.)

As Scott continues to shrink, the world and its outside concerns are put aside; his new world changes every time he is reduced, with fresh challenges around every corner. Scott's personal elevator to hell is filled with surprises.

I think this is why we sympathize with Scott regardless of his chilliness or veiled hostility. Everyone deals with inevitability—a loved one dies slowly in front of our eyes; we are unable to ease or end suffering; or even more personally, we have to accept the decay of our own body. Sometimes the potions work, and sometimes they don't.

This is the same kind of base fear that David Cronenberg trades in—how do we react when everything *within* us is changing? Especially when the social politics of the era draw the male/female line not in the sand, but rather in publications that blare out "32 Ways to Keep Your Husband Happy," and the Teflon-coated middle-class Americana of *Leave It to Beaver, et al.* Scott is upset that his role has changed as much as his size; no longer caretaker of Louise, he is (literally) reduced to a fraction of the man he was.

Jack Arnold had already proven himself as a first-class horror director with *It Came from Outer Space* (1953) and of course *Creature from the Black Lagoon* (1954). As with those films, his direction is sure, the pace is fast for maximum suspense, and he gets strong performances from the cast.

The other big stars of the film are the cadre of special effects, set design, and photography folks who create this incredible world; a combination of rear projection, forced perspective and oversized props fulfill the promise of the spectacular. Even by today's standards, the cumulative effect is one of awe—Arnold and Matheson have created a complete world to get lost in, and to disappear from. *The Incredible Shrinking Man* may not answer all of your big burning questions: Why are we here? Is there life after death? Are Scotts actually the best? It does however, couch these queries in a sci-fi horror classic whose stature will grow for generations to come.

━━━━━━━━━━━━━━━━

From hairy spiders to hairy Oliver Reed: Which is more frightening?
That is up to you dear reader, but be careful and beware...

The Curse of the Werewolf (1961)

Pity poor Leon. As played by legend Oliver Reed, whenever he gets randy and is away from his one true love, he finds himself under *The Curse of the Werewolf* (1961), Hammer Film's only werewolf film, and one of its finest early productions. And it's Ollie, so he is randy, like, all the time.

Released in June, *Curse* didn't do much at the box office, maybe because lycanthropes were seen as the black wolf of the horror family. With no ancient mythology to draw from, the werewolf story is illegitimate in

some people's eyes; it doesn't have the necessary esteemed literary "roots" like *Dracula* or *Frankenstein*. Oh well. Those same people would be seriously pissed with *Curse* then, as it takes a book from 1933 called *The Werewolf of Paris* by Guy Endore, guts it, and pretty much does its own thing, including moving all the action to Spain. (Hammer had these sets ready from a discarded production.)

But the truth is that *Curse* is one of the sturdier Hammer films of the day, using all of its formidable resources and the usual stable of creative stalwarts who guided the classic monsters to fresh pastures. It does however use a different tact to get there—*Curse* is an origin story. (They're not just for Marvel as it turns out.) This is probably one of the reasons that it isn't often discussed in similar breaths as director Terence Fisher's other monster mashes, *The Curse of Frankenstein* (1957) and *Horror of Dracula* (1958); those got down to business right away. *Curse* plays a different game, yet is just as enjoyable.

We begin in a small village in Spain. A beggar (Richard Wordsworth) wanders in, looking for food and shelter. He is sent to the Marqués Siniestro (Anthony Dawson), who is celebrating his wedding day and is also unusually cruel—after the Marqués makes the beggar dance for scraps and crawl on all fours like a dog, he throws him into jail to rot to death.

The beggar is cared for by the mute daughter of the jailer. After she is grown up, the beggar, who is now completely mad, rapes the girl and then dies. Soon, she is sent to "entertain" the Marqués, but spurns his advances and eventually kills him during the confrontation. She escapes into the woods, where she is found nearly dead by Teresa (Hira Talfrey), the housekeeper of Don Alfredo (Clifford Evans). She is also quite pregnant.

The poor mute woman dies giving birth to a son who Don Alfredo dubs Leon (as in lion? The name is right on the kitty-cat nose and I love it); and according to Teresa, doomed because he's born on Christmas Day. Yeah, I don't get it either; I thought that was considered "a good day" for Christians. Anyway, between calendar calamity and his dad being a homeless person, Leon is marked by the werewolf. (No biting please, we're Catholic.)

Let's sidebar this for a second: perhaps werewolves have an identity issue? And I don't mean religion, I mean canon; no wonder they get lost in the shuffle when one gets all weird with the iconography. They do stick with silver bullets, though.

As Leon reaches adolescence (a solid turn by Justin Walters), animals from the area are found dead with their throats ripped out—dogs, goats, Amway folk—and Don and Teresa discover that Leon is responsible. Bars on the windows prevent the young teen from heading out during the full moon, and a chat with the local clergy (John Gabriel) also offers a hint of salvation: true love can conquer the beast. This works well enough under the loving care of his Auntie Teresa and Uncle Don, until Leon becomes a man and leaves home to find his fortune, or at least his place in the world.

He soon finds love with the daughter of the local vintner, Cristina (Catherine Feller), again keeping the wolf at bay. But when his friend takes him to a house of ill-repute, too many women and too much wine make Leon a frisky fella, and one very hairy hellraiser. Waking up in his old bed is enough to let Leon and the family know that the curse has returned. He also has no alibi for the brothel, so it's off to jail he goes. A pity then, as Leon and Cristina spent the previous night together and he hadn't transformed.

No matter. Jail does not suit our young Leon, and we finally get to see Ollie in full gear—the same imagery that haunted the pages of older horror reference books that older writers perhaps read—and he goes on a terror for the final act, culminating in a bell tower climax befitting *Curse*'s Gothic aspirations. Will beauty save the beast?

That outcome is doubtful; instead it's inevitable, dark and direct. Hammer stalwart Fisher drops the romanticism at the last minute, leaving an ending without a passionate gesture to land on, instead offering one dead werewolf and unrequited love. Wah wah. It is possible that the sober and nihilistic ending of *Curse* did no favors with audiences of the day; or it could be that the unfantastical terror of *Psycho* (1960) had crowds looking for something grittier, more ... grown up.

This was not it. Somber, yes, but also melodramatic in Hammer's special way—heaving bosoms, sweeping gestures, you know the drill. Audiences were ready for suits and ties, sundresses and bouffants—even if they did end up bloody.

And you're probably blaming Reed for all of the drama, but this was his first leading role, and he was only starting to bring forth his heaving intensity. Not quite barrel of chest and eyes of bulge, but he was on his way, while managing a lot of sympathy for poor Leon.

The biggest complaint against *The Curse of the Werewolf* is that it takes an hour before Leon is shown in full, blood dripping glory. Hell, we don't get Ollie until halfway through the film. But the script by producer Anthony Hinds (under his writing name John Elder) and direction by Fisher is certainly strong enough—the story bears that out—that one gets swept along from the beginning. For those looking to expand their Hammer clan, do yourself a favor and head to the pound, adopt Leon, and give him the home he deserves.

From becoming a subatomic whisper to hanging with some freaky cult;
we believe in some tonal whiplash round these parts.
You will too after you've witnessed...

Messiah of Evil (1973)

Sometimes finding the entry point for writing about a film is the tough part; where to start, introducing a theme or hook to grab onto, and running with it. *Messiah of Evil* (1973) is a doozy. It's a film that works when it really shouldn't; it doesn't make any sense, and it is quite sloppy. It is also eerie, disquieting, gorgeous, and surreal, and this is why we're talking about it in the first place.

Messiah of Evil, aka *Dead People*, was done as a quick flick by the husband and wife team of Willard Huyck and Gloria Katz, who would make this right before completing the script for USC classmate and pal George Lucas' *American Graffiti* the same year. Does the film play like people desperate to make anything to prove what they can do? Absolutely. Does this slapdash approach benefit the finished film? Absolutely.

Okay, let's take a stab at the story: A sweaty man is running down a deserted street at night (it turns out it's future legendary director Walter Hill!) and he is offered reprieve from an adolescent girl hanging out by a pool. He lies down on the pool concrete, and when he's relaxed, the girl cuts his throat with a straight razor. Cue credits!

Our story proper starts with a young woman named Arletty (Marianna Hill) offering helpful voiceover narration, as she arrives at the California seaside town of Point Dune in search of her missing artist father. She pops in at the art gallery in town and is told they hadn't seen her father, but that a man and two women were by earlier in the day asking about him.

She tracks the three—Thom (Michael Greer), Laura (Anitra Ford), and Toni (Joy Bang)—to the local motel, where she finds them listening to an ominous story from the town drunk (Elisha Cook, Jr.) about a "dark stranger" returning to town after one hundred years during the "blood moon." Arletty leaves the motel, and is again warned by the drunk that something sinister has happened to the folks in Point Dune and that he is not as crazy as he sounds.

Arletty heads to her father's beach house—large, deserted, the walls covered in murals and oversized portraits of suited people. (Legendary art director Jack Fisk, take a bow.) It isn't long before Thom and the girls show up, claiming they were kicked out of the motel and have no place to stay; Arletty could use the company, so she lets them stay. Thom's girls (rightly)

believe that Arletty is interested in their man; I say if there's enough of him for two, there's enough for three. Free love and the 1970s man—no hang-ups, you dig?

Except Laura thinks that three's a crowd and decides to split town, but first stops in at the grocery store, where she is met by a group of pasty-faced locals making a meal of all the fresh, raw meat on display. When they spot Laura, they choose to upgrade their dining to free range.

Meanwhile back at the beach house, Thom continues to listen to audiotapes that Arletty's father had left there. They contain warnings of the "dark stranger" and his plans to return for … well, who knows what exactly? But next Toni heads out to catch a movie. How exciting! Once she gets her ticket, unbeknownst to her, the theater's outside lights are turned off, signaling no more movies for the night. Especially for Toni. As she starts to watch the film—*Kiss Tomorrow Goodbye*, the marquee says—the theater is empty; while she becomes engrossed further into the film, it fills up with the same townsfolk who interrupted Laura's shopping. By the time Toni realizes that she's surrounded, it's curtains for her.

Back to the beach house. Thom decides to go and find Toni, but all the stores are closed; a woman on the street asks for Thom's help, but he declines as she's bleeding from one of her eyes. (A regrettable side effect of whatever the hell is going on.) He then witnesses a shootout between the police and the townies from the theater, which becomes a shootout between the two cops, as one of them has that little redeye problem as well. Thom then hightails it back to the beach house.

Before he gets there however, Arletty is visited upon by her father (Royal Dano), who tells her to leave and warn the outside world; she responds by covering him in blue paint and then stabbing him to death with shears. Thom begins to get the same treatment—accidentally—when he arrives, but only gets it in the arm.

Even though she stabbed him, Thom still takes Arletty and they try to make their escape via the water; perhaps they can reach a boat, and survive their ordeal with the *Messiah of Evil*? Come to think of it, did they even encounter the Messiah? Or it? It's hard to make definitive statements about a film whose visuals are very coherent yet surreal, with a script that is utter mush. Perhaps they were shooting for a Lovecraft tone, and one could see that—a lot of moon gazing, disconnections from reality, an unknown specter—but it is simply beyond the scope of the small budget.

So instead, they make the most of those visuals. *Messiah of Evil* feels like a cross between *Phantasm* (1979) and *Dead & Buried* (1981), although neither had yet been made. Surreality buttressing up against the Town with a Secret is the simplest logline I can think of, although that certainly doesn't do it justice.

How about this: a couple of ambitious filmmakers—who love the aesthetics of foreign films—decide to make their cheap horror film with those trappings, and the results are … unique. Unlike say, the films of Dario Argento or Mario Bava however, *Messiah of Evil* really has no plot or direction; when it isn't being beautiful, it loiters.

But, it *is* often beautiful, in contrasted, breathtaking set pieces: first, we have the uncompromising brightness of the grocery store, with the pallor of the people popping off the screen. The opposite effect happens at the movie theater, as Toni is enveloped at first by the darkness, and then by its inhabitants. There is also the beach house itself: while not haunted, it is haunting, with its mysterious wall murals and sticky shadows in every corner. The film is a masterclass in the use of lighting and color as mood movements.

Huyck and Katz are without question accomplished screenwriters; writing for Lucas and Spielberg most certainly puts them in the upper echelon. *Messiah of Evil* is a calling card that they seemingly left on the boardwalk a long time ago; it's a testament to its lasting appeal—and flat-out weirdness—that horror fans are still picking it up.

━━━━━━━━━━━━━━

The previous film has a pro– um, sand stance if that's such a thing;
but you will never mistreat Mother Nature again,
not after getting a stern lecture from…

The Bees (1978)

I would absolutely love to know why we, as a civilization, demonize bees. I know the "when," more or less; I vaguely remember news reports in the 1970s mentioning chilling phrases, like "killer bee invasion," and "Irwin Allen presents." As a human on the planet, even as a kid, I knew—and was told in school—that the bee was beneficial to the world. But as a burgeoning horror fan, I was in *Animal Killdom* heaven: *The Savage Bees* (1976), *The Swarm* (1978), and from the same year, *The Bees* (1978)—why yes, the one featuring John Saxon, Angel Tompkins, and John Carradine wiss zee wurst German accent is what we'll be discussing, how'd you guess?

The Bees isn't that different from the others mentioned above. It's about the degrees of talent on hand, because you won't find many variations on the story itself—a swarm of bees is a swarm of bees. At least that was my original theory, but a rewatch of the film—this is serious business,

The Bees, New World Pictures, 1978

people—has reminded me of one jaw-dropping turn: these bees communicate, and they're pissed about a whole array of environmental topics. They don't communicate with just anyone though; only our three leads.

Let's not get too far ahead without some story first: Mexico. A bee farm run by Dr. Franklin Miller (Claudio Brook) and his wife Sandra (Tompkins). A local man and his son break in to steal honey. Instead, they upset the African killer bees that Franklin is trying to crossbreed and tame, and the son is killed by—you guessed it—a lot of angry bees.

This angers the locals, who in turn burn down Franklin's house, and he is—wait for it—stung to death by the killer bees. Meanwhile in the States, Sandra's Uncle Ziggy (Carradine) and his pal Dr. John Norman (Saxon) are working on the same thing; excited, they have Sandra smuggle in some of the African bees in her makeup kit back to America.

Sandra joins up with Uncle Ziggy and John to create a non-violent breed; however, the fatcats behind Big Honey (I have no other word to describe them) want it done sooner—more bees, more honey—and import their own South American killer bees to expedite the process. Naturally this goes as well as you think; the South American bees get loose and breed with the regular bees, and become a super smart hybrid—and pretty vicious.

How vicious? Well, they attack a Rose Parade, an airplane, picnics, you name it. If there is an excuse for the disco horror soundtrack to kick in, writer/director Alfredo Zacarias (*Demonoid*) will find it—oh yeah, kiss the kids goodbye too! No one is immune to being pelted with flying puffed wheat up in here, big or small. And if you know me, you know I hold no truck with saving kids in movies, what with it being make-believe and all.

Okay back to the story. While the world is under attack for being greedy bitches and wanting all the honey, our three heroes soldier on until they realize that the new strain is trying to talk with them. Communicate. Work shit out. So the gang heads to the United Nations to state their case, and a warning from the beelords: the people of earth shall rule alongside the bees … or perish. Which will Earth choose?

For the sake of the film, I'd like to believe that *The Bees* ends with mankind taking a minute, reflecting, and accepting their new co-leaders. The film does leave the question open, and with the state of the world today I could see someone issuing a strongly-worded letter or tweet to the bees, thanking them for the offer, but humans are higher level creatures, blah blah. This would be shortly followed by the bees decimating the population until there's nothing left but honeycombs and flowers. That sounds nice, come to think of it.

After that incredibly long-winded description I'm keen to point out that *The Bees* is even weirder than I thought. Instead of focusing entirely on the bees and their path of destruction, we get corporate espionage. Everyone is either sneaking bees out of countries, sneaking bees in, promoting bees without even as much as an interview, and shooting old men with atrocious German accents. (RIP Ziggy.) Why?

Well, why not? Without the boardroom shenanigans—which hold as much weight as a corporate takeover on *The Young and the Restless*— *The Bees* is no different from the others mentioned, plus more. And to be frank, this is the only bee film that tries to compromise and negotiate with the enemy—to find that common ground between man and insect that isn't a flyswatter. Idealistic? Sure. Really stupid? You bet.

Look, there is no good way to make bees scary; you have to mob them up, and to give them a purpose, a singular identity. And that never works, even here when late in the game the insects have a voice. Oh and it sounds like Brad Garrett mumbling through a vocoder. But I don't watch these films to be scared, merely entertained. And between Carradine's enunciations and proclamations, Saxon's swag, Tompkins' beauty, countless attacks, and the disco-soundtracked apocalypse, *The Bees* definitely entertains. And quit picking on them, or I'll send them after YOU.

═══════════════════

It's the end of the world as we know it—
and the middle section of his Apocalypse Trilogy—
and John Carpenter feels fine, as he summons forth the...

Prince of Darkness (1987)

A priest of the Brotherhood of Sleep dies, and another (Donald Pleasence) is present to bring forth the message to the world—well, to the Los Angeles scientific community, anyway—that Satan is back, and this time he's bringing his pappy back with him! Welcome to *Prince of Darkness* (1987), director John Carpenter's incredible paean to classic British sci-fi horror with his own peculiar bent.

My own history with the film dates back to its original release in theaters; a quickened pulse took me and my sis-in-law Steph to check it out during the opening week, and I was ... underwhelmed. What? I know. I found it slow, meandering, and unfocused at the time; and I am pretty much going to blame that initial viewing on youth and maybe a disinterest in the particular subject matter—how *do* science and Satan intersect?

Frankly, I just didn't care. I would like to think that as I've gotten older some measure of wisdom has been attained—not through any direct

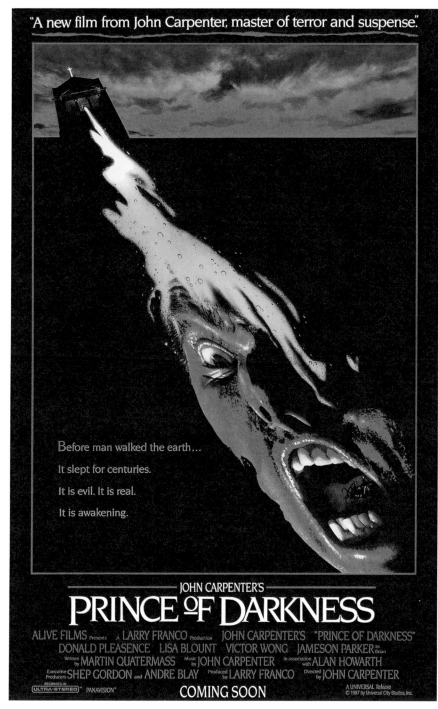

action on my part, but most likely through osmosis or some accident—because I could not have been more wrong about a film. (Except for *The Shining*. I'll never like it—I promise.)

Prince of Darkness is not only one of the best John Carpenter films, but also a personal favorite in the Apocalypse Sweepstakes because it deals with the precipice of the end, which is where all that juicy tension is.

And what tale is Mr. Carpenter laying on us this time? Check it: After Pleasence finds his dead priest, he goes to see Howard Birack (Victor Wong), a professor dealing with this kind of matter and antimatter, and their relationship to spirituality. Pleasence tells Wong the Brotherhood of Sleep has guarded the essence of the Anti-God from the world, captured as a green swirling cocktail in a giant canister. And according to their dreams, His return is near.

This matches up with Brian Marsh (Jameson Parker), a science grad student, suffering from the same, peculiar dream—a cloaked figure engulfs the doorway of a church while the crackling through fragile frequencies delivers warnings about the future of the Anti-God's upcoming reign. All the way in 1999. Wong, Parker, and some other student physicists, bicyclists, theologians, et al., bunk up in the church with Pleasence, along with a host of blinking machines, and a relentless synth score by Carpenter and Alan Howarth.

The Green Thermos of Evil is poked, prodded, and most dangerously, preened over by the students. This leads to one of them receiving a mouthful of mouthwash and turning demonic, surrounding Catholic baubles be damned. As the Los Angeles sky turns black, Alice Cooper appears as a scowling homeless man, and it brings up the biggest misstep in the film. It's not the casting of Cooper per se, but rather having the destitute as vessels of evil, which comes across as gross (intentional or not), and oddly out of character for an empathetic humanist like Carpenter.

As the students turn into infected church zombies one by one, gargling the devil's essence involuntarily—it's *magical*, gutterheads—and cutting throats and such, the film goes from slow burn and philosophically mathematical (or is that mathematically spiritual?) to ratchet-up rage and malice on the part of Satan's new followers.

On top of all that, our heroes have to prevent the legion of evil from bringing the Devil's Daddy to our realm through murky mirror water. (Carpenter is the best at being able to create the most with the least.) Is half of *Simon & Simon* enough to stop the *Prince of Darkness*?

The math would have you lean toward Satan, as would Carpenter. The true evil of his *The Fog* (1980) is the greed of the church, not the sailors they kill in cold, salted blood. A deity may seem like a fascinating failure to a humanist, and I'm inclined to agree; which one can do tangible good? The Brotherhood of Sleep comes across as much more batshit than the logic seekers. But then the inevitable perfect Venn diagram of demonic communique via computers and dot matrix printers competing with the Forever Cloud King sort of makes it all null and void.

Both philosophies wind up in the same position then—kind of like MacGuffins—once they've served their purpose they become a fading concern as the film turns into *Church Bingo of the Living Dead*. I'm okay with that. The first half offers the heady exposition and suppositions—intriguing stuff, it's like trying to pin string to a soul—and the second half offers a base release, a primitive terror trapped in a siege showdown. This is the horror version of the cop shop siege from *Assault on Precinct 13* or the farmhouse siege from *Night of the Living Dead*.

It is all of one Carpenter piece though, just separated like a stage play, with the first half heavy on prose and promise, and the second half ... the delivery. This has always been the main issue critics have with this film; some find the second half a bit of a slog after the buildup. Perhaps this is where my original malaise sprung from—wanting more get-up-and-go in the back end.

Definitely a "me" problem, though; countless rewatches have proven that the pacing is carefully calibrated to not pounce, but rather insinuate—until it's too late and the demons have infiltrated. Frankly, I find most Carpenters move at a deliberate pace; they know where they're going and when they're going to get there—but you may not, and by the time you do, you're already there.

There's a dourness to *Prince of Darkness* that I think has more to do with Carpenter's worldview than any sort of specific theme. Optimism in the face of evil or adversity has lifted a pall from certain parts of his filmography—*Starman* immediately springs to mind—but his films are where cynicism, mistrust, paranoia reach out and envelope all they encounter. It's interesting to see his follow-up film, *They Live* (1988), one of the most paranoid of them all, end with the aliens being exposed to the world. Now *that's* optimistic.

But meanwhile, in that decrepit church, things are going quite poorly—one *Simon* isn't much of a fighter without his TV brother, the scientific community is rapidly dwindling, and Cooper and his friends have decided to start up the evening service.

It was fun to see Carpenter tackle low-budget work again; it was a chance to write, direct, and have full creative control again after a few run-ins with the major studios (*The Thing, Christine, Starman, Big Trouble in Little China*). An agreement with Cooper's long time manager Shep Gordon's Alive Films gave Carpenter a three-picture deal holding all the reins.

Guess what? *Prince of Darkness* did well enough at the box office, certainly enough over its low budget, to see the sense in the deal. Working with Carpenter in this situation can be low risk, high reward and it definitely paid off here.

This was also the first collaboration between Carpenter and cinematographer Gary B. Kibbe, but it wouldn't be the last. He would be Carpenter's DP for the rest of his career (Kibbe passed away in 2000) with a couple of exceptions. His work on *Prince of Darkness* is ominous and gritty, with the same Panavision setup very much favored by Carpenter, lending a scope and size to an essentially one-setting film. But what a setting. And what a film; the performances are fine, but in a large group folks can end up fighting for the screen—Carpenter lets everyone get in a few good lines.

And there are a lot of them; lines that is. The film is very chatty especially in the first half. Do you see that screenwriting credit? Martin Quatermass? That's Carpenter himself paying homage to British writer Nigel Kneale, creator of the sci-fi character Bernard Quatermass and his numerous TV and film appearances; sort of a Doctor Who but more horrific. Anyway, those shows and films feature a lot of back-and-forth banter and dialog before bringing forth the action. And it's the same business with *Prince of Darkness*—it works because it possesses ideas; there really isn't sexual banter (okay, a little) but rather intriguing questions about how and where we come from. The end result will still be putrescence and doom; one just has food for thought on the way down. *All* the way down.

Festival Twelve:
Around the Weird in a Day

For those keeping tabs, this is Festival Twelve, aka The Last One. You should be terribly saddened that it is almost done. The good news is, you can reopen the book at the start and read it again. It's just that simple.

Around the Weird in a Day. The idea behind this festival was easy: let's look at some films from around the world, outside of our normal purview. Okay fine, my purview then; I have been focused for so long on films of North American origin, just because those are the films most easily accessed—or, at least they were.

Times have certainly changed; technology grows by leaps and bounds, making the world of communication closer and closer while opening up the film market's past for niche collectors. And there must be many of them—boutique Blu-ray labels such as Severin, Scream Factory, Vinegar Syndrome, and several others continually feed home viewers the films—many foreign—they didn't know they needed. At least now they have a choice.

And the choices are staggering nowadays, with streaming services as well as the boutiques offering up obscurities every week to watch, rent, or buy. Not only obscurities; hits like Netflix's *Squid Game* show that horror is universal—I know a lot of people think that that is love's designation, but nothing bonds better than blood.

Let's have a look at the films: first up we head off to Italy to pay our respects to Mario Bava and his *Blood and Black Lace* (1964); a lot of giallo elements were solidified here, and slashers paid attention too. There are a lot of Bavas I could have chosen as representative—of him and the subgenre he pretty much created—but I think this one does the trick.

Next, it's Great Britain and *Quatermass and the Pit* (1967); and more specifically Hammer Film, whose bloodied paw prints are all over this verbose, yet tense sci-fi thriller.

The Soviet Union offers up the phantasmagorical, and very funny,

VIY (1967), a trippy and surrealistic witch story whose visuals will become permanently embedded while you search for even more unique horror from the region.

How about a trip to Japan and *Evil Dead Trap* (1988)? If you like slashers and you like gialli, weirdness, and endings that don't make sense, boy oh boy pull up a chair and let down your hair. This one's a doozy.

And finally, we end up in beautiful Mexico, where this Mexican/Italian co-production takes place: *Santa Sangre* (1989) is a mesmerizing film by surrealist master Alejandro Jodorowsky (*El Topo*), and is a whirlwind of violence and beauty.

I think that's a fair list, yes? Small without a doubt, and far from complete—but that's what second volumes are for.

Grab your passport; we're on our way.

―――――――――

We start in the land of vineyards and beauty—
not your uncle's dive bar in Manitoba—but rather, Italy.
We specifically head into the fashion world,
where "cutthroat" takes on a new meaning...

Blood and Black Lace (1964)

Horror isn't all about mood, but it can be *a lot* about it; even a film that's trying not to evoke a specific mood will have one. *Blood and Black Lace* (1964) has no shame about its mood, its style, and its panache; it is simply built on a foundation of fabulousness and gorgeosity, courtesy of Mario Bava, the soon-to-be reigning king of Italian scares.

Mr. Bava had been directing documentaries and shorts since the late 1940s, but fully embraced horror with 1960s witchy *Black Sunday* and its mesmerizing Barbara Steele performance. From there he gave us plenty of horror classics, specializing in the giallo subgenre, which he essentially created.

"But what is a giallo?" you ask, and I'll give my answer to this question, the horror version of the stand-ups' inside joke *The Aristocrats*. Giallo is used as a descriptor for an Italian crime thriller with an intricate mystery; a police procedural with, usually, a lot of stabby work from a masked killer. This would seep over into what we know as a slasher, the North American phenomenon that can cut down on police involvement, and increase the more horrific elements of the story—more graphic violence, and less emphasis on style.

A FASHION HOUSE OF GLAMOROUS MODELS...
BECOMES A TERROR HOUSE OF BLOOD!!

But the lines have been blurred and the arguments continue to this day over what separates the two subgenres, so I'll just say this: slashers have more or less belonged geographically to North America, and gialli to European countries, especially Italy. (Giallo is Italian for yellow, the same color as the cheap crime novels popular in Italy at the time, and where the spirit of the genre comes from.) The North American slasher is foremost concerned with the body count, and the relationship between hero(ine) and villain; gialli tend to broaden the focus to be hero, villain, *and* the authorities. A small distinction, but gialli always seems to give equal time to law enforcement.

So anyway... *Blood and Black Lace* is most definitely a giallo. It's one of the first, and one of the best, after Bava's own *The Evil Eye* aka *The Girl Who Knew Too Much* from 1963, which put down a very large footprint for everyone to follow—including himself. But he was ready, and *Blood and Black Lace* codified many of the pillars of the burgeoning subgenre: the black-gloved killer, wearing a mask of some sort (here, a tan nylon stocking leaving the face a blank canvas with a black-brimmed hat), and usually a knife or straight razor.

Well thought-out, to be sure. But everything giallo was a stepping stone from Germany's very popular Krimi films of the 1960s, based on British writer Edgar Wallace's books, which were huge hits in Italy; these films offered up the blueprint for giallo. But Bava was certainly the figurehead, and *Blood and Black Lace* is still a breathtaking testament to style, beauty, and the ugly that bubbles right below the surface.

Story? I'll try my best. There is a large group of beautiful women who populate an Italian fashion house; one by one, they are removed from the earth by a trenchcoated and masked man, who is desperately trying to get his hands on a diary that one of the women owns. Secrets? Oh, there are secrets ... and plenty of bloodshed.

There's a lot of plot going on—or rather a lot of people. The police have several suspects to round up, including all of the beautiful women and men from the fashion house. Perhaps it's the owner, Contessa Cuomo (Eva Bartok), or her business partner, Massimo Morlacchi (Cameron Mitchell)? In addition, we also have a suspected junkie, a couple of suspicious ex-boyfriends—you get the idea; EVERYONE'S A SUSPECT. Until they die, that is, and you can cross them off the list. (It's *so* much easier guessing the killer this way.)

I'll be completely honest: I am terrible at solving mysteries. I used to have to look at the back of Encyclopedia Brown books in elementary school because I couldn't figure out who did it. (I still can't.) So is this a good one, then? A mystery, that is?

I have been assured by friends that it plays fair; it also uses a red herring technique that I thought was invented later on that century—so good on you, *Blood and Black Lace*, for fooling me above and beyond my normal realms of nescience. Well done!

But it's how a giallo *feels* that's important; the mood it evokes and the reactions that happen—says the guy who couldn't find the plot if it was buried up, well... The color scheme of the film is delightful and decadent, and would become a large part of Bava's appeal. The reds are bright and deep, framing everyone it captures in a ray of guilt and/or impending doom, and the purples bring a usually undeserved regalness. The shadows hide the monsters, at least for a while.

All this beauty and death; only in European cinema would the demolition of an entire dynasty (glamorous, but still) raise barely more than an eyebrow. There are hysterics, but the reactions are more akin to losing one's cell phone than the life of a best friend.

That disconnect brings charms though—a dry humor that stays at arm's length with bemusement, and the film has more than a whiff of poetic justice, as the rich find out they bleed like everyone else.

I actually would have liked to see more behind-the-scenes at the fashion house, instead of it just being a backdrop for murder: perhaps that's the point, though? The killer's mask is blank, leaving the expressions—of fear, and shock—for the audience to feel. But the vivid and lurid scenery of *Blood and Black Lace* is mere window dressing for a stylish thriller that is prêt-à-porter. How much is that dead model in the window?

———————————————

All roads from Rome lead to London—that's my pea brain segue.
In England a group of much-smarter-than-me science-type folk
have dug up something unearthly...

Quatermass and the Pit (1967)

There sure is a lot of confrontation and conversation in *Quatermass and the Pit* (1967): heated debates on the velocity of alien spaceships, subatomic vibrations, and other ephemera related to hostile foreign takeovers. This is what one used to call, derisively, "a thinking man's picture."

Of course, I see the problem with that statement. How DARE you assume that I go to a picture to think; perhaps I'm there just to immerse myself in sensory overload, and enjoy some snacks. Lame labels aside, this is a film that one must lean into, heed, and *engage*—in the same way one should engage with *any* film—eyes open, heart open.

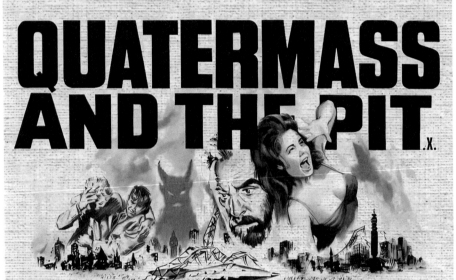

FORCE MORE POWERFUL THAN 1,000 H-BOMBS UNLEASHED TO DEVASTATE EARTH! WORLD IN PANIC! CITIES IN FLAMES!

QUATERMASS AND THE PIT .X.

JAMES DONALD · ANDREW KEIR · BARBARA SHELLEY
JULIAN GLOVER TECHNICOLOR A HAMMER FILM PRODUCTION presented by ASSOCIATED BRITISH PATHE LTD

Starring

JAMES DONALD · ANDREW KEIR
BARBARA SHELLEY · JULIAN GLOVER

Produced by   Directed by   Screenplay by
ANTHONY NELSON KEYS · ROY BAKER · NIGEL KNEALE
A SEVEN ARTS-HAMMER PRODUCTION

Yet *Quatermass and the Pit* is pretty much a "tell, don't show" kind of film—but intentionally so. Writer Nigel Kneale is fascinated by people trying to work things out with reasoning and logic, and setting aside emotional responses. But this is impossible to do, and part of what makes the film fun to watch.

Released as *Five Million Years to Earth* in North America, the film remained a UK box-office-success only. I get it, truly. For those not calibrated, this is a different speed of sci-fi, one that attempts to take a more highbrow approach to flying saucers and little green men—which will only get you so far. But Kneale's ideas are unusually intriguing and outside of the scope of the "regular" sci-fi of the day—more Red Scares, anyone?— and put mankind's very existence into question.

Storytime, then: it's the 1960s in London Town, and plans to expand the underground tube system have hit a snag—well several, really; it seems there are a bunch of five million-year-old skeletons buried beneath the system. Oh, and a Martian spaceship, impervious to any outside force. The British people are turning surly and violent—and that's with the telly off.

How do we know this? Because when legendary British scientist Bernard Quatermass arrives on the scene, he knows where it's at, baby. (Also the dossier and exposition dump at the start help too.)

The truth is, Quatermass (Andrew Keir) isn't called in until it's decided that the underground missile found is unlike anything seen on earth and that it isn't a bomb. Quatermass ascertains, with the help of Doctor Roney (James Donald) and his assistant from the Institute, Barbara (Barbara Shelley), that it is a Martian spaceship. When a diamond drill can't pierce the ship's skin, a secret compartment—similar to a hive— is revealed and shattered. Inside are two-foot-tall locust-like beings with horns—or rather *were*; these creatures are quite dead and have been for millions of years.

So here's a theory that noted scientist Quatermass comes up with after adding to the theorem along the way: the Martians fled their planet millions of years prior looking for asylum from an evil regime; they landed on earth and colonized with prehistoric man. Laden with abilities beyond human comprehension—we would call them magic, alchemy, sorcery, religion—they wove their new future into mankind in the hope of survival.

But now their plan has been exposed, and the strange vibrations coming from the ship whenever it is "attacked" (i.e., touched, poked, prodded, looked at funny) grow stronger and affect the good people of London, causing them to commit horrible acts of pushing, stabbing, and some death. Terribly sorry about that.

Quatermass and his team must figure out a way to destroy the

Martians' hold on London before they take over the world ... or are they already too late?

Kneale's Quatermass works were all done first via multipart serials for BBC Television, and then adapted by him for film; I can't speak for the first two films in the series, but I can say that *QATP*'s director Roy Ward Baker—marking his first of six efforts for Hammer—does his best to keep things moving with very limited sets. We go from the discovery site to the Minister's Office, to the site, to the pub around the corner, to the Institute, to the site, pub, etc. You get the idea. The occasional British vista reminds us of the outside world looming—undoubtedly watching as the turn of events unfold. But the film ramps up not only through Baker's assured and mobile direction, but through the performances of the main cast, especially Keir; he brings an authority—and empathy—to Quatermass. It is compelling to watch as his sense of reason is challenged by the military, which is inclined to do the most damage and can strike first.

But strike against what? Or whom? The problem with an alien invasion that's 5 million years old is you have no one to bill the damage to. This film leaves a lot of London looking worse for wear, and no solutions until science and Quatermass can save the day.

Quatermass and the Pit works well in a couple of interesting ways. First, for a very talkative film, it moves at a brisk pace. Roy Ward Baker should be credited with trying to remove as much TV influence as possible, offering a film that flows without repeating itself. Second, the implications and insinuations of Quatermass' colonization theory are fantastic, because it puts us underneath the microscope for a change instead of being the scientists looking through it.

The insidious—some would say blasphemous—notion that religion and humankind were derived from a literal alien species creates a frisson for those uncomfortable with being *the other*. Or *any* other for that matter; if it doesn't align with the sacred texts of [insert your deity here], they don't want to know. But what if there was no choice? I say accept your heritage; we're all green on the inside, anyway. (If you can't have God, you can always have God-Like; they're everywhere!)

Quatermass and the Pit isn't a cautionary tale on how to *prevent* an invasion; it's what to do after you discover one from millions of years ago. And as you'll see in this brilliant work, it's a messy proposition.

━━━━━━━━━━

I can't see Russia from my backyard, but I have seen their very first horror film from the comfort of my own home. A fine tradeoff, if you ask me.
Steady yourself for the horrors of...

Viy (1967)

My knowledge of Russian folklore is nil, nada, nyet; what I know
about Russian horror, even less. So we'll start with the first one they made,
Viy (1967), a twisted, funny, and macabre tale that corrals the fantastic
in the style of Sam Raimi and Guillermo del Toro: joyful yet tense, and
exploding with vivid imagery.

Based on Ukrainian-born Russian author Nikolay Gogol's 1835
novella, *Viy* is a goofy surrealist piece that manifests as 1960s Hanna-Bar-
bera on bath salts; imagine Fred Flintstone without any chill. He's prone
to bash in the head of an old yet seemingly harmless witch when she forces
him to pretend he was a horse and fly her around. Oh, let's not get too far
ahead in this fairytale. Flip back to the start of the story, shall we?

The setting: a Russian seminary. Praying is hard, and it's time for a
holy break. A small group of young, rambunctious seminarians head for
the countryside in search of some light mischief and raised spirits. Three
of them rest for the night at the farm of an old woman who allows them in,
yet oddly makes them sleep in different parts of the barn.

In the middle of the night, she makes a move on Khoma (Leonid
Kuravlyov), who resists while he can; but soon she hops on his back, and
has him soaring through the skies before a well-placed blow brings them
crashing to the ground. It takes Khoma approximately one second to grab
a stick and beat the woman to within an inch of her life; he stops when he
sees her turn back into a beautiful young witch. Oops.

Khoma runs back to the seminary, his clothes in tatters but his lips
still sealed due to his rumble in the jungle. That is until he's told that he has
to perform the last rites for a neighbor's daughter, dying after a very sudden illness. He's ordered to do so because the perishing young woman asks
for him specifically and if he doesn't, it will not bode well for his future
prospects. What's a poor drunken boy to do?

Off he heads in a covered wagon to the neighbor's estate, where upon
arrival he discovers she has passed. Plan B, as per her wishes, is for Khoma
to pray over her corpse for three consecutive nights in the church. Reluctantly agreeing—what choice does he have?—he heads into the church six
sheets to the wind, to face a casket, and a very pissed off and dead witch.

Much like the witch in her haggard form, *Viy* takes to the skies in its
third act; a phantasm of movement and mischief that plays like a half-re-
membered nightmare—taunting yet ultimately harmless.

That's certainly what is projected to audiences; the film is so broad
yet contained in its mania. It's like a cartoon ready to rip right through
its panels. Directors Konstantin Ershov and Georgiy Kropachyov energize
this comic with a playful style that never stops. The scenes in the church

are vertiginous, to say the least, with the camera swooping and spinning, capturing the madness without pinning it down.

The feeling this inspires in me more than anything is glee; *Viy* is a pure shot of cinema espresso. It's a canvas for small-wall creatures and giant stone ogres to come to life through the special effects of Russian director Aleksandr Ptushko, who was also rumored to have directed *Viy*'s effects scenes. It's trippy, and the Golem Green (ask for it at your local paint store) cinematography inside the church during the after-hours possession sessions is like the beautiful drawings of the retribution of the dead. Scored to oompa-loompa music, naturally.

Much has been made and already debunked of Gogol's "folklore" around the story of *Viy*. It wasn't some deep dive through Ukrainian mythology, but rather his own version—an addition to it, if you will.

I've also seen healthy debate as to the themes present in *Viy*, besides batshittery, that is, and it boils down to Khoma's latent homosexuality and his spurning the advances of the witch. Okay, sure.

I prefer to think the main message of *Viy* is "fuck around, find out." If you're going to beat a witch to death, you should be prepared for the consequences, even if they include flying coffins, loose limbs, and rock monsters. That, or maybe lay off the sauce a little?

And Khoma most definitely did not live happily ever after. The end.

Looking for murderous twins who set up Saw traps for Japanese reporters? What a coincidence—we happen to have one of those films! Make sure you're strapped in for the...

Evil Dead Trap (1988)

By the late 1980s, it was time for a change in horror; slashers had been tired for a while, and nothing else really seemed to grab hold. I would like to be able to say that Japan's *Evil Dead Trap* (1988) swooped in and saved the day, but it wouldn't be until the next decade that horror fans all over the world could witness this weirdo brew of giallo, slasher, and the supernatural.

No, we would have to order a videotape from the back pages of a 1990s *Fangoria* magazine if we wanted to watch a fuzzy copy of a copy. (But in widescreen, ooh.) That changed with the explosion of DVD sales in the early 2000s, giving foreign films a huge opportunity to be exposed to the rest of the world.

As horror fans, we were opened up to a whole new level of availabil-
ity, without sending away for a catalog—foreign cinema was finally on our
doorstep.

And we were oh so happy, because Asian horror was new to most of
us. Up until that point, it was a collector's commodity. One was not likely
to see a film like *Evil Dead Trap* on the Sunday afternoon flick on your
local TV station, nor would it be flooding the multiplexes. Word of mouth
was our delivery system.

So what exactly is all the hubbub about, specifically *Evil Dead Trap*?
How weird and different is it from what we were normally getting?

As it turns out, quite a bit; the film is heavily influenced by Italy's
Dario Argento—especially the aesthetic, which is lifted wholeheartedly
from his films. As for the story, it starts as a slasher, and ends as one messy,
supernatural sibling slaughterhouse. Let's get trapped, shall we?

Nami (Miyuki Ono) is a Japanese late-night cable host. She receives a
videotape showing a woman, gagged and bound, having her eye and bow-
els removed by a cloaked and masked man. Before the tape ends, Nami's
face appears on the screen. Intrigued, she begs her boss to let her find out
where it was filmed and follow up on the tape. He reluctantly agrees, and
she takes a nearly all-female crew with her on the trip.

One Volkswagen bus trip later, Nami and her friends wind up at a
huge abandoned facility off the beaten path, and as the audience needs
the film to move forward, they decide to split up and search for the crime
scene. Huzzah for stupidity!

First, we follow Nami. She comes across a well-dressed man, Masako
(Aya Katsuragi), who says he's looking for his brother Hideki—not looking
too hard, mind you—who disappears nearly as soon as he arrives. Meanwhile, two of the other crew members head off to make sweet, sweet love in
a disgustingly dirty warehouse; and while a two-for-one deal sounds about
right in the world of horror, we need kill fodder so one at a time, please.

And that's what we get—in various and sometimes elaborate ways;
there's archery on hand, the occasional impalement, and other moments
of shaky logic.

But who cares about logic in a film that is really geared to show off
some impressive practical and visual effects by Shin'ichi Wakasa and
Takashi Itô, and the confident direction of Toshiharu Ikeda, who splays
everything in blues when he isn't spraying the screen in reds. The weak
link is indeed the script, which is just a bunch of set pieces until the back
half of the film, where the story takes a turn for the supernatural—and
becomes a battle between two. Okay, three.

Remember how Masako was looking for his brother Hideki? Well, it
turns out Hideki is inside Masako and has been making him kill. Spoiler

alert: Yes, the guy wandering around the facility while everyone is murdered is in fact the killer. But not willingly—Hideki takes over when it's time to kill.

Until that back half, when Hideki decides to move out, as it were, and take on Nami himself; then it becomes Nami versus Masako and Hideki in a battle till the end. And another battle. Oh and one more. (This film has about seven climaxes too many.)

There are essentially two different films going on in *Evil Dead Trap*: getting rid of Nami's friends and then fighting Nami. But I really don't think there's that much disconnect between the two halves as many critics have pointed out—not when the whole film is unmoored from reality. The first half isn't some Netflix docudrama following a serial killer; it's a guy in a slicker and a mask, engaging in way too complicated traps for … whatever reasons.

Was this the birth of *Saw*? Possibly? The basic idea is certainly present if none of the moralizing; I couldn't tell you the brothers' motivation other than to destroy in elaborate ways.

Evil Dead Trap is disjointed, sure, but endearingly so. It's a film that wears its influences on its sleeve, with those influences being from other countries—Argento from Italy, Raimi from America—but ends up being its own particular beast, with a unique flavor.

The bottom line is this: is *Evil Dead Trap* derivative of other films by celebrated horror artists? Sure. And while it may consist of 95 percent perspiration and 5 percent inspiration, it came along at a time when some good old sweat—and copious amounts of blood and viscera—breathed some far away life into the genre.

All films are magical—some more than others.
This film is beautiful, terrifying, and haunting.
Welcome to Mexico, and welcome to...

Santa Sangre (1989)

The mind is at once unfathomable and all too familiar with the inner working of its personal host. It plays games and tricks, with parlor moves designed to confuse its subject; not out of malice—but rather, to offer protection. *Santa Sangre* (1989) is a film that looks at mental illness and psychological warfare through a lens of poverty, perversion, and longing. And it is simply stunning.

Santa Sangre, Mainline Pictures, 1989

I often make fun of "arthouse" films around these parts, but only for the laughs and for the obvious disconnect between most of what we watch and, say, *Howard's End*. A fine film to be sure, but never one to be confused with *Killer Rack*. So dignity of material comes into play when deciding what's arthouse, to be certain—mature themes only, thank you. This almost predestines the films to be dramas about Big Things.

Santa Sangre is about Big Things too; after all, what's more important than the human condition? But the film is arthouse because it feels untouched by corporations and bean counters, and wholly owned by legendary cult director Alejandro Jodorowsky (*El Topo*). It unfolds and doesn't feel forced. It happens, and we can't stop watching. And it's always with a strong sense of empathy for its characters, who could use all the help they can get.

Fenix (Adan Jodorowsky) is a boy who lives and works in his mom and dad's traveling Mexican circus. It's a colorful life but filled with familial danger under every inch of its tattered tent. Fenix is the Boy Magician, dad is the Knife Thrower, and mom is the Aerialist. Fenix's best friend, Aladin (Jesús Juárez), a dwarf featured in the show, is also his protector from a drunk and violent father, who tattoos an eagle across Fenix's chest to "make him a man."

Also losing out in the mom sweepstakes, Fenix's religious zealot of a mother (Blanca Guerra) turns out to be the head of a religious cult called "Santa Sangre"—"holy blood"—which worships an armless woman as its saint. This position makes her very unstable and unpredictable; when she witnesses dad (Guy Stockwell) having relations with the Tattooed Woman (Thelma Tixou), she pours acid on his doo-dads and his friend to boot. He in turn takes two of his knives and removes both of his wife's arms to keep her closer to her saint. He then cuts his own throat, in plain view of his son.

We meet up with Fenix (Axel Jodorowsky) around a decade later, much the worse for wear. Living in a mental facility and climbing a tree in his room, he's completely disconnected from society. Terrified of the outside world—for good reason—he is made to attend a movie in town with a group of fellow patients. A slick pimp (Teo Jodorowsky) convinces the group to use their movie money on cocaine and prostitution, which has me wondering what kind of allowance these patients have.

Fenix wanders off though and happens to see the Tattooed Woman dancing in the town square; unbeknownst to Fenix, she is now a prostitute. He also is unaware that she adopted Alma, the mute girl from the circus who was Fenix's friend and ally. He leaves without confronting the Tattooed Woman.

The trip to the outside world reinvigorates Fenix and he's eager for his next adventure. He doesn't have to wait long as his armless mother stands below his window, beckoning him; he grabs some rope and makes his way to the street, and runs off with her.

Soon the duo are performing a double for sold-out performances; with Fenix standing behind her and acting as her arms, Concha sings for the appreciative audiences that fill the local theater in town. A big success, things seem to be going well for Fenix; he gets to resume his complicated relationship with his mom, whose behavior can charitably be described as "smothering,"

Back at their manor, it's more of the same. Fenix sits behind her, puts his arms through her sleeves, and acts as his mother; whether knitting or playing the piano, his hands carry out her wishes.

As mother and son combos go, Concha and Fenix's codependency is up there with the horror greats like Norma and Norman, Ethel and Junior, Rosemary and Beelzebaby; its literalness is a clue to its puzzle and part of its poetry.

When Concha wants Fenix to kill a flirty member of their new troupe, he flinches because he doesn't want to, but feels he must appease mom—one last time. So he has an idea: he'll find a muscular woman who can physically overpower him and stop him from killing. And he does; he meets up with an amorous bodybuilder and takes her back to his place. Meanwhile, a grown-up Alma searches for Fenix after her adopted tattooed mother violently meets her demise...

The rest I will not indulge; but needless to say, *Santa Sangre* has a lot to say about redemption, and the diligent pursuit thereof. Fenix does not want to kill, but his bounty is laid before him in the finale. A graveyard visit to his backyard reveals that Fenix has been much busier than we originally thought as multiple women rise from their shallow earth to bellow from the beyond.

The key to *Santa Sangre* working is in the portrayal of Fenix; nearly every frame is with him. It is to the credit of Jodorowsky and his co-writers Claudio Argento (Dario's brother) and Roberto Leoni that Fenix is presented as very sympathetic.

From a young age, Fenix is made to play with the tattered cards he's dealt, reshuffled over decades and generations of abuse and addictions; to say the circus isn't an environment for a child would be an understatement.

This is a story of fighting against a rotted heritage in the hopes of some sort of salvation; Fenix finds his with the return of Alma, and breaks through the past. *Santa Sangre*, with its stunning imagery and captivating performances, is a horror film about searching for—and finding—the calm in the chaos. Regardless of our circumstance, we could all use a little bit of that.

The Past, Present
and Future of Horror:
Or, How to Hit Your Word Count
and Close Out the Book

I hope you've enjoyed this too brief journey through some horror history; and I do mean brief—60 films is nothing in a tapestry that weaves from the late 1800s to now. But if you're a horror enthusiast like me—new or old alike—perhaps you have had the opportunity to dig into whatever subgenres float your boat.

As I wrote earlier, I had a wonderful relationship with films from the time I was a little kid; my first big screen horror was *Burnt Offerings* in 1976 when I was six years old. Yes, that's a long time ago, thanks for noticing; but what my advanced physiology offers is a—sometimes muddled—appreciation to have been a kid who loved horror. My friends weren't allowed to go to horror movies with me when I was really young; instead, we would see regular Saturday matinee fare like already old Martin & Lewis pictures, or the latest Disney live action adventure. I enjoyed them all, truly; but not nearly as much as I did sneaking out with my older brother Jeff to see *Halloween* on a cold October night. He was babysitting me; we both wanted to see it. When he asked if I wanted to go, I already had my coat on. He told the theater owner that we got locked out of the house and our parents wouldn't be home for a couple of hours. Genius.

It worked. We came in during Michael's rainy escape from Smith's Grove, but we caught up soon enough, and were terrified along with everyone else in that theater. The walk home had us both shook, under the lonely streetlights which seemed miles apart from each other, with nothing but dark in between. An old house, where every door moaned and every cross breeze was a scream, offered no additional comfort.

But I had to have it. The horror—no matter how terrified, frightened, or nervous I was, I somehow just instinctively knew from a young age that

216

these couldn't harm me in any way. It was entertainment. That's not all the films were when I was a child, and definitely not as an adolescent. They were companions, friends, support: a horror film won't say they'll call you about going to a dance and then doesn't, or ignore you for other friends with a higher status. A horror film will never judge you.

I don't believe these to be trivial sentiments; everyone strives to connect to *something*—and when one does, it can cover a lot of necessary emotional needs as well.

Okay, before you think I'm going to be hawking a new-age way of peace through horror: RELAX. (That's the next book; it comes with a free wishing stone.) All I mean is that horror films—and books, shows, the whole shebang—offer respites from reality and conjure up creative pursuits of the unimaginable—from a safe distance of course.

Growing up, it's great to have horror by your side. That hasn't changed, of course; here I sit typing, and wondering what I'm going to watch next. Something new, recent, or older?

Now, my "older" and your "older" may be a little different; mine could mean some Hammer, yours could mean some Blumhouse. But I think it's great that horror fans right now have so many choices at their fingertips that they can go even further back from *my* older. Hell, I hadn't seen *Nosferatu* (1922) until a handful of years ago, and that's considered a landmark film. Which it is—simply mesmerizing. Point being, we all have a personal journey with horror; not in some creepy religious way (that's my third book, *My God, the Horror!*), but rather as seekers of entertainment. It doesn't have to offer traditional enlightenment—not to get stuck in the sacred, sorry—but truths can be found in all manner of horror films, from the "elevated" horror associated with A24, to the backyard and basement musings of an Andy Milligan.

We're living in an age of extreme anxiety. I don't think it's a coincidence that horror has never been more popular than it is; it truly is an escape valve for many, at least for a couple of hours. What's even more amazing is the quality of the quantity—there truly are a number of great films across a spectrum of tastes at the moment: the *Suspiria* remake, *Midsommar*, *Scare Me*, *Saint Maud*, David Gordon Green's *Halloween* trilogy, *A Quiet Place*, *The Night House*, *The Lighthouse*, *The Slumber Party Massacre* remake, *X*, and so many more. It really has been a spectacular era; you can't judge it until there's distance, but I think it will hold strong in horror fandom's eyes.

As for the future, where you and I will spend the rest of our lives, there's a few things I'm hopeful about—and for: I'd love to see the continual growth and exposure for queer filmmakers from the entire LGBTQ+ community. We've gotten a lot of queer horror, or rather, we've exposed the genre as the thematic melting pot of the subversive and sympathetic. We're at a point where we can celebrate the subversive hitting the surface and sort of ruling: *Chucky* is a big hit as a TV series, offering up a gay teenage romance that's sweet and funny while Chucky causes havoc. Then there are films like Christopher Landon and co-writer Michael Kennedy's hilarious *Freaky*, the *Fear Street* films on Netflix, the *Slasher* TV series, *American Horror Story* (Ryan Murphy must be mentioned), the new version of *Hellraiser* with transgender actress Jamie Clayton bringing forth a different Pinhead more in line with Clive Barker's original vision. Acceptance is on its own timetable, but things are moving in the right direction.

I'd dig it if we kept championing the POC creatives in horror; directors like Nia DaCosta (the *Candyman* remake), JD Dillard (*Sweetheart*), Remi Weekes (*His House*), and Jordan Peele blasting through the ceiling with his first three films: *Get Out*, *Us*, and *Nope*. I'm also going to keep cheering for the success of horror from all over the world—and if you haven't yet, I'd highly recommend taking a trip to another part of the map.

And finally, an unnecessary reminder for us all: keep spreading the word about the greatest genre around. What other art form offers tragedy, comedy, drama, romance, dismemberment, action, suspense, and immolation? (What other one would want to?)

And if you're still here, this is the end of *A Cut Below*. You made it! Thanks for sticking around; may Pazuzu offer you ill health and an elevating sleep mattress. Until we meet again, save me a spot in the cinematic shadows.

Index

"A" movies 1
Abby 12, 37
Academy Awards 21, 151
Ackland, Josh 75
Affleck, Neil 110
Alice, Sweet Alice 24–27
Alien 172
Allied Artists 26
Amalgamated Productions 170
Amicus 75, 82, 86
Anderson, Maxwell 23
Ansara, Michael 160
Argento, Claudio 215
Argento, Dario 27, 191, 211
Armstrong, R.G. 103
Arngrim, Stefan 52
Arnold, Jack 184
Arywitz, Mark 64
Ashton, James 46
Asylum 75, 79–82
Atkins, Tom 86
Avco Embassy 158

"B" movies 1
The Baby 143, 144–147
The Bad Seed (1956) 21–24, 28
Baker, Rick 104
Baker, Roy Ward 79, 206
Baker, Tom 78
Balsam, Martin 49
Band family (Albert, Richard, Charles) 2
Barbeau, Adrienne 88
Barker, Clive 218
Bartok, Eva 202
Basket Case 163, 173–176
Bava, Mario 191, 200, 202
Baxter, Meredith 9
Bayldon, Geoffrey 81
The Bees 180, 191–194
Ben 7–10
Benjamin, Richard 96
Bennett, John 75

Benson, Deborah 65
Beswick, Martine 84
Bing Crosby Productions 4, 9
Bishop, Wes 44
Black Christmas (1974) 54, 55, 60, 121
Blake, Richard 166
Bloch, Robert 54, 56, 75, 81
Blood and Black Lace 199, 200–203
Bolling, Tiffany 15
Bonner, Beverly 175
Borgnine, Ernest 7
Bottin, Rob 19
Brand, Neville 153
Breckinridge, John 169
Brolin, James 96
Bronson, Charles 65
The Brood 107, 112–115
Brook, Claudio 193
Brooke, Hillary 164
Brooks, Ron 84
Bryans, John 75
Brynner, Yul 96
"Bud" Cardos, John 13
Bunston, Doug 178
Burial Ground 140–142
Burman, Ellis 46
Burman, Rob 84
Burman, Tom 111, 160
Burnette, Dorsey 13
Burns, Marilyn 153
Burnt Offerings 107, 216
Burr, Jeff 84
"But what is a giallo?" 200–201

Caesar, Harry 84
Caillou, Allen 15
"Canadian tax breaks" 107, 121
Cannom, Greg 124
Cannon 65
Carpenter, John 194–198
Carradine, John 47, 191
Carrie 52, 101

Carter, Helena 164
Cash, Rosalind 84
Castle, William 35, 56, 60
Catholic Church 24, 37, 49
Cedar, Jon 158
Chicago International Film Festival 24
The Children (1980) 31–33
Christie, Julie 99
Chucky 218
The Church of Satan 46
Cineplex Odeon 82
Cinerama Releasing Corporation 81
Ciupka, Richard 123
Clark, Bob 60
Clavell, James 93
Clayton, Jamie 218
Collins, Roberta 153
Comer, Anjanette 146
Cook, Elisha, Jr. 188
Cooper, Alice 196
Cortese, Joe 103
Cosmatos, George P. 115
Crabtree, Arthur 172
Craig, Michael 78
Crawford, Joan 56, 58
Creepshow 72, 82, 86–89
Creepy 76, 86
Crichton, Michael 96
Criswell 167
Cronenberg, David 93, 104
The Curse of the Werewolf 180, 184–187
Curtains 107, 121–124
Curtis, Tony 158
Cushing, Peter 75, 76, 81, 129

DaCosta, Nia 218
Dane, Lawrence 115
D'Angelo, Beverly 49
Dano, Royal 190
Danson, Ted 88
Dante, Joe 17
Davis, Gene 67
Davison, Bruce 7, 9
Dawson, Anthony 186
Day of the Animals 4, 12, 16
Death Bite 120
Death Wish 47, 65, 67, 157
Del Grande, Louis 115
Deliverance 62, 64
Demon Seed 97–100
DeNoble, Anthony 27
De Palma, Brian 143
The Devil Rides Out 38–41
The Devil's Rain 16, 38, 44–47
Dillard, JD 218
Dillman, Bradford 17
Dimension Pictures 13

Donald, James 205
Donaldson, Lesleh 123
Duffell, Peter 76
Dunham, Joanna 75

Eaten Alive 143, 151–154
Ebert, Roger 65, 81, 112
Eden, Daniel 52
Eggar, Samantha 112, 121
Eilbacher, Lisa 68
Elias, Jeannie 36
Elliott, Denholm 75
Englund, Robert 153
Erickson, Leif 164
Ershov, Konstantin 207
Essoe, Gabe 46
Evans, Clifford 186
Evil Dead Trap 200, 209–212
The Evil Eye 202
Evilspeak 101–103
The Exorcist 12, 21, 24, 37, 49, 118, 158

Fear No Evil 38, 50–53
Feller, Catherine 187
Ferrer, Jose 49
Ferrer, Mel 153
Fiander, Lewis 28
Fiend Without a Face 162, 170–172
Finley, William 149, 150, 151
Fisher, Terence 41, 186
Fisk, Jack 188
The Fly (1958) 91–94
Fonda, Peter 44, 118
Ford, Anitra 188
Francks, Don 110
Franks, Chloe 75
Franz, Arthur 164
Friday the 13th (1980) 33, 54, 55, 62, 64, 137, 138
From a Whisper to a Scream 72, 82–85
Frost, Lee 44
Fruet, William 120
Fuest, Robert 46

Gabriel, John 186
Garofalo, Joseph 103
Gary, Lorraine 12
George, Christopher 12, 69, 71
Girdler, William 10, 12, 37, 143, 158
Godzilla (1954) 3
Gogol, Nikolay 207
Goldblatt, Mark 19
Goldblum, Jeff 49
Golden Globes 9, 151
The Golden Turkey Awards 167
Gordon, Shep 197
Gornick, Michael 89

Graham, Gerritt 100
Grant, Arthur 40
Greer, Michael 188
Griffin, Lynn 123
Grizzly 10–13, 16
Guerra, Blanca 214
Gulager, Clu 84
Guza, Robert, Jr. 123

Habif, James 156
Hallier, Lori 110
Halloween (1978) 54, 55, 123, 137, 181, 216
Hammer Film 38–40, 79, 126, 129, 180, 186, 199, 206
Harper, Jessica 149, 150
Harris, Ed 88
Harry, Debbie 104
Heckart, Eileen 21
Hedison, David 93
Henenlotter, Frank 163, 173
Henkel, Kim 154
Henry, Gregg 65
Herrier, Mark 60, 61
Hill, Joe 86
Hill, Marianna 146, 188
Hindle, Art 112
Hinds, Cindy 112
Hitchcock, Alfred 26, 27, 55, 58
Hoffman, Elizabeth 52
Holbrook, Hal 88
Holland, John 52
Hollingsworth, Laura 35
Hollywood Meatcleaver Massacre 143, 154–157
Hooper, Tobe 143, 151–154
Hopman, Gerald 46
House of Mystery 76, 86
The House That Dripped Blood 73–76
Howard, Clint 90, 101
Howarth, Alan 196
Hunt, Jimmy 164
Huyck, Willard 188

Ikeda, Toshiharu 211
The Incredible Shrinking Man 180, 181–184
Invaders from Mars 162, 164–166
Irving, Gregg 64
Irwin, Mark 120
Itô, Takashi 211

J. Gillis, Barry 178
Jackson, Michael 7
Jaeckel, Richard 12
James, Anthony 107
Jaws 10, 17
Jensen Farley Pictures 121

Jodorowsky, Adan 214
Jodorowsky, Alejandro 214
Jodorowsky, Axel 214
Jodorowsky, Teo 214
Johns, Glynis 78
Johnson, Tor 169
Jones, Carolyn 153
Jones, Claude Earl 103
Jordan, Andrew 178
Joyner, C. Courtney 84
Juárez, Jesús 214
Judd, Edward 78
Jurgens, Curt 78
Just Before Dawn 62–65
Justin, Larry 156

Kalmanowicz, Max 33
Karlson, Phil 10
Katsuragi, Aya 211
Katz, Gloria 188
Keene, Kerrie 120
Keir, Andrew 205
Kelly, Nancy 21
Kelman, Paul 110
Kennedy, Arthur 49
Kennedy, George 65
Kennedy, Michael 218
Kibbe, Gary B. 198
King, Joel 64
King, Stephen 73, 86, 88, 89
Kingdom of the Spiders 13–16
Kiser, Terry 84
Kneale, Nigel 198
Knight, Keith 115
Krimi films 202
Kropachyov, Georgiy 207
Kuravlyov, Leonid 207

L. Fast, Alvin 154
LaLoggia, Frank 50
Lanchester, Elsa 6
Landon, Christopher 218
LaVey, Anton 46
Leder, Herbert J. 172
Lee, Christopher 41, 75, 156
Lee, Evan 157
Lee, Joanna 169
Lehman, Lew 35
Lemmon, Chris 65
Leoni, Roberto 215
LeRoy, Mervyn 23
Lewis, Geoffrey 68
Lieberman, Jeff 62
Lindfors, Viveca 88
The Living Dead at Manchester Morgue 132–135
Locke, Sondra 6

Lom, Herbert 81
Lowry, Jane 26
Lugosi, Bela 167
Lupino, Ida 46
Lyman, Craig 33

Magee, Patrick 81
Majors, Lee 56
Manfredini, Harry 33
The Manitou 12, 143, 158–161
Manley Blau, Beatrice 146
Manlove, Dudley 169
Mann, Daniel 6
Manzy, David 146
March, William 23
Marshall, E.G. 88
Marshall, Herbert 93
Massey, Anna 78
Massey, Daniel 78
Matheson, Richard 40, 183, 184
McAllen, Kathleen Rowe 52
McCall, Joan 12
McCarthy, Kevin 17
McCormack, Patty 21
McFarland, Megan 84
Media Entertainment 2
Menzies, Heather 19
Menzies, William Cameron 166
Meredith, Burgess 160
Messiah of Evil 180, 188–191
MGM 65, 96, 97, 170,
Mihalka, George 111
Miles, Sylvia 49
Miller, Dick 17
Mitchell, Cameron 84, 202
Moll, Richard 101
Montana, Lenny 103
Montgomery, Lee 9
Moreno Films 101
Morse, Barry 81
Motion Picture Production Code 23
Moviestore Entertainment 82
Der müde Tod (Weary Death) 72
Murphy, Ryan 218
My Bloody Valentine 107, 108–111

Neumann, Kurt 93
New World Pictures 17, 35, 112
Nielsen, Leslie 88
Night of the Living Dead 2, 30, 125, 128, 132, 138, 172, 197
Norstar Releasing 121

Oates, Warren 44
Of Unknown Origin 107, 115–118
The Omen (1976) 21, 24, 43, 49
Ono, Miyuki 211

Orbach, Jerry 49
Ormsby, Alan 60, 61
Owens, Patricia 93

Paramount 108
Paris, France 149
Parker, Jameson 196
Parker, Kim 170
Parker, Lara 44
Parkins, Barbara 81
Paynter, Robert 124
Peele, Jordan 218
Peeping Tom 3, 54
Pertwee, Jon 75
Phantom of the Paradise 143, 147–151
Pieces 55, 69–71
Piranha 17–19
The Pit 33–36
Pitt, Ingrid 75
The Plague of the Zombies 126–129
Plan 9 from Outer Space 162, 167–169
Pleasence, Donald 194
Polsky, Abe 146
Popcorn 58–62
Porter, Nyree Dawn 75
"portmanteau" 72
Post, Ted 146
Powell, Robert 81
Prather, Joan 46
Price, Vincent 82, 93
Prince of Darkness 181, 194–198
Prine, Andrew 12
Psycho 2, 23, 40, 56, 75, 143, 153, 187
Ptushko, Aleksandr 209

Quatermass and the Pit 199, 203–206

Rabid 106, 112
Race with the Devil 38, 41–44
Raines, Christina 49
Ralston, Gilbert 6, 10
Rampling, Charlotte 81
Randall, Dick 71
Ransome, Prunella 28
Ratman's Notebooks by Stephen Gilbert 6
Reed, Oliver 107, 112, 118, 120, 184, 187
Reeve, Spencer 40
Reeves, Kynaston 170
Reynolds, Larry 110
Richards, Kyle 153
Riggs, Dan 178
Ritvo, Rosemary 27
Roberts, Tony 60
Roberts, William 68
Robinson, Richard 15
Roeg, Nicolas 27

Roman, Ruth 146
Romero, George 73, 78, 86, 125, 126, 132,
135, 138, 140, 172,
Rosemary's Baby 38, 40, 41, 100
Rosenberg, Max 75, 81, 82
Ross, Gaylen 88
Rosson, Harold 21
Rustam, Mardi 154

Santa Sangre 200, 212–215
Sarandon, Chris 49
Satanic Panic 41, 99
Saturn Award 50
Saxon, John 191
Sayles, John 17
Schifrin, Lalo 160
Schoelen, Jill 60
Scotia International 144
Scott, Darin 84
The Sentinel 38, 47–50
Serrador, Narciso Ibáñez 30
Shadow, John 71
Shatner, William 13, 44
Sheinberg, Sid 12
Sheldon, David 12
Shelley, Barbara 205
Sheppard, Paula 26
Shields, Brooke 26
Shivers 106, 112
Shore, Howard 114
Simon, J.P. 71
Simpson, Peter 123
Sinclaire, Crystin 153
"slashers" 50, 52, 54, 58, 60, 65, 69, 71, 107,
110, 199, 200, 202, 209
Slugs 71
Smith, Dick 49, 118
Smits, Sonja 104
Snyders, Sammy 36
Sole, Alfred 26
Spasms 107, 118–121
Spielberg, Steven 17
Stark, Don 103
Starrett, Jack 43
Stevens, Andrew 68
Stevens, Stella 160
Stockwell, Guy 214
Strait-Jacket 56–58
Strasberg, Susan 158
Strode, Woody 15
Stuart, Ian A. 35
Stuart, Randy 181
Subotsky, Milton 75, 82
Susan Smith, Terri 175
Swit, Loretta 44
Syms, Sylvia 81

Tales from the Crypt (1972) 75, 82
Talfrey, Hira 186
Tangerine Dream 120
10 to Midnight 65–68
The Texas Chain Saw Massacre (1974) 54,
143, 151, 153
Things 163, 176–179
Thomas, Terry- 78
Thompson, J. Lee 67
Thompson, Marshall 170
Thorson, Linda 123
Tixou, Thelma 214
Todd, Richard 81
Tombs of the Blind Dead 129–132
Tompkins, Angel 191
Travolta, John 46
Tweed, Shannon 115
20th Century–Fox 38, 91, 126, 148, 164
Tyrell, Susan 84

Unheimliche Geschichten (Uncanny
Stories) 72
Universal 106

Vampira 167
Van Hentenryck, Kevin 175
Vaughn, Robert 90, 99
Vault of Horror 75, 76–79
Vernon, John 123
V/H/S 73, 79
Videodrome 90, 104–106
Villard, Tom 60
Villiers, James 81
Virgo International Pictures 151
VIY 200, 207–209

Das Wachsfigurenkabinett (Waxworks)
72
Wakasa, Shin'ichi 211
Walken, Christopher 49
The Walking Dead 125
Wallace, Dee 60
Wallace, Edgar 202
Wallach, Eli 49
Walston, Ray 60
Walters, Justin 186
Warner Bros. 12, 21, 115
Warner-Pathé 38
Waxman, Al 120
Weaver, Fritz 88, 99
Weekes, Remi 218
Weller, Peter 115
The Werewolf of Paris by Guy Endore 186
Weston, Eric 103
Westworld 94–97
Whatever Happened to Baby Jane? (1962)
56

Wheatley, Dennis 38
Whitlock, Albert 49
Whitman, Stuart 153
Who Can Kill a Child? 28–30
Willard 4–7
Williams, Grant 181
Williams, Paul 143, 149, 150
Wincott, Michael 123
Winner, Michael 47, 67
Winnipeg, Canada 149
Wong, Victor 196

Wood, Ed 35, 167–169
Woods, James 104
Wordsworth, Richard 186
Writer's Guild of America 151
Wynn, Keenan 16, 19, 46

Zacarias, Alfredo 193
Zaillian, Steve 15
Zenor, Suzanne 146
Zombie 135–139